W9-ADN-803

Shakespeare's Romances

Shakespeare's Romances

A STUDY
OF
SOME WAYS
OF THE
IMAGINATION

BY HALLETT SMITH

THE HUNTINGTON LIBRARY · SAN MARINO, CALIFORNIA

1972

Copyright 1972
The Henry E. Huntington Library and Art Gallery
San Marino, California
Library of Congress Catalog Card Number 72-79314
Designed by Ward Ritchie
Printed in the United States of America
by Anderson, Ritchie & Simon

Research, though toilsome, is easy; imaginative vision, though delightful, is difficult; and we may be tempted to prefer the first. Or we note that in a given passage Shakespeare has used what he found in his authority; and we excuse ourselves from asking why he used it or what he made of it. Or we see that he has done something that would please his audience; and we dismiss it as accounted for, forgetting that perhaps it also pleased him, *and that we have to account for* that. *Or knowledge of his stage shows us the stage convenience of a scene; and we say that the scene was due to stage convenience, as if the cause of a thing must needs be single and simple. Such errors provoke the man who reads his Shakespeare poetically, and make him blaspheme our knowledge. But we ought not to fall into them, and we cannot reject any knowledge that may help us into Shakespeare's mind because of the danger it brings.*

A. C. BRADLEY

Contents

Preface

The term "Romances" is sometimes applied to those plays Shakespeare wrote at the end of his career which are neither histories nor tragedies and can be called comedies only if one uses the broad classification adopted by Shakespeare's first editors, Heminges and Condell, in the Folio of 1623.[1] These plays include *Pericles, Cymbeline, The Winter's Tale, The Tempest* and *The Two Noble Kinsmen;* of these the first and last are thought to be partly by somebody other than Shakespeare. It is generally conceded that these five plays as a group have elements in common, and that as a group they differ in significant ways from Shakespeare's earlier work. The reasons alleged for this difference are various: some have thought that the influence of the younger playwrights for the King's Men, Francis Beaumont and John Fletcher, pulled Shakespeare in a new direction, but there is no proof that the experiments of the collaborators antedated Shakespeare's first venture in this kind of drama. Others have thought that Shakespeare, at the age of forty-four, having written thirty-two plays in the past sixteen years, was tired and simply wrote these plays to help his company, without really putting his heart into it. They point out that he does seem to be living in Stratford rather than London in 1610, and that it would not be unreasonable to picture him as a retired successful man, enjoying the financial rewards of his two decades in the theater in London, and basking in the company of his daughter Susanna, her husband, Dr. John Hall, and their daughter Elizabeth. Others maintain that the special character of Shakespeare's romances is to be explained by external theatrical conditions rather than by anything personal to the poet himself. In 1608 Shakespeare's company acquired the Blackfriars theater, where boys had been acting for a dozen years; after some delay due to the plague the King's Men played there in the winter at the "private," indoor theater and in the summer in their usual place on the Bankside, the Globe. Audiences at the Blackfriars were more exclusive than those at the Globe; presumably they shared the court taste for spectacle and theatrical display and the Blackfriars had scenic facilities to appeal to this taste. A weakness of this argument is that *Pericles,* the first of the romances and in some respects the model for the others, was almost certainly composed before the King's Men occupied Blackfriars. In any event, we know that the romances were performed at the Globe as well, so the plays had to be conformable to its stage.

The term "romances" for these late plays is not wholly satisfactory. An early comedy, *Two Gentlemen of Verona,* might perfectly well be called a romance, and *As You Like It* is in large part a dramatization of a prose romance, Lodge's *Rosalynde.* But the alternatives are even less satisfactory. These plays are not tragicomedies in the sense that Italian plays bearing that label or some of the plays of Beaumont and Fletcher are tragicomedies. The term "last plays" is vague — should it include *Coriolanus* and *Antony and Cleopatra?* — and it would have to include *Henry VIII,* which because of its subject matter is different from the others. Further, that title implies that Shakespeare knew they were his last plays so he made a kind of farewell or testament of them. I do not believe this to be true.

My aim is to show that the romances are a natural outgrowth of Shakespeare's experience in writing comedy and tragedy. This aim is not very different from that of Northrop Frye in *A Natural Perspective,* except that he confines himself to comedy. I also wished to approach as nearly as I could to the question of Shakespeare's imagination — how did it change from his early period to his late period? One way to deal with this problem is to compare the way he used his source in writing *As You Like It* with the way he used a similar source in writing *The Winter's Tale.* But the imagination is not necessarily observed as well when we watch Shakespeare transforming a novel into a play as it might be in a somewhat freer situation, so it seemed advisable to consider in juxtaposition two of his works usually thought to be most imaginative, the early comedy *A Midsummer Night's Dream* and the late romance *The Tempest.*

My interest in Shakespeare's imagination underlies what I have done in all of the following chapters. I have not taken up the subject systematically because it seems to me that the materials for doing that are simply not available. We have no notebook with jottings from the books he read, as John Livingston Lowes had for Coleridge. But it is now possible to do more sensitive work with the sources than it used to be; in this area one must of course speak of the great contributions of Geoffrey Bullough, Kenneth Muir, and Jacob Isaacs. The latter's study of "Shakespeare's Earliest Years in the Theater"[2] came to my attention after I had done most of my work on his latest years in the theater, and it gives me great satisfaction to realize that Shakespeare too could have used that curious motto of Mary Queen of Scots, "In My End is My Beginning."

The last plays are full of theatrical spectacle and elaborate devices. They were written, most of them, when the company for which Shakespeare wrote had the Blackfriars, a private, enclosed, lighted theater, available to it. They were of course also written with an eye to possible production at the Jacobean court, and this involved the use of the kind of display featured in the masques which enjoyed such popularity there. But these plays were put on, let it not be forgotten, at the Globe as well as the Blackfriars and some possible great hall, and the Globe was also important. What elaboration Shakespeare could give to the regular stage he had been writing for all his career I have considered in a chapter on verbal scene painting or "landscape" in connection with the actual setting and properties which the audience literally saw.

I have tried to give an appropriate context for reading or seeing these late plays by opening with a chapter on the romance tradition as it was available to Shakespeare. Other critics have done this, to some extent, but there is still so much misconceived commentary on the romances that I felt it necessary to start from the beginning — the romantic tale which was so common in Shakespeare's generation and so uncommon in ours. His last plays are a return to a kind of thing popular in his youth, and we must acclimatize ourselves in this tradition if we are to see his final works in the right context.

Another critical problem is the heroines of the last plays — those girls with semi-symbolic names like Marina, Imogen, Perdita and Miranda. Romantic and Victorian criticism idealized them, and more recent comment has turned the other way. The relationship between innocence and the pastoral environment of these plays needs to be re-realized.

After much in which I have relied upon other critics for guidance and insight, I have finally been compelled to express my opposition to two tendencies which, innocent enough in themselves, seem to me to have been carried too far and to have resulted in some serious misreadings of the last plays. So I have included two appendices, one on the Myth and Archetype criticism of the romances, and the other on Topical Significances and Occasions alleged for these plays. I am enouraged in my dissent by several voices: Allardyce Nicoll wrote in 1960, "It may be suggested that much of the current interpretation of the romances either imposes on these plays a purpose not in Shakespeare's mind when he wrote them or else, if the interpretation be regarded as valid, indicates a failure on his part to achieve that purpose."[3] Philip Edwards wrote, in 1957, in reviewing J. C. Maxwell's edition of *Pericles,* "Maxwell is a little on his guard against interpretations of the Last Plays which treat them as symbolic or mythopoeic representations of fundamental human experience. He could afford to be even more suspicious; the tide is running strongly against those who, thinking to make the last plays big by ignoring 'surface levels,' have succeeded only in deflating them."[4] Most of all I rejoice to be in the company of the late John Crow, whose article "Deadly Sins of Criticism, or, Seven Ways to get Shakespeare Wrong" the author himself called "this piece of platform buffoonery" but which seems to me the wisest thing written about Shakespeare commentary in my time. I cannot quote from it because I would have to quote the whole thing.[5]

I hope I will not be thought to mention, and to quote, too many critics for the pleasure of disagreeing with them. As a scholar, it is my business to be familiar with everything of importance that has been published on the subject I pretend to discuss — though this is all but impossible if the subject is Shakespeare, or even his romances. But as a critic, I subscribe to the doctrine enunciated by John Dryden in 1677

— and he, too, referred to an earlier critic: "Criticism, as it was first instituted by Aristotle, was meant a standard of judging well; the chiefest part of which is, to observe those excellencies which should delight a reasonable mind."

My obligations to others are great. The splendid staff of the Huntington Library and many distinguished scholars from all over the world who have worked there have been my benefactors. I am particularly indebted, for encouragement and criticism, to James Thorpe and Jenijoy LaBelle.

HALLETT SMITH

Shakespeare's Romances

Chapter 1
THE ROMANCE TRADITION
AS IT INFLUENCED SHAKESPEARE

My plea is that readers of Shakespeare should focus their eyes more sharply upon the matter in hand and exchange wonder for curiosity.

George Rylands, *Words and Poetry*

The Latin romance called *Apollonius of Tyre,* a work of the third century, was extremely popular in the Middle Ages, nor has it completely lost that popularity since: it is still alive as a folktale in Greece.[1] There is a fragment of a version of it in Old English and a version in Middle English. It was retold by John Gower in Book 8 of *Confessio Amantis* and it was the 153rd story in *Gesta Romanorum,* which was translated into French and then by Lawrence Twine into English under the title *The Patterne of Painefull Aduentures* in 1607. Gower and Twine, in turn, are the principal sources of Shakespeare's *Pericles.* The Apollonius story has a wider significance for the whole area of Shakespeare's romances, however. It is so characteristic a piece of romance narrative that we should examine its plot in some detail before we see how it relates to a number of the plays:

Antiochus, king of Antioch, has a beautiful daughter who is sought by many suitors. Antiochus himself falls in love with her; he rapes her and she accepts the incestuous relationship. Suitors for her are required to answer a riddle based on the daughter's situation or lose their heads; presumably any who answered it correctly would also lose their heads. Apollonius, a prince of Tyre, makes the attempt and successfully solves the riddle. Antiochus, however, tells him he has failed but may return in a month and try again. Apollonius returns home but Antiochus sends his steward after him to kill him. Apollonius realizes his danger and flees in a ship richly laden with gold and food supplies. Apollonius arrives at Tarsus, where he encounters a fellow Tyrian named Hellanicus who remains faithful to him; Apollonius finds a famine at Tarsus, which he is able to relieve with his cargo; the city gratefully erects a monument to him. He departs on his wanderings, but is shipwrecked on the shore of Pentapolis, where he is aided by a fisherman. He goes to the gymnasium, where he wins the favor of Archestrates, the king, who invites him to dinner. There the king's daughter meets him, falls in love with him and secures him as her music teacher. Three of her persistent suitors demand that she choose among them. Archestrates sends to her (she is in bed suffering from lovesickness) by Apollonius to get her answer. She replies to her father that she will take the shipwrecked one, who is finally recognized to be Apollonius. The king is pleased, dismisses the three suitors, and proceeds to marry his daughter to Apollonius. After some months, when Apollonius's wife is pregnant, he learns that Antiochus and his daughter have been struck by lightning while in bed and that the kingdom is being held for Apollonius, his successor. He hastens to leave, but his wife is unwilling to stay behind even though her time of delivery approaches. She takes with her a nurse, Lycoris. In a storm at sea she gives birth to a daughter and is thought to have died in childbirth. She is put into a waterproof chest and cast into the sea. The chest drifts ashore at Ephesus, where she is revived by a physician, Chaeremon, or rather, by one of his assistants. Her identity is revealed by documents and by the gold left in the chest with her, and she is put into the charge of the priestesses of Diana at Ephesus.

Apollonius meanwhile turns his course to Tarsus, where he leaves his daughter and her nurse in charge of his old friends there, providing amply for her education. He vows not to cut his hair or fingernails until he gives his daughter in marriage, and departs for Egypt to be a merchant. Tarsia, the daughter, grows up to be beautiful and accomplished, but her foster-mother is jealous because she so far outshines her own daughter, and orders a slave to kill her. When he is about to do so, pirates appear and take her away. They take her to Mytilene, where she is sold at auction to a brothel keeper who outbids the prince, Athenagoras, but who promises him the privilege of being her first customer. He, and all succeeding customers, are overwhelmed by Tarsia's appeals and she retains her virginity. Finally she is adopted by Athenagoras.

Apollonius finally returns to Tarsus to claim his daughter, but is told by the false foster parents that she died. He goes into deep mourning and sets off for Tyre. The ship is blown off course, however, and finds haven at Mytilene. There Athenagoras encounters him, learns from the sailors that his name is Apollonius, recalls that Tarsia had said that was her father's name, and sends her to minister to him in his melancholy. She makes several attempts, on one of which he strikes her down, but finally her account of her life makes him recognize her as his long-lost daughter. After a touching reunion, he gives her in marriage to Athenagoras.

He sets sail for home, but is warned in a dream to go to Ephesus to the temple of Diana and there to tell his story. He takes his daughter and son-in-law with him; his narrative prompts the revelation of his wife as the chief priestess of Diana and the happy reunion of husband, wife and daughter. Apollonius then goes to Tarsus, punishes the false foster parents by having them stoned to death, and continues on to Pentapolis, where he has a reunion with his father-in-law Archestrates and shows him his long-lost daughter and his granddaughter. He also rewards the fisherman who had come to his aid and the faithful Hellanicus who helped him in Tarsus. At the death of Archestrates he and his wife inherit the throne, which he passes on to a son. He ends his life happily as ruler of Antioch and Tyre.[2]

Now this story had a direct influence on Shakespeare in two of his plays, the early *Comedy of Errors* for the plot of "hapless Ægeon," and of course in the late romance *Pericles*, through the channel of Gower and of Twine's *Pattern of Painful Adventures.* But the reader of Shakespeare's romances will notice that there are also relationships with other plays. This plot deals with separated parents and children; so do *Cymbeline, The Winter's Tale,* and, in a way, *The Tempest.* In this story there is a shipwrecked hero with whom a princess falls in love, just as Miranda falls in love with the shipwrecked Ferdinand in *The Tempest*. An important turn in the plot results from a warning given in a dream or vision; the same statement can be made about *Cymbeline, The Winter's Tale,* and *The Tempest*. Here we read how a queen, supposedly dead, is found to be alive and is reunited with her husband and daughter; what else is this but the conclusion of *The Winter's Tale?*

The Winter's Tale, as we know, is a dramatization of Greene's *Pandosto*. But, as Geopp has shown, there is "striking similarity between the Leontes-Hermione-Perdita-Florizel story and the corresponding Apollonius-Archestrate-Tharsia-Athenagoras pattern."[3] The four points of correspondence Goepp finds are the following:

1. The hero's relation to his family. (The motivation is different.)
2. The disappearing wife, supposed dead.
3. The heroine (Tharsia-Perdita) is ordered slain, escapes, finds a lover, is reunited with her parents. (In *Pandosto* the mother really dies; not in Shakespeare.)
4. There are traces of a second incest-motif, besides the Antiochus one; Pandosto woos his own daughter, not knowing who she is; there are traces of the same situation in the Apollonius plot. (Shakespeare of course suppresses this part of Greene.)

Moreover, it is clear that Shakespeare knew other romances which are related to the Apollonius saga. Some of these constitute part of the Constance legend. They deal with an accused queen; the most prominent version in English is Chaucer's *Man of Law's Tale*.

One of the versions of the Constance legend which there is reason to believe Shakespeare knew is *Valentine and Orson*. It was popular as a romance, and a man almost Shakespeare's contemporary, Robert Ashley the translator, said that he read it as a boy.[4] A pageant on the subject had been part of the coronation ceremonies of Edward VI in 1547. There was at least one play, and there may have been several, based on the story, acted in the popular theater during Shakespeare's active life in London. One was played by the Queen's Men and entered in The Stationers' Register in 1595. It may or may not be the basis for the play by Hathway and Munday played by the Admiral's Men in 1598. And a play by the Queen's Men was licensed to William White on March 31, 1600.

The Valentine and Orson story goes as follows:

The sister of King Pepin is accused of adultery and banished by her husband. Her twin sons are exposed; one is carried off by a wild beast and the other, his parentage unknown, is brought up at court and called Valentin. His brother, Orson, grows up in the forest as a wild man. Eventually Valentin fights and conquers him, but they become companions and set out to find Valentin's parents. Valentin has become a champion warrior and is beloved by King Pepin's daughter, but he modestly declines because of his uncertain birth. The brothers seek to rescue a captive maiden who can only be won by a prince who has never been suckled by a woman. The wild Orson qualifies and marries the maiden. The brothers fight against the Saracens on their father's side. Their birth, their relationship, and the whereabouts of their mother (she is held captive by a giant) are revealed to them by supernatural means in a castle. Valentin marries the lady of the castle. The two brothers proceed to rescue their mother; her name is cleared and the family is reunited.[5]

The idea of wolves or bears suckling children was clearly in Shakespeare's mind when he wrote *(Winter's Tale* II. iii. 185 ff.):

> Come on, poor babe.
> Some powerful spirit instruct the kites and ravens
> To be thy nurses! Wolves and bears, they say,
> Casting their savageness aside, have done
> Like offices of pity.

Of course he may have thought of the legend of Romulus and Remus for the wolf as nurse, but this image may have been coupled in his mind with a recollection of the bear as nurse in Valentine and Orson.[6]

Dickson thinks that absolute proof that Shakespeare knew Valentine and Orson comes from *Macbeth.* Two motifs are especially similar; a murderer entering a bedchamber to commit a murder, fearing to do it and leaving the knife there, and the banquet scene, which is not in Shakespeare's main source, Holinshed. "Like Spenser, Shakespeare remembered particularly from our story the figure of the wild Orson, and transmuted by his imagination, it became the ghost of Banquo."[7]

The point here is that Shakespeare's environment was full of legend and folktales which supplied the stuff of romance to him. It had long done so.

Shakespeare's knowledge of lost plays or of folktales which he heard rather than read cannot of course be documented in the usual way sources are documented. But the manner in which he altered some of his sources sometimes points very clearly to influence from romance material. An example is the pseudo-Clement, which dates from the second century A.D. One of the irrelevant stories told about St. Clement can be summarized as follows:

He had two elder brothers, Faustus and Faustinius, who were identical twins. Their mother was importuned by the advances of her brother-in-law. To escape from him without accusing him to her husband she went on a journey, taking the twin children with her. The father stayed in Rome with Clement. In a storm at sea the twins were lost and the mother was cast ashore on the island Aradus, where she lived as a beggar-woman, and, later on, with St. Peter's help, went to Laodicea. The twins were rescued by pirates, who gave them different names and sold them. In the course of time — we are not told how it came about — we find them together in prosperity at Laodicea. Many years after their disappearance the father and Clement set off in turn in search of the lost family. Eventually they all meet in Laodicea. Their recognition and reunion ends the story.[8]

Now some details of the *Comedy of Errors* are closer to the pseudo-Clement than to the *Menaechmi:* the twins are separated by a shipwreck, and Ephesus, which is not mentioned in Plautus, is evidently the scene of the romance.[9]

As Miss Trenkner concludes, "Shakespeare found the non-Plautine elements of the *Comedy of Errors* in current tales. By dovetailing these into Plautus' plot, he returned to the primary source from which the Greek original of the *Menaechmi* is derived." It has sometimes seemed mysterious that Shakespeare, in dramatizing Greene's *Pandosto,* could

6

make it more like Greek romance than the original itself. It should not be mysterious if we recall how much of the world of fiction was available to him in folktales and subliterary versions.

The brothel scenes in *Pericles,* which have been said by Raleigh and others to be uniquely Shakespearian, have of course a pretext in the story of Apollonius as told by Gower, but they are greatly elaborated. Miss Trenkner summarizes: "The popular theme of virgins who defend their honour is a common favourite of Greek romance. To accomplish it the heroine pretends to be ill, takes, as she thinks, poison, kills her attacker, or saves herself by courage, and so on. The theme was peculiarly well suited to Christian legend, in which it was easily applied to the characters of the saints. A situation frequent in these stories is that in which the heroine is rescued from a brothel. In Greek romance and in the *controversiae,* as in the legends of saints and in medieval collections and the novelle of the Renaissance, in all of which we find virgins turned over to prostitution, it is invariably virtue which triumphs."[10]

Some of these romantic tales were early dramatized. One such is the legend of Placidas, who after his conversion was Eustachius and became St. Eustace. Listed in the records as "Placy Dacy, alias Saint Eustacy," it was given at Braintree, in Essex, in 1523, 1525 and 1534 to raise money for repairs to the church. The story is briefly this: Placidas, a Roman general, loses the emperor's favor and is forced to flee. On his flight he first loses his wife and then his twin sons, one of whom is carried away by a lion and the other by a wolf. The boys are brought up by peasants in the same village, but they do not know each other. Finally they are united with their father and then find the mother living in poverty. The reunion provides the usual happy ending. The story is chapter CX of *Gesta Romanorum* and is in Caxton's *Golden Legend.* In 1566 appeared John Partridge's *Placidas,* a version of the narrative in pedestrian fourteeners.[11] That there were many such plays is certain. Our difficulty is that many of them have not survived.

The Placidus-Eustace legend has a relative in the first novella of Barnabe Riche's *Farewell to the Military Profession,* a book which we know Shakespeare was familiar with because he used the second story in it as a source for the main plot of *Twelfth Night,* and the fifth may

7

have provided hints for *Merry Wives* and the punishment of Malvolio in *Twelfth Night*.[12]

The story has been summarized as follows:

Sappho, Duke of Mantona, a military leader under the Emperor Claudius, is deprived of his dignities and banished, together with his wife and children. The duke and his small son are separated from his wife and daughter. The son is lost by straying; and the father is reduced to the position of sexton in a village church, where he serves for fifteen years. Sappho is then recalled by the emperor, restored to his former dignities, and made leader of the emperor's force against the Turks. He is victorious in his military campaigns, discovers his wife and daughter, who had supported themselves as seamstresses during the separation, and then, as the judge who is about to pass sentence of death upon a young soldier in his army for having stolen a nobleman's daughter, Sappho identifies the soldier as his lost son. Thus the family is united.[13]

Sappho, and stories like it, were told to illustrate the vagaries of fortune and to encourage the virtue of patience in adversity.

All of these go back directly or indirectly to the *Aethiopica* of Heliodorus, dating from around the third century A.D., or *Clitophon and Leucippe* of Achilles Tatius, or the pastoral *Daphnis and Chloe* attributed to Longus. The first of these was translated in part by James Sanford under the title *The Historie of Chariclea and Theagines Gathered for the most part out of Heliodorus a Greeke Author,* and appended to his amorous and tragical tales out of Plutarch in 1567. Two years later came the complete translation by Thomas Underdowne, called *An Aethiopian Historie, Written in Greek by Heliodorus.* It was republished in 1587, "newly corrected and augmented," and again in 1605. Achilles Tatius was translated as *The Loves of Clitophon and Leucippe* in 1597 by William Burton, the elder brother of Robert Burton, the anatomist of melancholy; he dedicated his translation to the Earl of Southampton, sometime Shakespeare's patron. *Daphnis and Chloe* was translated by Angel Day from the French of Jaques Amyot in 1587. They were all accessible, and they were all popular, both with writers and with readers.

"I may boldely say it because I haue seene it," says Stephen Gosson

8

in 1582, "that the Palace of pleasure, the golden Asse, the Aethiopian historie, Amadis of Fraunce, The Rounde table, baudie Comedies in Latine, French, Italian and Spanish, have beene throughly ransackt to furnish the Playe houses in London."[14] The Greek romances would have been scorned by the enemies of the stage, like Gosson, and they are generally regarded as naive and preposterous works now, hardly worthy of serious literary consideration, but that was not the Elizabethan view. Sidney remarks that Xenophon wrote an absolute heroical poem about Cyrus, and he adds, "So did Heliodorus in his sugred invention of that picture of love in Theagines and Cariclea. And yet both these writ in prose: which I speak to shew, that it is not riming and versing that maketh a poet."[15]

The classicist Ben Jonson, who thought Pericles (which is Apollonius of Tyre) a mouldy tale, recognized that Heliodorus, Achilles Tatius, and Longus constituted the staple of romantic legend:

> The truest Lovers are least fortunate,
> Look all their Lives, and Legends; what they call
> The Lovers' Scriptures — Heliodores or Tatii!
> Longi! Eustathii! Prodromi! you'll find it![16]

That Shakespeare knew the story of Theagenes and Chariclea in some form is evident from a reference in *Twelfth Night:*

> Why should I not (had I the heart to do it),
> Like to th' Egyptian thief at point of death,
> Kill what I Love?
>
> (V. i. 120-22)

He may have known it from the stage. There was a play called *Cariclea,* now lost, presented at Court on Christmas, 1572. In 1578 at Bristol a play called *The Queen of Ethiopa* was acted, and there is some evidence that there was a play by Thomas Dekker called *The White Moor,* also based on the Theagenes and Chariclea story.[17]

The influence of Greek romance on Elizabethan fiction was profound, and where but to Elizabethan fiction was a playwright to go for his material? Walter R. Davis has pointed out that the importance of Greek romance in its effect upon Elizabethan fiction was twofold:

9

that it provided a technique for elaborating plot and providing action and suspense, and that it "reinforced interest in a vision of the world governed purely by chance, time and fortune, a medieval vision to which it brought new intensity and a new direction."[18] There is also a tremendous expansion of space and time, so that the plot is very much fuller of action. William Warner's *Pan His Syrinx* (1584, 1597), which Davis calls "the main example of a full-blown Greek romance in English" presents "a world of chance, in which human purposes are both powerless and irrelevant and action is void of meaning only to reject it." *Pan His Syrinx* retains much of the euphuistic rhetoric which was fashionable in the eighties, but in the second edition, 1597, the author pruned much of it. What Warner added to the set discourses of the Lylian novel was material from the Greek romances, largely Heliodorus. His events are often sensational, not to say decadent. Cannibalism and incest are the spice to episodes of separation of lovers, mistaken identity, recovery of lost children or parents, and reunions after shipwrecks, slavery, and torture.[19]

The principal importer of Greek romance into English fiction was Robert Greene. His *Pandosto: The Triumph of Time,* 1588, provided Shakespeare with the material for *The Winter's Tale,* and the relationship between these two works is discussed in a later chapter. But it needs to be noticed here that Greene was deliberately searching for romance material. S. L. Wolff demonstrated that when he borrowed from Boccaccio, in *Perimides,* for example, he took those stories from his Italian source which were most like Greek romance in motif and perhaps derived from now lost Greek romances.[20]

Greene's *Arbasto* (1584) has as its subtitle *The Anatomie of Fortune.* This sounds as if it is really a romance, though it is still as much the anatomy of love as of fortune. But even to the extent that it is a tale about fortune, there is a special Elizabethan handling of the theme which removes it from the strict area of Greek romance. "The nature of action in a world governed by fortune is not one of pure chance or accident, as in the Greek romances, but rather one of irony, of the constant falsification of expectations and overturn of intentions. Experience does not so much test ideas here, as demonstrate that life, dominated as it is by passion and luck, is absurd."[21]

Menaphon (1589) is usually considered Greene's masterpiece. "He creates interest in plot by beginning *in mediis rebus,* by spacing elements for suspense, and by framing the whole with an obscure oracle announced at the beginning and the end. For once the narrator is unobtrusive, refuses moralizing comment, and lets action and characters speak for themselves. And *Menaphon* is filled with verse — it contains more verse than any other of the romances — and that of high quality. The influence of Greek romance, acquired through or combined with that of Sidney's *Arcadia* (as its running title 'Arcadia, the Reports of the Shepheardes' and its verse suggest), is in part responsible for its excellence, for in it we see imitation of the narrative technique as well as the themes of Heliodorus."[22]

Menaphon is a story of separated spouses, the princess Sephestia and her husband Maximus. Sephestia and her baby son, Pleusidippus, survive shipwreck and are helped by the king's chief shepherd, Menaphon. Sephestia changes her name to Samela and becomes a shepherdess. Menaphon falls in love with her, though Pesana, a shepherdess, is in love with him. Melicertus, another shepherd, falls in love with Samela, too, thinking how like his dead love, Sephestia, she is. Samela wonders if Melicertus can really be a shepherd. These are the ironies.

"Thus Fates and Fortune dallying a doleful Catastrophe, to make a more pleasing Epitazis, it fell out thus." So Greene describes his narrative method. Epitazis, or epitasis, means "that part of a play where the plot thickens."[23] Now of course the plot must be thickened by the passage of time. Pleusidippus at the age of five shows greatness of spirit and qualities of leadership. He is abducted by pirates and taken to Thessaly, where he grows up in court and wins the favor of the princess Olympia. One time there is a debate about which country produces the most beautiful maidens and a courtier who has been there says Arcadia does and shows a portrait of Samela. Pleusidippus falls in love with the picture of his mother and departs for Arcadia. The king of that country, Democles, who has exiled his daughter Sephestia sixteen years before, is now a licentious widower. He hears of the beauty of the shepherdess Samela and disguises himself as a shepherd to pursue her. So we have the situation of the beautiful princess, in disguise as a shepherdess, pursued by her unrecognized fiancé — whom

11

she has already agreed to marry as soon as the oracle at the beginning of the story is fulfilled — by her son, and by her father. There is a siege, and there would be a Sohrab-Rustum combat except that a mysterious stranger reveals the identity of the principals and shows how that all-but-forgotten oracle has been fulfilled; all ends happily. Menaphon, since he cannot have Samela, is content to take Pesana, as Phebe takes Silvius in default of Ganymede in *As You Like It.*

The romances of Lodge and Greene have immediate and obvious relevance to Shakespeare, since he dramatized one of each, but a more profound and interesting relationship is that with Sidney's *Arcadia.* Shakespeare's most direct borrowing from Sidney is of course in the Gloucester plot of *King Lear,* and it may be that the very existence of the late romances flows from that influence. The original version or *Old Arcadia* was probably composed between 1577 and 1580; it was revised at various times before he left for the Netherlands in 1585. No part was published until 1590, but it circulated widely in manuscript and was known to Green and Lodge.

Sidney mixed the genres of heroic and pastoral, of tragic and comic, of prose and verse, in his *Arcadia,* and he gave the whole narrative a five-act structure and a combination of serious main plots and comic subplots. It is not difficult to see why a dramatist would find it interesting.

Sidney praises Heliodorus, it will be recalled, in the *Apologie for Poetrie,* as "Heliodorus in his sugred invention of that picture of love in *Theagenes and Chariclea.*" But Sidney brought into his work a large element from the *Diana* of Montemayor, a highly wrought pastoral-chivalric romance.[24]

The episode of the Paphlagonian king, which Shakespeare took for the subplot of *King Lear,* demands closer attention. Wolff's account of the borrowing goes as follows:

> The first is the episode of the "paphlagonica" or "Galatica" (*Arc.,* II. x, 143^V-146), founded upon Helidorous's story of Claasiris, Petosiris, and Thyamis (*Aeth.,* I. xix; VII. ii, vi, viii, xi): One of two brothers (Petosiris; Plexirtus) by slander usurps the birthright of the other (Thyamis: Leonatus), causes his banishment, and attempts his life. Their father, too, goes into exile. The injured brother

returns to his native country, fights for and regains his birthright, and forgives the usurper. The father also returns, formally invests the true heir with his rights and immediately dies. Sidney added greatly to the point and pathos of Heliodorus's tale by having the King himself turned against the good son and seeking his life; by having the King blinded by the wicked son; and by inventing the passage where the old man begs to be led to the top of a rock that he may end his life by leaping down. Sidney also ministered to the surviving mediaeval and chivalric ideas of his time by making the wicked son a bastard. He thus somewhat recast his original, or at least gave it a tone foreign to Heliodorus. Probably it was this new tone which attracted Shakespeare, who, in the underplot of Gloucester and his sons, in *King Lear,* retained, though with changes again, the features which Sidney added, and added besides, much new matter of his own. The result is a complete transformation of the plot and personages of the Greek Romance. In Shakespeare's underplot, and in the characters of Gloucester, Edgar and Edmund, it is difficult to trace any part of the story as told in the *Aethiopica,* or to recognize the old priest of Memphis and his two sons.[25]

The degee to which Sidney transformed pastoral romance from Montemayor and Greek romance from Heliodorus is not our immediate business, though the fact that he made of this composite genre something more weighty and serious, especially as he revised his *Arcadia,* is naturally of interest to anyone who is trying to trace the ways of Shakespeare's imagination and who finds that an important clue to the late romances lies in *King Lear.* It becomes more and more evident, as the subject is studied, that the *Arcadia* influenced *King Lear* profoundly, not merely in the material for the subplot, but in the main plot as well; not merely in plot, but in image, in thought, and in total meaning. Indeed, it seems that four attitudes toward Providence which are displayed in *King Lear* come from Sidney's *Arcadia.*[26]

What led Shakespeare to select the story of the Paphlagonian king as a subplot to the story of King Lear as told in *The True Chronicle History of King Leir,* Holinshed's *Chronicle,* Spenser's *Faerie Queene,* and *The Mirror for Magistrates* is of critical interest and importance. In no other play does the subplot so intensify the meaning of the main plot. And the answer seems to be that in a way the King in Sidney was another Lear, more like Lear than like Gloucester:

> who (dronke in my affection to that vnlawfull and vnnaturall sonne of mine) suffered myself so to be gouerned by him, that all fauors and punishments passed by him, all offices, and places of importance, distributed to his fauourites; so that ere I was aware, I had left my self nothing but the name of a King: which he shortly wearie of too, with many indignities (if any thing may be called an indignity, which was laid vpon me) threw me out of my seat, and put out my eies; and then (proud in his tyrannie) let me goe, nether imprisoning, nor killing me: but rather delighting to make me feele my miserie; miserie indeed, if euer there were any; full of wretchedness, fuller of disgrace, and fullest of guiltines.[27]

In responding to that very popular book, *The Countess of Pembroke's Arcadia,* Shakespeare was embracing a genre which was to dictate the character of his late plays. As Wolff says, "the reader receives the impression that Sidney has learned the very accent of Greek Romance; once more he feels that Sidney has deliberately written Greek Romance in English."[28]

The vogue of the romantic play is a matter of record, but relatively few of the plays are extant. In the list of thirty known romantic plays of the period 1570-1585, only three survive: *Clyomon and Clamydes, Common Conditions,* and *The Rare Triumphs of Love and Fortune.* From just after this date we have *Mucedorus,* which seems to be, on the basis of printed editions, the most popular Elizabethan play.[29]

Clyomon and Clamydes can be dated only conjecturally, but it probably comes from about 1576. Its earliest edition is 1599, the title page of which states that it has been sundry times acted by her Majesty's players. This presumably refers to the company founded by Walsingham in 1583. It had, then, some vogue over a period of more than twenty years. A passage in the prologue gives some indication of its appeal:

> Wherein the forward chances oft, of Fortune you shall see,
> Wherein the cheerful countenance, of good successes be;
> Wherein true lovers findeth joy, with hugie heaps of care,
> Wherein as well as famous facts, ignomius placed are;

14

Wherein the just reward of both is manifestly shown,
That virtue from the root of vice might openly be known.

The play has some odd similarities with some episodes in Shakespeare's romances.

Bryan Sans-Foy, a cowardly knight, is in love with Juliana, princess of Denmark, who has assigned her lover Clamydes the task of killing a dragon, which he does. But while he is resting, Bryan charms him asleep for ten days, steals his armor and his silver shield and the dragon's head to go to Denmark and claim the princess. (Cloten in *Cymbeline* is a coward who dresses in his successful rival's clothes and goes to seek the lady.) Neronis, the princess whom Clyomon is in love with, is abducted by the king of Norway in disguise as a merchant. She escapes to the forest and wears page's clothing. She finds the grave of Norway, whom Clyomon has killed, and sees Clyomon's arms hung up above it. She naturally thinks it is Clyomon's grave. (So Imogen thinks Cloten's headless body is that of her husband, Posthumus, because the body is dressed in Posthumus' clothes.) Neronis is about to kill herself with Clyomon's sword when Providence descends and makes her read the verses that tell her that Clyomon has killed Norway. (Posthumus is wishing for death when he sleeps and is reconciled to life by a visitation of the ghosts of his parents and of Jupiter, who leaves a prediction with him.) Clyomon finds her dressed as a page as he is going to combat for her. She gives a French name, Coeur-d'Acier (cf. Imogen's du Champ). In another scene Clyomon, the victim of a storm at sea, is put ashore by mariners and is relieved by Neronis (cf. *Pericles*). He will not reveal his name but is known only as the Knight of the Golden Shield.

David Bevington calls the play "a rollicking and professionally acted popular drama." He calculates that it may be played by ten actors, three of them boys, and he supposes that it is elaborate enough in staging to require a permanent London theater. This seems clear enough if the descent and ascent of Providence were performed in the original production.[30]

Clyomon and Clamydes does not rely solely on romantic plot events for its theatrical appeal; there is a Vice called Subtle Shift, the subtlety of whose humor may be judged by his first entrance. He falls backward onto the stage as if he had just pulled himself out of the mud, and he starts to go back into the puddle to retrieve what he thinks is one of his legs, but it is really only his boot.

A play of about the same time, with similar romantic material in it, is *Common Conditions.* It has been thought in the past that the two plays are by the same author, but the recent edition of *Clyomon* by Betty J. Littleton argues persuasively against the attribution (p. 253). The Vice whose name gives the title to *Common Conditions* is much more of an intriguer than Subtle Shift; many of the events are of his contriving, whereas Shift is almost completely a comic character. The play includes an exiled Duke, and his exiled son and daughter, who are separated, he to become a wandering knight, she to be married to a Phrygian prince, wrongly suspected, exiled again, captured by pirates and finally rescued and put under the care of a wealthy knight who is really her father unrecognized. The device of non-recognition is carried further when her brother arrives on the scene, does not recognize her and falls violently in love with her. The play ends inconclusively, with the epilogue explaining that there was insufficient time to proceed further.[31]

The third surviving romantic play is *The Rare Triumphs of Love and Fortune,* which was performed before Queen Elizabeth at Windsor on December 30, 1582, but was not published until 1589. Its plot has been summarized as follows:

> *Love and Fortune* tells of the love of Princess Fidelia for the seeming orphan Hermione, (a man, not a woman as in *The Winter's Tale*) who has been brought up at the court by her father, King Phizantius. Fidelia's rash and boorish brother, Armenio, learning of their lovesuit, provokes trouble and secures the banishment of Hermione. Hermione sends a servant to instruct Fidelia to meet him at a secret place but the plan is betrayed to Armenio who follows her. Fidelia eventually receives hospitality in the cave of Bomelio, a former courtier who was banished by Phizantius because of the calumnies of a faithless friend. The plot proceeds through a series of crude and improbable episodes until the lovers are re-united and the contending parties reconciled.[32]

16

This summary suggests parallels with *Cymbeline,* and Nosworthy believes that Shakespeare knew the play; he guesses that the King's Men considered reviving it, as they did revive *Mucedorus,* and that Shakespeare read it then and remembered it when he wrote *Cymbeline* and again when he wrote *The Tempest.* Bomelio, a hermit who lives in a cave, practices magic; he turns out to be Hermione's father. Interspersed with the romantic material are mythological scenes, particularly at the beginning and the end. These are like an older interlude, *Love and Riches,* performed at Greenwich May 6, 1527.[33]

Mucedorus was revived sometime between 1603 and 1610 and additions by another hand were provided for it. The title page of the first edition, in 1598, calls it *A Most pleasant Comedie of Musedorus the kings sonne of Valentia and Amadine the Kings daughter of Arragon, with the merie conceites of Mouse. Newly set foorth, as it hath bin sundrie times plaide in the honorable Citte of London. Very delectable and full of mirth.* Though it is advertised as a comedy, and though Mouse is a clown rather than a Vice like Subtle Shift or Common Conditions, the material of the play is as much romance as any of the three plays so far considered. Mucedorus disguises himself as a shepherd and saves the heroine from a bear when the villain Segasto, his rival, deserts her and runs away. Segasto gets a military hero, Tremelio, to kill the shepherd, but Musedorus kills him instead and is banished. Amadine is captured by Bremo, a wild man, and again she is rescued by Mucedorus, who kills her captor and discloses himself.

> *Mucedorus:* In tract of time a man may alter much;
> Say, Ladie, doe you know your shepheard well?
> *Amadine:* My Mucedorus! hath he set me free?
> *Mucedorus: Mucedorus* he hath set thee free.
> *Amadine:* And liued so long vnknowne to *Amadine!*

When Mucedorus publicly reveals the fact that he is no shepherd but the son of the King of Valentia, Segasto repents and surrenders his pretensions to Amadine and all ends happily.

Leo Kirschbaum argues that the text of *Mucedorus* which has come down to us is a bad quarto and that it gives no dependable version of what the play itself was actually like.[34] He doubts that there was a revival by the King's Men, the only evidence for which is Jones's title page of 1610. All we can be sure of is that there was a revival by some company between 1603 and 1610. In any event, the play was fantastically popular with the *reading* public, seventeen editions having been published, more than any other play of the period. George F. Reynolds[35] points out that the popularity of the play dates from its revival by the King's Men in 1610; reasons for its popularity are the parallel popularity of Sidney's *Arcadia,* the merry conceits of the clown, Mouse, and perhaps the novelty of having the part of the bear taken by a real bear. On the question of the source of the play, Reynolds says "it may also be in point to notice the growing popularity of the *Arcadia,* since it does give in unconsecutive passages amounting to about 500 words the basic situation of *Mucedorus.* In it Mucedorus disguised as a shepherd rescues the princess Pamela from 'a horrible foul bear' (shortly before the first eclogue) and much later elopes with her."[36]

J. C. Maxwell suggests that the author of Acts I and II of *Pericles* may be the same as the author of the additions in the 1610 Quarto of *Mucedorus.* This is a most interesting idea; if it could be shown to be true, the whole story of Shakespeare, the King's Men, and the revival of old romantic plays (and Shakespeare's authorship of new ones) would become clearer.[37]

The recent full study of the late plays and their relation to the tradition is Carol Gesner's *Shakespeare and the Greek Romance: A Study of Origins* (Lexington, Kentucky, 1970). Miss Gesner devotes a chapter to the Greek romances themselves, a chapter to the continental tradition, then one to the derived tradition as it can be seen to influence the earlier plays, and finally two chapters on "Shakespeare's Greek Romances," by which are meant *Pericles, Cymbeline, The Winter's Tale,* and *The Tempest.*

In *Pericles,* she finds, Shakespeare and his collaborator used two versions of the Apollonius story, that in Gower's *Confessio Amantis* and that in Twine's *Painful Adventures.* All this has been well known for some time, but Miss Gesner sees the combination as strengthening the concentration of Greek romance elements. "Thus *Pericles,*" she says, "drawing upon both Gower and Twine, unites the two versions of romance which during the Middle Ages developed independently, probably from the same classical source" (p. 88). She notices that Shakespeare's work is different from what he had done earlier, and that the old Apollonius story has been transformed: "By use of the archaic romance materials with their inevitable circular movement from prosperity and well-being through adversity to joy and prosperity again — a stringing out of events which seem to end where they began rather than the development of plot out of character — he has infused the play with an air of oft-repeated ceremony and ritual, giving it the tone of old myth, the quality of pageant and spectacle reenacting the predictable cycles of life" (p. 88).

Cymbeline has of course a more complicated background, since its material is drawn from more than two sources. She finds that all three elements of the *Cymbeline* plot are related to Greek romance: the wager story with Imogen's troubles, the kidnapped princes, and the war with Rome. The links with Chariton, Xenophon of Ephesus, and Longus are, she thinks, indirect, but she finds less distance between the play and Greek romance in the case of Achilles Tatius and Heliodorus. "There seems to be evidence that Shakespeare gathered materials directly from the *Aethiopica* in writing *Cymbeline,* and it is logical to conclude that he derived them from the very widely read translation of Thomas Underdowne" (p. 98). If *Cymbeline* is viewed as Shakespeare's attempt to write a Heliodoran romance, several problems in the understanding of the play can be cleared up. Imogen and Posthumus are "married" by hand-fasting, but the marriage has not been consummated; this is like Chariclea and Theogenes, who are married but vow to preserve their virginity until she is restored to her parents.[38] The comic banter between Posthumus and his jailers and the oracular dream in V. iv is the stuff of Greek romance. The wager plot, the striking of the heroine, the mysterious submission to Rome even after the English have won the battle — all these are standard fare in Heliodorus. In essence, she says that only the Holinshed materials cannot be called Greek romance. But even then, a shadowy historical background for the love story was traditional, and what so obvious as a source for that as Holinshed, from which the historical material for *King Lear* was taken?

In *The Winter's Tale* Shakespeare was dramatizing Greene's *Pandosto,* so there is no need to search for other sources. But the interesting thing is that Shakespeare, when he deviated from his source, did so in the direction of the Greek romances. The most obvious example is the keeping of Hermione alive, instead of having her really die, as Greene does with his Bellaria.

S. L. Wolff claimed as long ago as 1910 that Longus' *Daphnis and Chloe* was a source for the pastoral episode in *The Winter's Tale.* Miss Gesner follows him and also claims that it is a source for *The Tempest.* Ariel's appearance as a water nymph, the storm, and the marriage masque in Act IV, all look as if they came from Longus, not, she thinks, in Angel Day's English version, but in the French of Jaques Amyot. In summary, "It is in *Pericles, Cymbeline, The Winter's Tale,* and *The Tempest* that we finally see the ancient genre deliberately utilized and lifted to new dimensions, turned from a rather inconsequential literature of escape to a new vision of reality, a vision created artistically by moving from the world of reality to a world of romance, wherein the compound of primitive Greek materials and the psychological crudity and immaturity of the genre make possible, when combined with great poetic power of expression, symbolic interpretation of the characters and events" (p. 140).

Whether this symbolic interpretation was Shakespeare's or is merely the fancy of modern critics will be the subject of a later chapter. But there can be no disagreement about the pervasive atmosphere of romance in the dramatic and literary milieu in which Shakespeare worked. He breathed it. There is no puzzle as to why Shakespeare wrote *Pericles, Cymbeline, The Winter's Tale,* and *The Tempest.* It would have been passing strange if he had not.

Chapter 2

INNOCENCE AND THE PASTORAL
WORLD

The idealized country of Arcadia, a product of the imagination of
Virgil,[1] was partly a matter of landscape and partly a matter of manners and morals. The most eminent of the Greek romances, *Daphnis
and Chloe,* contributes a setting:

> It was the beginning of spring, and all the flowers of the lawns,
> meadows, valleys and hills were now blowing. All was fresh and
> green. Now was there humming of bees, and chanting of melodious
> birds, and skipping of newborn lambs; the bees hummed in the
> meadows, the birds warbled in the groves, the lambs skipped on the
> hills. And now, when such a careless joy filled those blest and happy
> fields, Daphnis and Chloe, as delicate and young folks will, would
> imitate the pleasant things they heard and saw. Hearing how the
> birds did chant it, they began to carol too, and seeing how the lambs
> skipped, tripped their light and nimble measures. Then, to emulate
> the bees, they fell to cull the fairest flowers, some of which in toysome
> sport they cast in one another's bosoms, and some platted garlands
> for the nymphs.[2]

A later example is equally idealized. It is from Boccaccio's *Genealogy of the Pagan Gods:*

> There the beeches stretch themselves, with other trees, toward heaven; there they spread a thick shade with their fresh green foliage; there the earth is covered with grass and dotted with flowers of a thousand colors; there, too, are clear fountains and argent brooks that fall with a gentle murmur from the mountain's breast. There are gay song-birds, and the boughs stirred to a soft sound by the wind, and playful little animals; and there are the flocks and the herds, the shepherd's cottage or the little hut untroubled with domestic cares; and all is filled with peace and quiet. Then, as these pleasures possess both eye and ear, they soothe the soul; then they collect the scattered energies of the mind, and renew the power of the poet's genius, if it be weary, prompting it, as it were, to longed-for contemplation of high themes, and yearn for expression.[3]

Finally, there is the well-known description of the country in Sidney's *Arcadia:*

> There were hills which garnished their proud heights with stately trees; humble valleys whose base estate seemed comforted with refreshing of silver rivers; meadows enameled with all sorts of eye-pleasing flowers; thickets, which being lined with most pleasant shade, were witnessed so to by the cheerful deposition of many well-tuned birds; each pasture stored with sheep feeding with sober security, while the pretty lambs with bleating oratory craved the dam's comfort. Here was a shepherd boy piping as though he never would be old; there a young shepherdess knitting and withal singing, and it seemed her voice comforted her hands to work and her hands kept time to voice's music.[4]

Despite the idealized conditions of the green world, the forest, the mountains of Wales, or the sheep farms of Bohemia, all was not perfect there. Refinement, gentility, civility — the virtues of court or city — were lacking, as were of course the attendant vices. Orlando is surprised when he finds that the banished Duke offers him hospitality and gentleness:

Speak you so gently? Pardon me, I pray you.
I thought that all things had been savage here.

(*AYLI* II. vii. 106-07)

Imogen, in disguise as a page, draws a sword, as Orlando does, to reinforce her demand for food in the Welsh mountains (*Cymbeline* III. vi. 25). The natives there were considered rude and wild; they were said to mutilate the bodies of their slain enemies, or even worse, their women committed this atrocity (*I Henry IV* I. i. 38-46). Olivia, commenting on the brawling of her uncle, Sir Toby, says he is "Fit for the mountains and the barbarous caves / Where manners ne'er were preach'd."[5]

Of course there were contrasting examples. People living in the wilds may well be gentle if they have gentle blood. Guiderius and Arviragus, the princes who suppose themselves to be Welsh youths named Polydore and Cadwal, have "honor untaught, / civility not seen from other" (*Cymbeline* IV. ii. 178-79). And Orlando, though he had been denied a polite and gentle education by his brother, was somehow "inland bred" and instinctively knew the values of civilized life. Of course, as the debate between Touchstone and Corin shows, the manners of one world are not appropriate to the other, though civil, humane behavior is to be applauded, even in the wilds.

Madeleine Doran well sums up Shakespeare's position:

> Nothing suggests that Shakespeare is a cultural primitivist.... This theme of civilized man, both in his own nature and in his relation to other men, is one of Shakespeare's most persistent themes, variously presented. Sometimes the terms are "Nature" and "art" (as in *Love's Labour's Lost* and *The Winter's Tale, Cymbeline* and *The Tempest*) ...sometimes (as in *As You Like It, The Winter's Tale* and *The Tempest*) the court and "the green world." But these terms are by no means interchangeable parts; the terms alter as the focus shifts. If Shakespeare appears to be on the side of "naturalists" against the "artsmen," he is not therefore on the side of primitive rudeness against civilization.[6]

In this pastoral world there may be wild beasts, who are under no controls except those of nature; the clown in *The Winter's Tale* knows that bears are only curst (fierce) when they are hungry, and even the courtly people in *As You Like It* are familiar enough with lions to know that "'tis / The royal disposition of that beast / To prey on nothing that doth seem as dead." And there are pirates, in *Daphnis and Chloe,* in *Pericles,* and in many other romances. There may be villains, escaped from the court circle somehow, often in pursuit of someone, like Cloten in the Welsh mountains in *Cymbeline.* But whatever else there is, there must be an innocent heroine.

"Shakespeare's heroines," one critic has said,

> may be roughly divided into two types, the independent, princessly young women who take positive action, like Rosalind; and the very young, helpless, innocent, like Perdita, and, above all, Miranda. It is not unreasonable to see here the two main types of heroine; one, the "modern," a woman fertile in resource and response, something of a help-meet (rather like Milton's Eve, a ripe woman); the other, the "medieval" heroine, who is, even in her physical charm, a very young girl. The childlike innocence, gaiety, and helplessness of the "medieval" heroine call forth a response far different from that aroused by the "modern" heroine. The early heroine is not an equal, not a mate. She is above her worshippers and yet, in a sense, because she is passive and needs protection, she is inferior to them. Child and divinity, she links in us two sets of feelings less often combined in later literature, the feelings both of Prospero and Ferdinand: the desire to cherish and protect, the desire to reverence and worship. Although there is here no question of physical type, Miranda may well be said to represent the essential appeal of the earlier heroine, her youth, purity, gaiety — a precious symbol of an early, innocent, fresh world, a symbol more powerful in the mind of earlier centuries than it is in ours.[7]

It is this fading of the image that leads such critics as H. B. Charlton to dismiss the general run of romance heroines as "charming nonentities."[8] But Shakespeare was modifying the character of his heroines in his earlier comedies in the direction of the romance heroine. Viola in *Twelfth Night,* for example, "has none of the vehement determination of the Italian heroine (of the sources). . . . She foreshadows

Perdita and Miranda in the romantically adolescent quality of her part."[9]

It has often been said that Shakespeare may well have been influenced by the heroines of Greene's plays as well as his prose romances, and, since there has been some critical confusion on this subject, a brief look at Greene's innocent heroines may be profitable. The two major ones are Margaret, the keeper's daughter of Fressingfield in *Friar Bacon and Friar Bungay* (1589-92) and Dorothea in *James IV* (1590-91). Margaret is described by the Prince of Wales after he has fallen in love with her:

> When as she swept like Venus through the house,
> And in her shape fast folded up my thoughts,
> Into the milkhouse went I with the maid,
> And there amongst the cream bowls she did shine
> As Pallas 'mongst her princely husewifery.
> She turn'd her smock over her lily arms
> And dived them into milk to run her cheese;
> But, whiter than the milk, her crystal skin,
> Checked with lines of azure, made her blush,
> That art or nature durst bring for compare.[10]

She surprises Lacy, Earl of Lincoln, into confessing his true identity when he has been masking as a farmer's son:

> *Lacy:* The Earl of Lincoln! Why, it cannot be.
> *Margaret:* Yes, very well, my lord, for you are he.
> The keeper's daughter took you prisoner.
> Lord Lacy, yield; I'll be your jailer once.[11]

When she receives the earl's proposal she is charmingly modest:

> *Lacy:* I meant, fair girl, to make thee Lacy's wife.
> *Margaret:* I little think that earls will stoop so low.
> *Lacy:* Say, shall I make thee countess ere I sleep?
> *Margaret:* Handmaid unto the earl, so please himself;
> A wife in name, but servant in obedience.[12]

She offers her own life in place of Lacy's when the prince threatens him with death, and says she will not outlive him anyway:

25

> *Margaret:* Why, thinks King Henry's son that Margaret's love
> Hangs in the uncertain balance of proud time,
> That death shall make a discord of our thoughts?
> No; stab the earl, and fore the morning sun
> Shall vaunt him thrice over the lofty east,
> Margaret will meet her Lacy in the heavens.[13]

When Lacy sends her a letter falsely asserting that the King has ɔrdered him to marry a noble lady instead, she first denounces Ate, who wraps Fortune in her snaky locks, then the stars, and, in a reply to a request for an answer, says she will go to Framingham to be a nun. When Lacy appears and tells her the letter was only sent to test her, she first says she must keep her vow, then gives up in a maidenly way:

> *Margaret:* The flesh is weak. My lord doth know it well,
> That when he comes with his enchanting face,
> Whatso'er betide, I cannot say him nay.
> Off goes the habit of a maiden's heart;
> And, seeing Fortune will, fair Framingham,
> And all the show of holy nuns, farewell.
> Lacy for me, if he will be my lord.[14]

A recent commentary on Greene admits Margaret's charm but says she is a failure as a character on two counts. In the first place, she is a milkmaid, a keeper's daughter, but "at moments Greene seems to forget her English simplicity and makes her acquainted with the classics"; in the second place, she is not intended to be stupid, but her tame submission to Lacy's cruelty, in the Griselda tradition, makes her unbelievable as a character. As for the first of these charges, simple maids in Arcadias who are destined for higher rank know their appropriate classical stories. Witness Perdita, whose foster-father and foster-brother do not suggest a household permeated by classical learning, but she can refer to Proserpina and Dis, Juno, Cytherea and Phoebus with easy familiarity.[15]

As for the second objection, it can perhaps be answered in the words of Daniel Seltzer:

No realistic motivation [for the sending of Lacy's letter] would have been necessary, for Greene's audiences would have found the logical emphasis where it in fact occurs, in Margaret's response. Unlike those Elizabethan and Jacobean plays in which the testing of the Griselda figure is motivated by a cynically realistic view of the world . . . the testing of fidelity in pastoral tragicomedy simply reinforces the natural nobility of the lady of low station — whether she is actually a country girl or a real princess disguised as a shepherdess. The testing is therefore a hyperbolic statement of a character already perceived by the audience, and although suspense is not removed by making the threat to constancy too feeble, the test and its results, on all levels of action, prove the lady worthy of noble love.[16]

Dorothea, the much-wronged heroine of *James IV,* is also felt to to be an incredible paragon by Kenneth Muir: "Even if we make due allowances for the belief in the theory of wild oats and for the medieval (and Elizabethan) admiration for Patient Griseldas, such facile forgiveness, such inhuman lack of resentment, takes away from the reality of the characters. She shrinks into pasteboard."[17] Dorothea's husband, King James, is unfaithful to her, but her defence of him is his youth:

Ah, Douglas, thou misconstrest his intent,
He doth but tempt his wife, he tryes my loue:
This iniurie pertaines to me, not to you.
The King is young; and if he step awrie,
He may amend, and I will loue him still.
Should we disdaine our vines because they sprout
Before their time? or young men, if they straine
Beyond their reach? no; vines that bloom and spread
Do promise fruites, and young men that are wilde
In age grow wise.[18]

He tries to get her murdered; her father, the English king, hearing that she has been murdered, invades Scotland to revenge his daughter's death. Lady Anderson, who has nursed her back to health, advises her to join her father, but she replies

27

Ah, Ladie, so wold wordly counsell work;
But constancie, obedience, and my loue,
In that my husband is my Lord and Chiefe,
These call me to compassion of his estate:
Dissuade me not, for vertue will not change.

This is, one must admit, incredible. But Greene, like the Shakespeare he called an upstart crow who imagined himself the only shake-scene in a country, presents the incredible and has a character comment on its incredibility. Lady Anderson says:

What woonderous constancie is this I heare!
If English dames their husbands loue so deer,
I feare me in the world they haue no peere.[19]

In Shakespeare's world of Bohemia, Perdita is the model of innocence. At the sheepshearing feast she is in costume, but she feels self-conscious about it, and declares that she would swoon if she saw herself in a mirror (IV. iv. 14). When she is drawn, by her own rhapsody on spring flowers, to an expression of physical love for Florizel, she blushes and apologizes:

Methinks I play as I have seen them do
In Whitsun pastorals. Sure this robe of mine
Does change my disposition.

(VI. iv. 133-35)

And it is Perdita who tells her brother to forewarn Autolycus to use no scurrilous words in his tunes (IV. iv. 215).

Shakespeare's audience would assume that a sheepshearing feast, like a Whitsun pastoral, involved at least some atmosphere of the bawdy, and the servant reflects this when he naively says that Autolycus' song is "without bawdry, which is strange." The comic irony is that of course the audience knew the words to "Whoop, do me no harm, good man" and were well aware that it was a ribald song.

Perdita's world is contrasted with the courtly world, which her foster-father somehow knows of as "getting wenches with child, wronging the ancientry, stealing, fighting," and where waiting-gentlewomen are involved in "some stair-work, some trunk-work, some behind-door-work" (III. iii. 59-75). She is virginal and shrewd; her maidenly modesty might make her mistrust Florizel's flattery were it not that he has been shown to be an unstained shepherd, not a courtier. Perdita has been likened to Pastorella in the sixth book of *The Faerie Queene*. Pastorella is described by Spenser as follows:

> And soothly sure she was full fayre of face,
>   And perfectly well shapt in euery lim,
>   Which she did more augment with modest grace,
>   And comely carriage of her count'nance trim,
>   That all the rest like lesser lamps did dim:
>   Who her admiring as some heauenly wight,
>   Did for their soueraine goddesse her esteeme,
>   And caroling her name both day and night,
> The fayrest *Pastorella* her by name did hight.
>
> Ne was there heard, ne was there shepheards swayne
>   But her did honour, and eke many a one
>   Burnt in her loue, and with sweet pleasing payne
>   Full many a night for her did sigh and grone:
>   But most of all the shepheard *Coridon*
>   For her did languish, and his deare life spend;
>   Yet neigher she for him, nor other none
>   Did care a whit, ne any liking lend:
> Though meane her lot, yet higher did her mind ascend.[20]

Both Pastorella and Perdita are foundlings, brought up by shepherds, loved by a knight or prince who assumes a shepherd's role to succeed as a suitor, and finally restored to their parents. Both are also, amid much wickedness, the innocent ones.

Rosalind, in her Arden, was only a visitor. She could mock lovers and world-weary travellers and even her own exiled father because she was secure, once she knew that the man she had fallen in love

29

with was in love with her. Songs of experience were her music, not songs of innocence.

Perdita's most splendid speech is the focus of her innocence:

> O Prosperina,
> For the flow'rs now, that, frighted, thou let'st fall
> From Dis's waggon! daffadils,
> That come before the swallow dares, and take
> The winds of March with beauty; violets, dim,
> But sweeter than the lids of Juno's eyes
> Or Cytherea's breath; pale primeroses,
> That die unmarried, ere they can behold
> Bright Phoebus in his strength (a malady
> Most incident to maids); bold oxlips, and
> The crown imperial; lilies of all kinds,
> The flow'r-de-luce being one!
>
> (IV. iv. 116-27)

Here are the fused elements of virginity, fragility, beauty and maidenly modesty. What in moral terms would be called innocence has been translated into the poetry of flowers and of classical mythology.

Shakespeare's imagination associated flowers with strewing them on a grave (cf. Ophelia in her mad scene). In his earlier romance, *Pericles*, his lost heroine, Marina, makes her first grown-up appearance strewing flowers over her nurse's grave:

> No; I will rob Tellus of her weed,
> To strow thy green with flowers. The yellows, blues,
> The purple violets, and marigolds
> Shall as a carpet hang upon thy grave
> While summer days doth last. Ay me! poor maid,
> Born in a tempest when my mother died,
> The world to me is a lasting storm,
> Whirring me from my friends.
>
> (IV. i. 13-20)

Perdita's flower speech derives from this, and, though there is no reason in the plot for mentioning graves (as there is in *Pericles*) the association persists:

30

O, these I lack,
To make you garlands of, and my sweet friend,
To strew him o'er and o'er!
Florizel: What, like a corse?
Perdita: No, like a bank, for love to lie and play on
Not like a corse; or if — not to be buried,
But quick and in mine arms.

(IV. iv. 127-32)

Dr. Jenijoy LaBelle has discovered another source, which she kindly communicated to me: "Perdita's flower speech derives from Marina's speech in *Pericles,* but it also derives from Autolycus's opening song in the preceding scene:

Autolycus: When *daffadils* begin to peer,
With heigh! the doxy over the dale!
Why, then *comes* in the *sweet* o' the year;
For the red blood reigns in the winter's *pale.*

(IV. iii. 1-4)

Perdita: *daffadils,*
That *come* before the swallow dares, and take
The winds of March with beauty; violets, dim,
But *sweeter* than the lids of Juno's eyes
Or Cytherea's breath; *pale* primeroses ...

(IV. iv. 118-22)

The same four words are used in both passages and in precisely the same order. In Autolycus's song are the fused elements of lechery, heartiness, and bravado. All that is fragile in Perdita's speech is made earthy in his: the sweet breath of a goddess becomes the red blood of a wench: dying unmarried is replaced with tumbling in the hay. This multiplicity of points of view is one of the distinguished characteristics of Shakespeare's imagination."

Related to both the *Pericles* and *The Winter's Tale* passages is another in *Cymbeline,* which comes between them in date. It is the comment of Arviragus on the supposedly dead Fidele.

With fairest flowers
While summer lasts and I live here, Fidele,
I'll sweeten thy sad grave. Thou shalt not lack
The flower that's like thy face, pale primrose, nor
The azur'd harebell, like thy veins; no, nor
The leaf of eglantine, whom not to slander,
Out-sweet'ned not thy breath.

(IV. ii. 218-24)

Here the innocent heroine is not the speaker of the lines but the subject of them, and Shakespeare saw the incongruity of putting such a speech into the mouth of a rugged young hunter-warrior, so he had the speaker's brother say

Prithee have done;
And do not play in wench-like words with that
Which is so serious.

(IV. ii. 229-31)

The only innocent heroine who is not shown in some kind of Arcadia is Marina, and her innocence is demonstrated in the opposite way, by showing her in a brothel.[21] The contrast between a young woman "enskyed and sainted" and a corrupt environment had been exploited in *Measure for Measure,* where the innocence of a novice nun, Isabella, is set against the foil of Vienna stews and prisons. Marina, like Desdemona before her, does not even understand some of the language used to her. Somehow the central symbol of *Pericles,* "the world to me is a lasting storm, / Whirring me from my friends," allows only the flower speech as a hint of the pastoral world.

The storm and the simple environment, the opposite of the court, are combined in *The Tempest.* And here, on the enchanted island, Shakespeare can present the most innocent of his heroines, Miranda. Her education has been entirely at her father's knees, and she has only the faintest memory of any other life. She has the confidence of the truly innocent — she would sin to think but nobly of her grandmother: "good wombs have borne bad sons." She cares nothing for compari-

sons between Ferdinand and other men; when her father teasingly
suggests that "To th' most of men this is a Caliban, / And they to him
are angels" she replies "my affections are then most humble. / I have
no ambitions to see a goodlier man" (I. ii. 481-83). Yet her enthusi-
asm is not exclusive. When she sees the court party, she exclaims

> O wonder!
> How many goodly creatures are there here!
> How beauteous mankind is! O brave new world
> That has such people in't!
>
> (V. i. 181-84)

Her father drily remarks " 'Tis new to thee," but this is not to imply that innocence is invalidated by experience. The play called
The Tempest concludes with calm seas, auspicious gales and sails so
expeditious that they will reunite the denizens of the enchanted island
with the royal fleet and the normal world.

Such innocence as Miranda's, which comes from isolation from a
world where Antonios and Sebastians are more common than Gon-
zalos, is also a perquisite of childhood, and it is thought of in a pastoral figure as Polixenes describes the boyhood of Leontes and himself
in an early scene of *The Winter's Tale:*

> We were as twinn'd lambs that did frisk i' th' sun,
> And bleat the one at th' other. What we chang'd
> Was innocence for innocence; we knew not
> The doctrine of ill-doing, nor dream'd
> That any did. (I. ii. 67-71)

Shakespeare returns to this theme in the second scene of *Two Noble
Kinsmen,* where he needs to blacken Creon and yet save, in the eyes
of the audience, his two nephews, Palamon and Arcite. Arcite proposes that they escape from the evil environment they are in:

> Dear Palamon, dearer in love than blood,
> And our prime cousin, yet unhard'ned in
> The crimes of nature — let us leave the city
> Thebes and the temptings in't before we further
> Sully our gloss of youth.
>
> (I. ii. 1-5)

After some discussion of the question whether one must necessarily lose one's virtue in an environment of sin, the two young men agree that the source of all the evil in Thebes is their uncle, Creon. Accordingly, Arcite again proposes that they leave the court for the country:

> Clear-spirited cousin,
> Let's leave his court, that we may nothing share
> Of his loud infamy; for our milk
> Will relish of the pasture, and we must
> Be vile, or disobedient — not his kinsmen
> In blood unless in quality.

(I. ii. 74-79)

Yet the innocence of Palamon and Arcite will shortly be changed to that different stage, where sexual attraction makes a kind of lapse into maturity, as it did for Polixenes and Leontes. So the theme is transferred to Emilia, and she, like Polixenes, relates it as a narrative of the past — her childhood friendship with "the maid Flavina":

>   but I
> And she (I sigh and spoke of) were things innocent,
> Lov'd for we did, and like the elements
> That know not what nor why, yet do effect
> Rare issues by their operance, our souls
> Did so to one another. What she lik'd
> Was then of me approv'd, what not, condemn'd,
> No more arraignment. The flow'r that I would pluck
> And put between my breasts (O then but beginning
> To swell about the blossom), she would long
> Till she had such another, and commit it
> To the like innocent cradle, where, phoenix-like,
> They died in perfume. On my head no toy
> But was her pattern; her affections (pretty,
> Though happily her careless [wear]) I followed
> For my most serious decking. Had mine ear
> Stol'n some new air, or at adventure humm'd [one]
> From musical coinage, why, it was a note

34

Whereon her spirits would sojourn (rather dwell on)
And sing it in her slumbers. This rehearsal
(Which [ev'ry] innocent wots well, comes in
Like old importment's bastard) has this end,
That the true love 'tween maid and maid may be
More than in sex [dividual].[22]

Imogen is unlike the other heroines of the romances in that she is married, has to defy her father and a wicked stepmother, repulse a loathsome suitor, and journey across country alone, but she has some of the attributes of the Arcadian innocent. She wishes she were one, while she is at court:

Would I were
A neat-herd's daughter, and my Leonatus
Our neighbour shepherd's son!

(*Cymbeline* I. i. 148-50)

She even wishes, in a prophetic-ironic way, that she were with her stolen brothers, who, she seems to divine, are living in the mean estate;

Had I been thief-stolen,
As my two brothers, happy! but most miserable
Is the [desire] that's glorious. Blessed be those,
How mean soe'er, that have their honest wills,
Which seasons comfort.

(I. vi. 5-9)

With the exception of Marina, Imogen is the most *pathetic* of the innocent heroines in the romances. Her enforced parting from her husband is portrayed imaginatively, rather than actually, as she tells Pisanio how she would have said farewell:

I would have broke mine eye-strings, crack'd them, but
To look upon him, till the diminution
Of space had pointed him sharp as my needle;
Nay, follow'd him, till he had melted from
The smallness of a gnat to air, and then
Have turn'd mine eye, and wept.

(I. iii. 17-22)

Cowden-Clarke records that when Keats read this passage aloud his voice faltered and his eyes filled with tears.[23]

Imogen is symbolically treated in the scene in her bedroom, where Jachimo notices that she has been reading the tale of Tereus and stopped at the point where Philomel gave up. Some critics have called this a symbolic rape of Imogen; that is perhaps going too far, but it is fair to say that we are to feel that she is an innocent victim.

She goes to a green place on the way to Milford Haven where she thinks her husband is. We are introduced to it as morally superior to the court by old Belarius, who has known both (III. iii. 1-78). The passage is as much a commendation of pastoral over court life as Meliboee's discourse to Sir Calidore in *The Faerie Queene* (VI. ix. 20-25). It has a different emphasis, however, because the two sons of Cymbeline, having aspiring minds suitable to their births, long for a greater arena to compete in. When Imogen, disguised as Fidele, joins them, there is an instant attraction between brothers and sister which Belarius ascribes to "worthiness of nature, breed of greatness" (IV. ii. 25). Imogen comments on their kindness, and notes that she has learned the fallacy of court notions about the country:

> Gods, What lies I have heard!
> Our courtiers say all's savage but at court.
> Experience, O, thou disprov'st report!
> Th' imperious seas breed monsters; for the dish
> Poor tributary rivers as sweet fish.
>
> (IV. ii. 32-36)

The rhyme shows this to be a gnomic pronouncement. Imogen's discovery is somewhat like Orlando's in *As You Like It* (II. vii. 106 ff.).

Pastoral innocence is not so specifically attributed to Imogen as it is to Perdita and Miranda. It is because Imogen is entrusted with a Patient Griselda role and the plot moves around her in a most complicated way. Still, the Welsh mountains are a kind of Arcadia, their values are superior to the values of court, and Imogen-Fidele is associated with the virtues of the simple life. There are some indications that Imogen's name was really Innogen. It is so in Holinshed, and

Dr. Simon Forman, who saw the play in 1610, spells the name that way. Moreover, the quarto edition of *Much Ado* (1600) a play which was much in Shakespeare's mind when he wrote *Cymbeline* ten years later, lists an Innogen as the wife of Leonato. If the name is Innogen, an association with Innocence is obvious, as G. Wilson Knight points out.[24]

Innocence, Marvell sings, is the dear sister of Fair Quiet. And Fair Quiet is not found in city or court or castle. She is found in Arden, or Arcadia, or Bohemia, or the mountains of Wales, or on some enchanted island.

Chapter 3
FROM COMEDY TO ROMANCE

Now bless thyself. Thou mettest with things dying, I with things newborn.
The Winter's Tale

In one of his earliest comedies, *The Comedy of Errors* (c. 1592), Shakespeare drew upon the romantic story of Apollonius of Tyre for the plot involving

> Hapless Ægeon, whom the fates have mark'd
> To bear the extremity of dire mishap!
>
> (I. i. 140-41)

He is an old man, the father of twin sons both named Antipholus. They were separated in a shipwreck when infants, and their mother was lost in the same disaster. At eighteen years of age Antipholus of Syracuse starts out, with his servant, to find his lost twin brother. He has been gone five years as the play opens, and old Ægeon has gone in search of *him*. He has wandered over sea and land and has finally come to Ephesus, where he is arrested as a merchant violating an international agreement. He is a pathetic figure, but so is his wandering son, Antipholus of Syracuse:

> I to the world am like a drop of water
> That in the ocean seeks another drop,
> Who, failing there to find his fellow forth
> Unseen, inquisitive, confounds himself.
> So I, to find a mother and a brother,
> In quest of them, unhappy, lose myself.
>
> (I. ii. 35-40)

39

There were many versions of the Apollonius of Tyre story, but the one Shakespeare used was in Gower's *Confessio Amantis,* and as such had a quaint and antique flavor. The strange, incredible adventures undergone by the victims of fate were not, however, so incredible to the Elizabethans as they seem to us. As Geoffrey Bullough puts it, "To a Tudor audience aware of enmities between city states in Italy and elsewhere and the perils of sea-traders, Ægeon's (= Apollonius') predicament was no romantic fancy. Shipwrecks were as common in life as in romances, and the father's graphic account of the loss of his babes and wife excites both sympathy and expectation that we shall meet them soon."[1] We do meet them, at the end of this short play, when the Abbess of Ephesus discloses that she is really Emilia, Ægeon's long-lost wife, and as such she is able to straighten out the identity of the twin brothers. The mistaken identity plot, taken from Plautus, is of course farcical, but Shakespeare returns in the conclusion to the pathos and wonder that has enveloped the Ægeon (Apollonius) story all along:

> *Ægeon:* Not know my voice! O time's extremity,
> Hast thou so crack'd and splitted my poor tongue
> In seven short years, that here my only son
> Knows not my feeble key of untun'd cares?
> Though now this grained face of mine be hid
> In sap-consuming winter's drizzled snow,
> And all the conduits of my blood froze up,
> Yet hath my night of life some memory,
> My wasting lamps some fading glimmer left,
> My dull deaf ears a little use to hear:
> All these old witnesses — I cannot err —
> Tell me thou art my son Antipholus.[2]

Antipholus' musings over the search of one drop of water for another, the loss, the quest, the confusion, have their answer in the summary of Gonzalo at the end of *The Tempest.* The finding of what is searched for means also the finding of one's self:

O, rejoice
Beyond a common joy, and set it down
With gold on lasting pillars: in one voyage
Did Claribel her husband find at Tunis,
And Ferdinand, her brother, found a wife
Where he himself was lost; Prospero, his dukedom
In a poor isle; and all of us, ourselves,
When no man was his own.[3]

Shakespeare returned to the Apollonius story for the material of the first of his late romances, *Pericles,* something like fifteen years later than *The Comedy of Errors.* He also turned to other old and neglected interests, but our concern at the moment is the continuity of some features of romance through the comedies. One of the subjects usually said to be characteristic of the romances is the subject of crabbed age and youth — essentially a comic subject. The old man in Shakespeare's last plays is reminiscent of the *senex iratus* of classical new comedy.[4] Simonides in *Pericles,* Cymbeline, Leontes and Polixenes in *The Winter's Tale,* and Prospero in *The Tempest* are representative of the type, though Simonides and Prospero only pretend to be difficult and are really on the side of the lovers all the time. The comic old man may of course appear in a tragedy, but he is comic none the less. Old Capulet in *Romeo and Juliet* is classified for the audience immediately when, on his first entrance, he cries, "Give me my long sword, ho!" and his wife replies "A crutch, a crutch! why call you for a sword?" His essentially comic role is maintained when he squabbles with the Nurse. In *Hamlet* there is something of the same effect in the verbal parries between Hamlet and Polonius; though in the action Polonius through his spying and intriguing is a menace to Hamlet, in the dialogue he is the comic *senex.* It is possible, of course, to treat the conflict between the generations tragically, as Shakespeare does in *King Lear,* but in that play there are two members of the younger generation, Cordelia and Edgar, who minister to their elders and show how, even in the most sinister environment, the generation gap can be bridged by love.

In the problem comedies Shakespeare explored some of the darker corners of the relationship between the generations. In *All's Well* he makes the old sick king recall the words of Bertram's late father,

> "Let me not live," quoth he,
> "After my flame lacks oil, to be the snuff
> Of younger spirits, whose apprehensive senses
> All but new things disdain; whose judgments are
> Mere fathers of their garments; whose constancies
> Expire before their fashions."   (I. ii. 58-63)

Despite this view, it is the younger generation who must sacrifice themselves in the problem comedies, as in the tragedies. Their sacrifice, however, leads to their redemption and salvation in the end.[5]

It may seem to be straining matters to suggest that there is any significant conflict between youth and age in *Measure for Measure,* since other conflicts are so much more important. Claudio and Juliet, the young lovers, are indeed at odds with the world represented by the old Duke, his deputy Angelo, and the ancient lord, Escalus. But Isabella is young, too, a novice, on the side of virtue and mercy, as is the aged Escalus. The issues are different. But there is much in the play about coldness of blood, the property of age, generally, and the warm feelings of youth. "Does your worship mean to geld and splay all the youth of the city?" asks Pompey, and when Escalus answers no, he concludes "Truly, sir, in my poor opinion, they will to't then" (II. i. 242-45). This is comic philosophizing upon the sexual drives of young people. Shakespeare continues it in the same vein in *The Winter's Tale,* when the old Shepherd says "I would there were no age between ten and three-and-twenty, or that youth would sleep out the rest; for there is nothing in the between but getting wenches with child, wronging the ancientry, stealing, fighting —" (III. iii. 59-63). It is familiar enough sentiment; it echoes a verse in the mad Ophelia's bawdy ballad,

> By Gis and by Saint Charity
> Alack! and Fie for shame!
> Young men will do't if they come to't
> By Cock, they are to blame.   (*Hamlet* IV. v. 59-62)

Dr. Johnson said, of *The Two Gentlemen of Verona,* "In this play there is a strange mixture of knowledge and ignorance, of care and negligence. The versification is often excellent, the allusions are learned and just; but the author conveys his heroes by sea from one inland town to another in the same country; he places the Emperor at Milan and sends his young men to attend him, but never mentions him more; he makes Protheus, after an interview with Silvia, say he has only seen her picture, and, if we may credit the old copies, he has by mistaking places, left his scenery inextricable. The reason of all this confusion seems to be, that he took his story from a novel which he sometimes forsook, sometimes remembered, and sometimes forgot."[6] *Two Gentlemen of Verona* is an early play which in some interesting ways prefigures the late romances. It has a romance plot, derived mainly from Montemayor's *Diana,* but it is clearly of a mixed kind, and its inconsistencies, which have been remarked on since the time of Dr. Johnson, have led to a variety of explanations, some of them involving revision or composition in more than one stage.[7]

Whether the play was written at various times, whether it was written all at once but in haste (this is E. K. Chambers' view), or whether some lost play on the Felix and Felismena story was a source Shakespeare used, it now seems clearly evident that in constructing the play he was fusing sources, in a more complex way than he followed when he adapted two Latin comedies to make *The Comedy of Errors.* He certainly used Montemayor's *Diana,* and I think there are enough verbal echoes to indicate that he used the translation by Bartholomew Yong, though, since that work was not published until 1598, he would have had to read it in manuscript. (Yong says in his preface that the translation had been finished sixteen years before.)

The story in Montemayor had no Valentine in it, and for that Shakespeare drew on the familiar literature of the friendship theme, reaching far back in antiquity but represented to him most vividly in Chaucer's *Knight's Tale,* Elyot's *Governour* and in a play by Richard Edwards called *Damon and Pythias.* But a third element was of importance: the long poem by Arthur Broke called *Romeus and Juliet* which he was to exploit later as the source for a romantic tragedy.[8]

The confused geography, and several other curious features of the play, are easily understood if we observe that he turned from his Montemayor material occasionally to *Romeus and Juliet.* The fact that there is no emphasis, except in the title, on the fact that Verona is the scene of the opening of the play, may not seem so strange when we reflect that Verona is the scene of the tragic love story. The curious mistake of the Duke, saying "Verona here" (III. i. 81) when he means Milan, shows the influence of Broke. The rope ladder which Valentine proposes to use for his elopement is Romeus's ladder. Valentine, banished from Milan, doesn't say where he is going, but he tells the outlaws he is going to Verona. Silvia, however, (IV. iii. 23-24) says he is in Mantua and she finds him in a wood, presumably near there. Why Mantua, of all places? Why, because Mantua is where Romeus went when he was banished. Valentine's lie to the outlaws as to why he left Milan seems odd. He could have given the true cause, "practising to steal away a lady, an heir, and near allied unto the Duke" (IV. i. 48-49), but he says he killed a man, in fair fight. It is Romeus' reason for banishment. That Shakespeare gave to the third outlaw Valentine's real offense may be another instance of the "thrift" which characterizes his use of source material.[9] The tale of Titus and Gissipus in Elyot's *Governour* which contributed to the friendship theme of Valentine and Proteus solves the plot by the use of the bed trick. Shakespeare does not use it here. He saves it for *All's Well That Ends Well* and *Measure for Measure.* Another instance of the elimination of a motif in the source and the saving of it for future use is the matter of a lady falling in love with a page who is really another lady in disguise. Harold Jenkins remarks, "In *The Two Gentlemen of Verona,* of course, the lady fails to fall in love with the page at all, which is really a little surprising of her, since she had done so in Shakespeare's source. It is almost as though Shakespeare were reserving this crowning situation, in which the mistress loves the woman-page, for treatment in some later play. At any rate, in *Twelfth Night,* he takes care to throw emphasis on it from the first. Viola is got into her page-boy clothes before we are half-way through the first act."[10] The disguised woman motif is so common that it is impossible to say that Shakespeare took it from one specific source. It occurs in Montemayor's *Diana,* of course; Felismena describes it as if it were novel:

44

But being in the mids of my mishaps, and in the depth of those woes which the absence of Don Felix caused me to feele, and it seeming to me that my greefe was without remedie, if he were once seene or knowen of the Ladies in that court (more beautifull and gracious then my selfe,) by occasion whereof, as also by absence (a capitall enemie to love) I might easily be forgotten, I determined to adventure that, which I thinke never any woman imagined: which was, to apparell myselfe in the habit of a man, and to hye me to the Court to see him, in whose sight al my hope and content remained: which determination, I no sooner thought of, then I put in practise, love blinding my eies and minde with an inconsiderate regarde of mine owne estate and condition. To the execution of which attempt, I wanted no industrie, for, being furnished with the helpe of one of my approved friends, and treasouresse of my secrets, who bought me such apparell, as I willed her, and a good horse for my journey, I went not onely out of my countrie, but out of my deere reputation (which [I thinke] I shall never recover againe) and so trotted directly to the Court, passing by the way many accidents, which (if time would give me leave to tell them) woulde not make you laugh a little to heare them.[11]

This idea of a young woman disguising herself as a boy was also present in *Romeus and Juliet,* where it is suggested by Juliet:

What letteth but in other weed I may myself disguise?
What, shall I be the first? Hath none done so ere this,
To 'scape the bondage of their friends?

Romeus rejects the idea, saying he will take her from Verona to a foreign land

Not in man's weed disguised, or as one scarcely known,
But as my wife and only fere, in garment of thine own.

But when Friar Lawrence sends to Romeus the fatally delayed letter, he revives the suggestion:

Then shall he carry her to Mantua away —
Till fickle fortune favour him, — disguised in man's array.[12]

On the stage, of course, nothing could be simpler than to have a boy actor impersonating a woman resume his boy's clothes as a disguise beyond his disguise. A good deal of solemn nonsense has been written about the supposed psychological effects of this device upon the Elizabethan public. It was a familiar device in prose romance, and it readily adapted itself to the stage. The old play *Clyomon and Clamydes*, first produced in the seventies but not printed until 1599, shows Neronis, Daughter to the Queen of the Strange Marshes, escaping in page's clothing from the court of Norway to seek her lover, the Knight of the Golden Shield, in the forest.

So Shakespeare's disguised ladies, Julia in *Two Gentlemen,* Portia and Nerissa in *The Merchant of Venice,* Rosalind and Celia in *As You Like It,* Viola in *Twelfth Night,* Imogen in *Cymbeline,* all come from an elaborate and mixed tradition. The value of the device for Shakespeare, aside from its obvious utility in providing a plot complication which could easily be untied by the simple expedient of the girl's removing her disguise, is that it provided a double personality for the girl in disguise — her real one and her assumed one. This is connected with what Bertrand Evans calls "discrepant awareness."

The Two Gentlemen of Verona is important to an understanding of the romances because it is a kind of early romance itself and because the developments from it that can be observed in later plays throw some light on the nature of his imagination. The relationship of *TGV* to *Romeo and Juliet* is obvious enough from the fact of their having a common source, Broke's poem, but the extent of the relationship is greater than one would expect.

That the material of *Two Gentlemen* was in Shakespeare's mind when he wrote *The Merchant of Venice* is suggested by the resemblance between Launce in the earlier play and Launcelot Gobbo in the later, and by the language Launce uses when he first complains about his dog Crab: "He is a stone, a very pebble stone, and has no more pity in him than a dog. *A Jew* would have wept to see our parting."[13]

A transformation in the later play may be noticed if we compare the signs of a man in love as given by Speed when he describes his master Valentine: he wreathes his arms, he relishes love songs, he walks alone, he sighs, he weeps, he fasts, he watches or stays awake at night, and he speaks puling (*TGV* II. i. 17-31). The signs of a man in love which Rosalind in disguise says she learned from her uncle are equally conventional, but different. He has a lean cheek, a blue and sunken eye, an unquestionable spirit, a neglected beard, unguarded hose, an unbanded bonnet, an unbuttoned sleeve, and an untied shoe. Everything about him shows a careless desolation (*AYLI* III. ii. 392-403). Other less comprehensive descriptions of the lover can of course be found in *Romeo and Juliet* and *Hamlet*.

The realization that *Two Gentlemen* is an important forerunner of later plays is expressed in another way by Northrop Frye:

> *The Two Gentlemen of Verona* is an orthodox New Comedy except for one thing. The hero Valentine becomes a captain of a band of outlaws in a forest, and all the other characters are gathered into this forest and become converted. Thus the action of the comedy begins in a world represented as a normal world, goes into a metamorphosis there in which the comic resolution is achieved, and returns to the normal world. The forest in this play is the embryonic form of the fairy world of *A Midsummer Night's Dream,* the Forest of Arden in *As You Like It,* Windsor Forest in *The Merry Wives of Windsor,* and the pastoral world of the mythical sea-coasted Bohemia in *The Winter's Tale.* In all these comedies there is the same rhythmic movement from the normal world to green world and back again.[14]

Frye goes on to say, wittily, that the second world, or green world, is absent from the so-called problem comedies, "which is one of the things that makes them problem comedies." Nevertheless, the problem comedies had their profound influences on the romances which followed them.

For our purposes, we will consider the problem comedies to be *Much Ado About Nothing, All's Well that Ends Well,* and *Measure for Measure. Much Ado* is often not included in this group because of the merry wit of its Beatrice-Benedick plot, but the Claudio-Hero part of it has the elements which make the problem comedies problems — a hero who gets the heroine to the applause of the characters in the play but to the less than complete satisfaction of the audience, at least the modern audience; a rather murky moral atmosphere against which a slandered or rejected heroine shines in luminous virtue and perseverance, and a wonderfully strange series of events to bring about the plot resolution.

Hero can no more understand her false accusation than can Imogen in *Cymbeline,* but the accusation is made to her directly, not by letter or messenger. The effect on her is really expressed by Claudio, who says what he had thought she was and laments the supposed change:

> O Hero! what a Hero hadst thou been
> If half thy outward graces had been plac'd
> About thy thoughts and counsels of thy heart!
> But fare thee well, most foul, most fair! Farewell,
> Thou pure impiety and impious purity!
> For thee I'll lock up all the gates of love,
> And on my eyelids shall conjecture hang,
> To turn all beauty into thoughts of harm,
> And never shall it more be gracious.
>
> (*Much Ado* IV. i. 100-08)

Then she swoons, and protests her innocence after she revives. Imogen cries out in answer to the slander,

> False to his bed? What is it to be false?
> To lie in watch there and to think on him?
> To weep 'twixt clock and clock? If sleep charge nature,
> To break it with a fearful dream of him
> And cry myself awake? That's false to's bed, is it?
>
> (*Cymbeline* III. iv. 40-44)

Both Claudio and Posthumus believe slanders which are supported by some testimony which they should have suspected but did not. Both find the revelation of the slander enough to turn them against all womankind. Both suppose that their slandered ladies are dead. But Shakespeare makes one significant difference between the two cases. Posthumus repents while still thinking Imogen guilty, but Claudio is guilty only of "mistaking."[15]

Much Ado is usually dated 1599; the other two problem comedies are three or four years later; *Measure for Measure* is dated by its performance at court on St. Stephen's night, 1604. *All's Well* is closely related to it, and, as G. K. Hunter says, it probably precedes it slightly: "in its added emphasis on reconciliation, on female purity, and on the achievement of humbled wisdom, *Measure for Measure* is a stage nearer the last plays, towards which, I take it, *All's Well* itself is pointing."[16] The conflict between youth and age, the somewhat magical aura surrounding the virgin Helena, the triumph of the life-principle over the death-principle, the promise of newborn things or of things about to be born, — these themes echo through the play.

Helena as a heroine is in some ways an anticipation of the innocent heroines of the romances. She is modest and humble. She cannot be deterred from pursuing her love. Shakespeare makes her speech defining her purposes into a touching revelation, such as those by Marina and Imogen and Miranda will be:

> Then I confess
> Here on my knee, before high heaven and you,
> That before you, and next unto high heaven,
> I love your son.
> My friends were poor, but honest, so's my love.
> Be not offended, for it hurts not him
> That he is lov'd of me. I follow him not
> By any token of presumptuous suit,
> Nor would I have him till I do deserve him,
> Yet never know how that desert should be.
> I know I love in vain, strive against hope;
> Yet in this captious and [intenible] sieve
> I still pour in the waters of my love
> And lack not to lose still. Thus, Indian-like,
> Religious in mine error, I adore
> The sun, that looks upon his worshipper,
> But knows of him no more.
>
> (*All's Well* I. iii. 191-207)

She is developed rather more than most Shakespearian heroines are by means of soliloquy, as at the beginning of the play:

I think not on my father,
And these great tears grace his remembrance more
Than those I shed for him. What was he like?
I have forgot him; my imagination
Carries no favo'r in't but Bertram's.
I am undone! There is no living, none,
If Bertram be away; 'twere all one
That I should love a bright particular star
And think to wed it, he is so above me.
In his bright radiance and collateral light
Must I be comforted, not in his sphere.

(I. i. 79-89)

This consciousness of spheres, of differences between one's hopes and one's apparent fate, underlies the attitudes in the romances.

Helena is separated from Bertram by rank; he is a count and she is a mere physician's daughter. When Shakespeare came to write *Cymbeline* he changed his source material taken from Boccaccio or *Frederick of Jennen* to make Imogen a princess and Posthumus a gentleman without noble rank, presumably because of the influence of *All's Well*. Cloten is able to describe him as

that base wretch,
One bred of alms and foster'd with cold dishes,
With scraps o' th' court,

(II. iii. 113-15)

though Shakespeare has been careful from the very beginning of the play to make clear the moral superiority of Posthumus to all other men at court and especially to Cloten. Even though introducing disparity of rank caused him some structural difficulties, it was worth it. The heroine of a romance ought to be a princess.

There is a good deal of talk about healing in *All's Well*; of course the plot turns on it. Whether healing is science, or magic, or the possession of a secret handed down like an inheritance, or some way related to the virtue of the healer — these are matters which carry over from Helena in *All's Well* to Cerimon in *Pericles*. And the notion of

50

miracles, whether they are still possible or not, a theme in *Cymbeline,*
The Winter's Tale and *The Tempest,* gets its first explicit expression
in the words of Lafew:

> They say miracles are past, and we have our philosophical
> persons to make modern and familiar, things supernatural and
> causeless. Hence it is that we make trifles of terrors, ensconcing
> ourselves into seeming knowledge when we should submit our-
> selves to an unknown fear.[17]

The denouements of *All's Well* and *Measure for Measure,* though
sometimes unpleasing to a modern taste, really depend upon the virtue
of forgiveness on the part of those sinned against — the women. So,
the wronged heroines of *Cymbeline* and *The Winter's Tale* are in a
sense more elaborate treatments of Helen, the skilled physician, and
Mariana of the Moated Grange.

In *Measure for Measure* the comic realism of the scenes involving
Mistress Overdone and Pompey prepares us for the brothel scenes in
Pericles, though in the later play a more immediate contrast between
virtue and vice is brought about by putting the innocent Marina into
the very bawdy house itself. But there are similarities. When the Duke
reproves Pompey for his way of life, the comic surprise is his resilience:

> *Duke:* Fie, sirrah, a bawd, a wicked bawd!
> The evil that thou causest to be done,
> That is thy means to live. Do thou but think
> What 'tis to cram a maw or clothe a back
> From such a filthy vice; say to thyself,
> From their abominable and beastly touches
> I drink, I eat, [array] myself, and live.
> Canst thou believe thy living is a life,
> So stinkingly depending? Go mend, go mend.
> *Pompey:* Indeed it does stink in some sort, sir.
> But yet, sir, I would prove —
>
> (*Measure for Measure* III. ii. 19-29)

Pompey is a frustrated Falstaff.

The comparable passage in *Pericles* is Marina's denunciation of
Boult:

Marina: Neither of these are so bad as thou art,
Since they do better thee in their command.
Thou hold'st a place for which the pained'st fiend
Of hell would not in reputation change.
Thou art the damned door-keeper to every
Custrel that comes inquiring for his Tib.
To the choleric fisting of every rogue
Thy ear is liable; thy food is such
As hath been belch'd on by infected lungs.

Instead of the comic response of Pompey, we have the grave reply of Boult:

Boult: What would you have me do? Go to the wars, would you? Where a man may serve seven years for the loss of a leg, and have not enough money in the end to buy him a wooden one?
Marina: Do anything but this thou doest. Empty
Old receptacles, or common shores, of filth,
Serve by indenture to the common hangman:
Any of these ways you are better than this;
For what thou professest, a baboon, could he speak,
Would own a name too dear.

(IV. vi. 171-90)

Earlier in *Pericles* there are verbal echoes of the Duke's speech, when Boult says that "She makes our profession as it were to stink" just after the exclamation "Abominable!" (IV. vi. 145).

It is no longer necessary to make a defense for the brothel scenes, as Walter Raleigh did in 1907, on the ground of Shakespeare's sympathy for all kinds of people whether they were morally respectable or not. But it was these scenes which were vital in the Raleigh picture of a Shakespeare who revealed himself in his works, not the impersonal, mysterious character of Browning's imagination or the complete business man of Sidney Lee's. *"Measure for Measure* and the Fourth Act of *Pericles* (which no pen but his could have written) prove Shakespeare's acquaintance with the darker side of the life of the town, as it might be seen in Pickt-hatch or the Bankside. He does not fear to expose the purest of his heroines to the breath of this infection; their virtue is not ignorance; ''tis in grain: 'twill endure wind and weather.' "[18]

It is not so easy to relate the major elements of *Measure for Measure* to the late plays because we must first interpret the meaning of that very ambiguous play. It will be obvious to some that the Duke manipulates the events in Vienna, by means of his disguise, in a way that foreshadows Prospero's manipulation of events in *The Tempest* by means of magic and his servant Ariel. And those who see a Christian meaning to the main plot of *Measure for Measure* will undoubtedly be readier to read a Christian allegory into *Cymbeline, The Winter's Tale* and *The Tempest*. Without going so far, we might agree with J. W. Lever that "self-knowledge, the essential quest in *Measure for Measure,* was the crowning achievement of the last plays."[19]

Chapter 4
FROM TRAGEDY TO ROMANCE

They looked as they had heard of a world ransomed or one destroyed.

The Winter's Tale

It has been suggested that the principal origin of Shakespeare's romances lies in his tragedy *King Lear*. Obviously enough, the subplot of that play, the Edmund-Edgar-Gloucester story, comes from a prose romance, Sidney's *Arcadia*. Clearly enough, also, there are plot motifs in the tragedy which appear, in modified form, in the romances: a king, separated from his daughter but reunited with her under strange circumstances *(Pericles, Cymbeline, A Winter's Tale)*; a storm *(Pericles, The Tempest)*; a man, suffering under many hardships, trying to learn patience and forgiveness *(Pericles, Cymbeline, The Tempest)*. And there are many images in common, such as that in *Cymbeline* which might be guessed by many to come from *Lear:*

> No more, thou Thunder-master, show
> Thy spite on mortal flies.
>
> (V. iv. 30-31)

It will be our concern here to trace, as best we can, the working of Shakespeare's imagination in the late romances compared to the way in which his imagination works in the great tragedies. It is sometimes said that the last plays or romances are not serious works of dramatic art like the tragedies. They may be beautiful — and who would deny beauty to *The Tempest?* But they are not profound, like *King Lear*.[1]

55

The relationship between the tragedies and the romances has not been clearly enough worked out so that one can tell whether such a comment is a mere fossil of the old Lytton Strachey doctrine that Shakespeare was, when he wrote the last plays, bored, or a version of Tillyard's idea that the romances are like the third play in a Greek trilogy.

It is important to notice that the story of the Paphlagonian king in Sidney's *Arcadia* influenced Shakespeare's handling of the main plot in *King Lear* as well as providing material for the subplot.[2] Other episodes in the *Arcadia* also influenced the playwright's handling of the duel between Edgar and Edmund and the device by which Edmund deceives Gloucester. More important still is the setting of the Paphlagonian king story in the *Arcadia*. It is told while Leonatus and his old father are taking shelter from a fierce storm. The princes, Musidorus and Pyrocles, are also there, and they find the old king and his son poorly arrayed and extremely weather-beaten. Leonatus begs them to convey the afflicted king to a place of rest and security. The bastard Plexirtus has taken away his father's kingdom and his eyesight, "the riches which Nature grants to the poorest creatures." It is evident that this source of the Gloucester plot had very significant influence on Shakespeare's treatment of the main plot which came from the old chronicle play *King Leir*.

The old play is, of course, not a tragedy. In it the invading forces from France conquer the army of the evil sisters and Leir is restored to his kingdom, over which he rules again for a couple of years and dies in peace. Shakespeare's is the only treatment of the story which ends tragically for the protagonist. In fact, some critics think that *King Lear* ought to be a tragicomedy, and that, up until the death of Cordelia, it is.[3] Though the forces of the French king, Cordelia's husband, are defeated by the English, the imprisonment of Lear and his loving daughter is presented as almost idyllic:

> We two alone will sing like birds i' th' cage;
> When thou dost ask me blessing, I'll kneel down,
> And ask of thee forgiveness. So we'll live,
> And pray, and sing, and tell old tales, and laugh
> At gilded butterflies, and hear poor rogues

Talk of court news; and we'll talk with them too —
Who loses and who wins; who's in, who's out —
And take upon 's the mystery of things,
As if we were God's spies; and we'll wear out
In a wall'd prison, packs and sects of great ones
That ebb and flow by th' moon.

(V. iii. 9-19)

The reunion of Lear and Cordelia is overwhelming in its pathos. Cordelia's tears have quenched the wheel of fire on which the old king was bound. His own language makes his awakening to find Cordelia a kind of resurrection:

You do me wrong to take me out o' the grave:
Thou art a soul in bliss, but I am bound
Upon a wheel of fire, that mine own tears
Do scald like molten lead.

(IV. vii. 44-47)

He has survived his purgatorial ordeal. Stripped of his crown, his knights, his regal robes, he has learned what it is to be merely human. He has lost his wits in the storm; his only companions were a wise and bitter fool and a Bedlam beggar. But he has regained his sanity with the recognition of his daughter:

Do not laugh at me,
For (as I am a man) I think this lady
To be my child Cordelia.

(IV. vii. 67-69)

If *King Lear* has an organic relation to the romances, we are obliged to consider not only that great tragedy but another drama which seems to have many things in common with it, the strange play *Timon of Athens*. Bradley pointed out that Lear's and Timon's denunciations of sexual vice and corruption are curiously similar.[4] Oddly enough the theme is natural and appropriate in *Timon*, for the speech is addressed to Alcibiades and two courtesans, but "Why," asks Bradley, "should Lear refer at length, and with the same loathing, to this particular subject? It almost looks as if Shakespeare were expressing feelings which oppressed him at this period of his life." Both plays have many references to lower animals; both have heroes who suffer from ingratitude and who are themselves unsuspicious, soft-hearted, and yet violent in their denunciations of mankind. The fool in *Timon* and the Fool in *Lear* are both described as "not altogether fool." Servants and lowly people in both plays are morally superior to their social betters. But most conclusive of all, to Bradley, is the resemblance in style and versification, which he considers strong evidence of proximity of date.

There is little evidence upon which to base the date of *Timon;* scholars divide into those who, like Bradley, favor a date very close to *Lear,* either before or after, and those, like E. K. Chambers, who place it after the Roman plays *Antony and Cleopatra* and *Coriolanus* and just before the romances. Clifford Leech favors a late date because he sees *Timon* as "containing the germ of the romances."[5]

This is of course another reason, entirely apart from its relation to *Lear,* why we should look at *Timon of Athens.* Northrop Frye links *Timon* with the romances by the ingenious device of considering the play a comedy: "It seems to me that this extraordinary play, half morality and half folk-tale, the fourth and last of the Plutarchan plays, is the logical transition from *Coriolanus* to the romances, and that it has many features making for an *idiotes* comedy rather than a tragedy. If we were to see the action of *Twelfth Night* through the eyes of the madly used Malvolio, or the action of *The Merchant of Venice* through the eyes of the bankrupt and beggared Shylock, the tone would not be greatly different from that of the second half of *Timon of Athens.*"[6]

Whether *Timon* was written before *Lear* and is an uncompleted first draft envisioning some of the themes of that majestic tragedy, or an afterthought, using material that had aroused Shakespeare's attention as he wrote the Roman plays, is not crucial to our present purpose. We need only to see how closely the imaginative world of *Timon* is related to the imaginative world of *Lear.* We may add to the similarities Bradley has pointed out. When Varro's second servant asks "Who can speak broader than he that has no house to put his head in?" (III. iv. 64) we are listening to the language of Lear's Fool. Timon's steward

Flavius is a faithful servant, like Kent. Timon meditates on nature before he digs for roots and finds gold. But the most striking example of all is a passage in Apemantus' speech to Timon at IV. iii. 221-31. In its imagery and rhetoric it is typically Shakespearean; one reason we think so is that it is so close to *Lear*. Another reason, of course, is that it exhibits that distinctive image-cluster of dogs-candy-fawning which Walter Whiter discovered.

> What, think'st
> That the bleak air, thy boisterous chamberlain,
> Will put thy shirt on warm? Will these moist trees,
> That have outlived the eagle, page thy heels
> And skip where thou point'st out? Will the cold brook,
> Candied with ice, caudle thy morning taste,
> To cure thy o'ernight's surfeit? Call the creatures
> Whose naked natures live in all the spite
> Of wreakful heaven, whose bare unhoused trunks,
> To the conflicting elements exposed,
> Answer mere nature; bid them flatter thee.

Maynard Mack has suggested that one defining source behind *Lear* is the shape of pastoral romance, only it is reversed. In the pastoral pattern the hero moves from civilization into the green world, undergoes a learning process there, undergoes a sort of ritual death and rebirth, and returns to the everyday world. *"King Lear* alludes to such patterns, it seems to me, but turns them upside down. It moves from extrusion not to pastoral, but to what I take to be the greatest anti-pastoral ever written."[7] Now of course in *Lear* the scenes on the heath in the storm are the scenes of Lear's purgation, of his education, of his acquiring wisdom as he ironically loses his wits. Likewise at Timon's cave by the seaside, in the woods, the hero vents all his satiric spleen on society and its hypocritical standards; he seeks for roots and finds gold; he gives it to whores whom he denounces, and the poet and painter who opened the play are beaten instead of rewarded. He finds death, which he sought, but ironically his influence brings peace and reconciliation to Athens under the victorious Alcibiades.

Malone noticed long ago that the magnificent scene in *Timon of*

Athens, IV. iii. in which Timon confronts Alcibiades and the whores, has some relationship to a passage in *Cymbeline:*

> *Jachimo:* Your lady,
> Is one of the fairest that I have look'd upon.
> *Posthumus:* And therewithal the best, or let her beauty
> Look through a casement to allure false hearts
> And be false with them.   (II. iv. 31-34)

This reflects Timon's advice to Alcibiades to spare none of the Athenians when he conquers the city:

> Let not thy sword skip one.
> Pity not honor'd age for his white beard,
> He is an usurer. Strike me the counterfeit matron,
> It is her habit only that is honest,
> Herself's a bawd. Let not the virgin's cheek
> Make soft thy trenchant sword; for those milk-paps
> That through the window bars bore at men's eyes
> Are not within the leaf of pity writ,
> But set them down horrible traitors.   (IV. iii. 111-119)

Nosworthy comments that "There is every reason for believing that *Timon,* or at least this particular scene, was fresh in Shakespeare's mind when he wrote *Cymbeline*."

One of the themes which has been said to link *Lear* with the romances is the theme of patience. The theme of patience is of particular importance in *Pericles,* the first of the romances. It is particularly noticeable if one compares the rather calm behavior of Shakespeare's Pericles with the frantic outbursts of Apollonius in Shakespeare's sources, Gower and Twine.[8] The word undergoes several changes of meaning or emphasis in *King Lear.* In the fourth scene of Act II it appears almost casually, without any but the most usual meaning. Regan is replying to her father's complaint about Goneril: "I pray you, sir, take patience" (l. 138). And Lear says, when he still has hope, "I can be patient, I can stay with Regan" (l. 230).

But some forty lines later, in the discussion of "need," in the magnificent speech which is prelude to the storm, the term becomes complex:

But, for true need —
You heavens, give me that patience, patience I need!
You see me here, you gods, a poor old man,
As full of grief as age, wretched in both.
If it be you that stirs these daughters' hearts
Against their father, fool me not so much
To bear it tamely; touch me with noble anger,
And let not women's weapons, water-drops,
Stain my man's cheeks! No, you unnatural hags,
I will have such revenges on you both
That all the world shall — I will do such things —
What they are yet I know not, but they shall be
The terrors of the earth! You think I'll weep;
No, I'll not weep.
I have full cause of weeping; but this heart
                          (Storm and Tempest)
Shall break into a hundred thousand flaws
Or ere I'll weep. O Fool, I shall go mad!

(II. iv. 270-86)

He first prays for patience, but as he elaborates it is clear that he means nothing like Christian patience but rather a masculine fortitude, a "noble anger" that would lead to notable revenge rather than humiliating defeat and show of feminine weakness. In the scene on the heath, after his defiance of the storm with his own thunder, Kent appears, and Lear says

No, I will be the pattern of all patience;
I will say nothing.   (III. ii. 37-38)

But of course he does not keep his promise. Shortly he breaks out in denunciation of the moral corruption of the world for which the "dreadful summoners" of the elements might be bringing punishment. This line is an instance, and a rare one, of the language of the old chronicle play *King Leir* carrying over into Shakespeare's mind at a very dramatic moment:

But he, the myrrour of mild patience,
Puts vp all wrongs, and neuer giues reply.[9]

The idea of patience permeates the Edgar-Gloucester plot as well. When Gloucester is persuaded that his life has been miraculously preserved after a fall from Dover cliff, he repents his attempted escape from his troubles:

> henceforth I'll bear
> Affliction till it do cry out itself
> "Enough, enough," and die.
>
> (IV. vi. 75-77)

and in reply Edgar says to him "Bear free and patient thoughts." One more calamity causes him to backslide. When told that Lear and Cordelia have been defeated and captured, he refuses to go further: "A man may rot even here." Edgar, who is almost an emblem of patience in this part of the play, corrects him:

> Men must endure
> Their going hence even as their coming hither,
> Ripeness is all.
>
> (V. ii. 9-11)

Shakespeare was not alone in celebrating patience as a virtue in the period when *King Lear* was being imagined and composed. In the first months of 1604 Henslowe paid Dekker and Middleton for a play he called "the pasyent man and the onest hore." *The Honest Whore* was entered on the Stationers' Register November 9, 1604, and when it was published the title page emphasized "The Humours of the Patient Man," Candido the linendraper. His speech in praise of patience is explicitly Christian, in contrast to Shakespeare:

> Patience my Lord; why tis the soule of peace:
> Of all the vertues tis neerest kin to heauen.
> It makes men looke like Gods; the best of men
> That ere wore earth about him, was a sufferer,
> A soft, meeke, humble, tranquill spirit,
> The first true Gentleman that euer breathd.[10]

Pericles offers many problems — of text, authorship, of intention and meaning — as well as of relationship to the earlier plays and the romances which followed. The romantic Apollonius story is one of loss and recovery, and it may have been a desire to work out at greater length the implications of this theme that led him to use it. Of course the story of Lear and Cordelia is one of recovery. The reunion of Pericles and Marina does not reach the heights of Lear's awakening; nothing does. But it is a reunion which invokes the music of the spheres.

The description of Cordelia when she first hears news of her father is based upon a passage in Sidney's *Arcadia,* and Steevens in the eighteenth century found many passages in *Pericles* which reflect language and images from the *Arcadia.* In fact, it may be that in changing the hero's name from Apollonius to Pericles Shakespeare was influenced by the name of Sidney's hero Pyrocles. Another influence was perhaps the Greek Pericles whom Shakespeare would have read about in North's Plutarch, particularly when he was collecting material for *Coriolanus.*

Cymbeline, aside from *Pericles* the first of the romances, has some obvious connections with *King Lear.* Both plays deal with a mythical period of English history, before Christianity. Both plays show an arbitrary and misguided king who is separated from his children. In both plays the innocent are driven into wild country, in refuge from the evil characters; in both plays the outcome of a battle brings about a paradoxical resolution of the plot. King Lear, in his awful curse on Goneril, invokes Nature as a goddess:

> Hear, Nature, hear, dear goddess, hear!
> Suspend thy purpose, if thou didst intend
> To make this creature fruitful.
> Into her womb convey sterility,
>
> (I. iv. 275-78)

In a very different context, Belarius in *Cymbeline* invokes the same goddess in wonder at the innate nobleness of the two young princes who do not know themselves to be royal.

> O thou goddess,
> Thou divine Nature; thou thyself thou blazon'st
> In these two princely boys! They are as gentle
> As zephyrs blowing below the violet,
> Not wagging his sweet head; and yet as rough,
> Their royal blood enchaf'd, as the rud'st wind
> That by the top doth take the mountain pine
> And make him stoop to th' vale. 'Tis wonder
> That an invisible instinct should frame them
> To royalty unlearn'd, honour untaught,
> Civility not seen from other, valor
> That wildly grows in them but yields a crop
> As if it had been sow'd.[11]

We have already noticed a similar figure with respect to the gods' treatment of men. The opening of Posthumus' vision shows his father singing

> No more, thou thunder-master, show
> Thy spite on mortal flies.
>
> (V. iv. 30)

which has some relationship to Gloucester's comment on Poor Tom and his son Edgar,

> As flies to wanton boys are we to th' gods,
> They kill us for their sport.[12]

When Posthumus believes that Imogen has cuckolded him, his wild rage resembles the madness of Lear:

> O, that I had her here, to tear her limb-meal!
> I will go there and do't, i' th' court, before
> Her father. I'll do something — *(Exit.)*
>
> (II. iv. 147-49)

and Philario remarks that he is "Quite besides the government of patience."

There are significant connections between *Cymbeline* and *Macbeth*. In the bedchamber scene, II. ii; Ingleby noted half a dozen verbal parallels, and Nosworthy comments "Shakespeare's mind would naturally tend to stray back to the earlier play with its somewhat similar presentation of trespass upon the royal person, assault upon sleeping innocence and resolution daunted (but not quenched) by fear and a troubled conscience."[13] The image that fused them together was the one of Tarquin approaching the sleeping Lucrece:

> Witchcraft celebrates
> Pale Hecat's off'rings; and wither'd murther,
> Alarum'd by his sentinel, the wolf,
> Whose howl's his watch, thus with his stealthy pace,
> With Tarquin's ravishing [strides], towards his design
> Moves like a ghost.
> (*Macbeth* II. i. 51-56)

and Jachimo, emerging from the trunk in Imogen's bedchamber, says

> The crickets sing, and man's o'erlabor'd sense
> Repairs itself by rest. Our Tarquin thus
> Did softly press the rushes ere he waken'd
> The chastity he wounded.
> (*Cymbeline* II. ii. 11-14)

The conclusion of Jachimo's soliloquy is even closer to the atmosphere of the Scottish tragedy:

> Swift, swift, you dragons of the night, that dawning
> May bare the raven's eye! I lodge in fear;
> Though this a heavenly angel, hell is here.

The second jailer in V. iv of *Cymbeline* resembles the porter in *Macbeth;* the Queen has some resemblance to Lady Macbeth, in character and the manner of her death. Some critics find her reminiscent of Goneril also, but she is perhaps essentially the wicked stepmother of folklore. Pisanio's speech on the receipt of Posthumus' letter associates images from *Macbeth* and *Antony and Cleopatra:*

No, 'tis slander,
Whose edge is sharper than the sword, whose tongue
Outvenoms all the worms of Nile, whose breath
Rides on the posting winds and doth belie
All corners of the world. Kings, queens, and states,
Maids, matrons, nay, the secrets of the grave
This viperous slander enters.   (III. iv. 33-39)

Finally, an image cluster is common to both plays:

Imogen: You look on me: what *wrack* discern you in me
Deserves your pity?
Jachimo: Lamentable! What
To hide me from the radiant *sun,* and *solace*
I' th' dungeon by a snuff?   (I. vi. 84-87)

The Bleeding Sergeant in *Macbeth* says

As whence the *sun* gins his reflection,
Ship*wracking* storms and direful thunders [break],
So from that spring whence *comfort* seem'd to come,
Discomfort swells.
                              (I. ii. 25-28)

It is not only the great tragedies of Shakespeare's mature period that seem to have some relation to the romances. Kittredge points out that there are tantalizing reminiscences of *Titus Andronicus* in *Cymbeline*. The threat Cymbeline makes to Lucius, of sacrificing him and the other prisoners to satisfy the souls of the fallen British, is like the demand of Titus' son (another Lucius) that the proudest prisoner of the Goths may be slaughtered and on a pile sacrificed *Ad manes fratrum*. The Queen in *Cymbeline* is not unlike Tamora, who also has wicked sons and deceives her gullible husband. Cloten's plan of rape and murder is an elaboration of Chiron's

Drag hence her husband to some secret hole,
And make his dead trunk pillow to our lust.
                    (*Titus Andronicus,* II. iii. 129-30)

Imogen goes to sleep while reading the tale of Tereus, and she turns down the leaf where Philomel gave up. "One is tempted to believe," concludes Kittredge, "that Shakespeare had been reading his own old-fashioned tragedy" when he wrote *Cymbeline*.[14] He might have added that a new quarto of *Titus Andronicus,* the third, was published in 1611, the year in which Dr. Simon Forman saw *Cymbeline* performed.

Antony and Cleopatra, though it shares distinctive traits with the other Roman plays, is in some respects transitional. Maurice Charney points out that the death of Antony is handled in a way different from the endings of *King Lear, Othello* and *Macbeth:*

> Finally, Cleopatra marks the moment of Antony's death with these words: "O, see, my women, / The crown o' th' earth doth melt. My lord!" (IV. xv. 62-63). Antony is not only her "lord" but the "crown o' th' earth"; the image attempts to objectify, to hyperbolize the personal dimension of the play. There is a peace and effortlessness in "melt," as if there were no barrier between life and death, and one could flow easily into the other. It is a fitting close for Antony. His end is not a "tragic" one as King Lear's is, or Othello's, or Macbeth's. Rather than being resolved, the conflict between Egypt and Rome ceases to exist, and the hard "visible shapes" of Rome are dissolved into an ecstatic, poetic reality. In this sense *Antony and Cleopatra* looks aheads to the mood of Shakespeare's last plays.[15]

It is very tempting to try to explain the differences between the tragedies and the romances by some biographical speculation. The period in which the romances were written corresponds roughly to the period when Shakespeare seems to have retired to Stratford. Moreover, in 1608, the year when he wrote *Pericles* and the year when his company acquired, but did not yet occupy, the Blackfriars theater, Shakespeare received news of the birth of his first grandchild, Elizabeth Hall, the daughter of his daughter Susanna and her husband Dr. John Hall. One recent biographer thinks that this was the inspiration for the heroines of the romances: "The theme of *Pericles* was appropriate, no doubt the reason why he had chosen it, for the birth of the heroine Marina was the shadow of that of his granddaughter, and the prayer of Pericles for the fresh-new seafarer, the poor inch of nature, that of himself for Elizabeth: 'Now mild may be thy life! Happy what follows!' There can be little doubt that Elizabeth Hall was a main inspirer of the writing of his last romances, and that Marina, Imogen, Perdita and Miranda are projections, whether conscious or unconscious, of Susanna's daughter."[16]

The picture of Shakespeare in happy retirement at the ripe old age of forty-four and upwards, not an hour more nor less, is a sentimentally appealing one. It has a venerable history; the first systematic account of Shakespeare's life, Nicholas Rowe's in his edition of Shakespeare in 1709 said, "The latter Part of his Life was spent, as all Men of good Sense will wish theirs may be, in Ease, Retirement, and the Conversation of his Friends."

But this hardly accounts for the difference in kind, and perhaps difference in quality, which is sometimes felt to mark off the romances from the tragedies which just preceded them. One critic accepts the inferiority of the romances as obvious: "Their imaginative and dramatic inferiority to the tragedies is very likely due to the premature oncoming of the dramatist's old age. His hand preserves its cunning, but his imaginative insight is less penetrating. Evil and pain have lost much of the destructiveness and of the agony which in his tragedies he had found them to have. He is still aware of their rifeness, but they do not press themselves so urgently on his consciousness. He feels and finds a benignity in old age, a benignity which grew in him in a similar way and through similar causes as it had grown in his own Countess of Rousillon. In his romances, with their depiction of kindly charity, reconciliation, forgiveness and tolerant sympathy, he expresses the serene calmness of a mind which accepts life trustfully in the confidence that it is primarily and naturally an embodied impulse toward human goodness."[17]

I have tried to make the point that the romances evolve in a natural way from the tragedies, as indeed they do also from the comedies. There is a tendency toward reconciliations in *Coriolanus* and *Antony and Cleopatra,* as well as in *King Lear.* In showing that a tragic world was essentially one in which the appearance was good but the underlying reality was evil, Shakespeare was surely aware of the opposite possibility, which he exploited in the romances, a world in which the

68

appearance is evil but the reality is good.[18] In the tragedies where reconciliation is allowed, it is overshadowed by the awful realization of the sacrifice of the good. Remove that sacrifice and you have the temper of the romances. In the wise words of J. W. Mackail, "romance has a constructional or artistic quality of its own, differing from that of tragedy or comedy ... it is this quality, and not the serene temper of the group of the late romantic plays, nor their happy endings, on which criticism may most profitably lay stress."[19]

Chapter 5

AS YOU LIKE IT AND ROSALYNDE

Believe, then, if you please, that I can do strange things. I have, since I was three year old, convers'd with a magician, most profound in his art and yet not damnable.

As You Like It

If Shakespeare's *As You Like It* had not survived in print but instead was another "lost" play, like *Love's Labor's Won,* and the references to it gave some hint that the lost play was a dramatization of Lodge's *Rosalynde,* what would we conjecture the lost play to be like?

We might suppose, knowing *A Midsummer Night's Dream, Much Ado About Nothing,* and *Twelfth Night,* that Shakespeare would have made much of the comedy of love which is partly developed in Lodge's romance; that he would transform the Forest of Arden from a wholly typical euphuistic romance landscape into something more natural and at the same time more exotic. The shepherds would probably be more recognizably English shepherds, there would be winter and rough weather, but, when the plot required it, there would be a hungry lioness. Tucker Brooke used to say that Shakespeare's romanticism, in contrast to Goethe's, turned inward, back toward Warwickshire instead of to the exotic south; the comparison was between "I know a bank where the wild thyme grows" and the German "Kennst du das land wo die citronon blühen?". There are lemon trees in Lodge's Forest of Arden but no citrus fruit whatever grows in Shakespeare's.

We might suppose also, remembering *The Two Gentlemen of Verona,* that Shakespeare's portrayal of exiles or outlaws in a forest would inevitably reflect the imagery and atmosphere of Robin Hood. This supposition would be strengthened if we kept in mind the theatrical history of the last years of the sixteenth century; pastoral plays were popular and in the years 1597-1600 Robin Hood seems to have enjoyed a special vogue. Ashley Thorndike traced the relationship between *As You Like It* and the Robin Hood plays long ago,[1] and more recently Frank Kermode has remarked, "Characteristically, Jonson chose the Robin Hood legend as the theme of his *Sad Shepherd*. This hero of the dead golden world of England echoes throughout Elizabethan pastoral."[2] Actually, when we look at the play which has survived, we find that there are four scenes: (II. i; II. v; II. vii; and IV. ii) which have no counterpart in Lodge and deal entirely with the banished Duke and his foresters.

If we looked back at *The Comedy of Errors* and *The Two Gentlemen of Verona* we might guess that Shakespeare would have done some adjusting of plot and characters to provide more symmetry, though we might not have been able to guess specifically that he would make the two dukes brothers (as he was to do later in *The Tempest*) and consequently present the audience with the spectacle of two pairs of brothers, of different generations, at odds; two fathers, one natural and the other unnatural, and two heroines who are cousins and finally marry the two younger brothers.

Our awareness of the difference between a prose narrative and a play might lead us to the conclusion that the playwright would compress, especially since the long, euphuistic speeches in *Rosalynde* were in the outmoded style of Lyly, not the newer style of the nineties. It would be a fair but fortunate guess if we estimated the 37,500 words of the romance to be cut to the 21,305 words in the play. We should be able to predict, also, that the play would be able to present the various love plots of the comedy as occurring simultaneously, by interspersing scenes, whereas the novel must narrate them sequentially or make use of the old "meanwhile back at the ranch" formula. These are matters of structure, and a great deal of investigation of Shakespeare's structural craftsmanship has been undertaken in recent years.

What song the sirens sang is not, according to Sir Thomas Browne, beyond all conjecture. So, perhaps the lost *As You Like It* might have been, in the ways I have suggested, crudely reconstructed. But what can conjecture *not* supply? Those creations of the imagination which have no source in *Rosalynde* or the earlier comedies — the characters of Jaques, Touchstone, Audrey and William (poor fellow, there is little to him, but the author, who is entitled to his views on this subject, lets us hear that William is a fair name). Fortunately *As You Like It* was not lost. It is alive, on the stage and in the study. By comparing it with *Rosalynde* we have an opportunity to observe Shakespeare's imagination at work.

In the first sentence of *Rosalynde* Shakespeare found his theme. It was a theme he had treated before, comically. "There dwelled adjoyning to the citie of *Bourdeaux* a Knight of most honorable parentage, whom Fortune had graced with manie favours, and Nature honored with sundrie exquisite qualities, so beautified with the excellence of both, as it was a question whether Fortune or Nature were more prodigall in deciphering the riches of their bounties."[3] What came from Nature and what came from Fortune was the subject of endless discussion, and the subject was so popular that the audience would catch the point of Dogberry's handling of it when he tries, in his own way, to praise his neighbor Seacole, fit to be constable because it is said that he can read and write. "Come hither, neighbor Seacole. God hath bless'd you with a good name. To be a well-favor'd man is the gift of fortune, but to write and read comes by nature (*Much Ado* III. iii. 13-16). Dogberry has a marvelous talent for getting things, or words, backward, but even the courtly Celia needs some correction as to what is the result of nature and what is the gift of fortune:

> *Celia:* Let us sit and mock the good husewife Fortune from her wheel, that her gifts may henceforth be bestow'd equally.
> *Rosalind:* I would we could do so; for her benefits are mightily misplac'd, and the bountiful blind woman doth most mistake in her gifts to women.
> *Celia:* 'Tis true, for those that she makes fair she scarce makes honest, and those that she makes honest she makes very ill-favoredly.
> *Rosalind:* Nay, now thou goest from Fortune's office to Nature's Fortune reigns in the gifts of the world, not in the lineaments of Nature. (*AYLI* I. ii. 31-42)

73

But the dialogue goes on, in a courtly wit-combat between the two cousins, as if there were no end to the subject. In fact, there is no end, because a "deep contemplative" fool, alone in the forest, rails on Lady Fortune in good set terms without knowing that in the process he is arousing the admiration of the melancholy philosopher Jaques (II. vii. 12 ff.).

The theme of conflict between Nature and Fortune has affected Shakespeare's delineation of characters and the handling of the plot.[4] He leaves obscure (compared to Lodge) the basis for the Oliver-Orlando conflict and the Frederick-Rosalind conflict and by so doing makes the Nature-Fortune conflict more prominent. Duke Senior, who came from the realm of Fortune, the court, to the realm of nature, Arden, can "translate the stubbornness of Fortune into so quiet and so sweet a style" (II. i. 19-20) that he wins the admiration of Amiens, his fellow exiles, and the audience.

Here is an example of Shakespeare's habit of picking up a small clue of idea or language, one which echoed in his memory from earlier experiments, and making something substantial of it. Another is the snake in Oliver's narrative of how Orlando saved his life while he was sleeping under the oak tree.

> about his neck
> A green and gilded snake had wreath'd itself,
> Who with her head nimble in threats approach'd
> The opening of his mouth; but suddenly,
> Seeing Orlando, it unlink'd itself,
> And with indented glides did slip away
> Into a bush, under which bush's shade
> A lioness, with udders all drawn dry,
> Lay couching, head on ground, with cat-like watch
> When that the sleeping man should stir; for 'tis
> The royal disposition of that beast
> To prey on nothing that doth seem as dead.
>
> (IV. iii. 107-18)

There is no snake in Lodge's *Rosalynde,* only the lion. But the situation is one in which the watcher deliberates whether to waken the

74

sleeper or not (in the novel he deliberates a long time and makes a speech to himself). So, in a passage written years before, Shakespeare had used such a situation in a figurative sense, when, in *II Henry VI,* Salisbury is telling the King of the Commons' determination to guard him.

> They say, in care of your most royal person,
> That if your Highness should intend to sleep,
> And charge that no man should disturb your rest
> In pain of your dislike, or pain of death,
> Yet notwithstanding such a strait edict,
> Were there a serpent seen, with forked tongue
> That slyly glided toward your majesty,
> It were but necessary you were wak'd,
> Lest being suffer'd in that harmful slumber,
> The mortal worm might make the sleep eternal.
>
> (III. ii. 254-63)

Shakespeare often transfers hints he finds in Lodge from one context to the other. These details have been noticed, and are usually regarded as trivial, but nothing which may give us any clue as to the working of Shakespeare's imagination (in the treatment of his sources) is irrelevant here. Let us consider the wrestling. In Lodge the narrative is comparatively direct and straightforward:

> At last, when the tournament ceased, the wrestling began; and the Norman presented himself as challenger against all comers. But he looked like Hercules when he advanced himself against Achelous, so that the fury of his countenance amazed all that durst attempt to encounter with him in any deed of activity, till at last a lusty franklin of the country came with two tall men, that were his sons, of good lineaments and comely personage. The eldest of these, doing his obeisance to the king, entered the list, and presented himself to the Norman, who straight coped with him, and as a man that would triumph in the glory of his strength, roused himself with such fury that not only he gave him the fall but killed him with the weight of his corpulent personage. Which the younger brother seeing, leaped presently into the place and, thirsty after the revenge, assailed the Norman

with such valor that at the first encounter he brought him to his knees; which repulsed so the Norman that, recovering himself, fear of disgrace doubling his strength, he stepped so sternly to the young franklin that taking him up in his arms he threw him against the ground so violently that he broke his neck and so ended his days with his brother. At this unlooked for massacre, the people murmured and were all in a deep passion of pity; but the franklin, father unto these, never changed his countenance but, as a man of courageous resolution, took up the bodies of his sons without any show of outward discontent.[5]

In the play this is all narrated by LeBeau, but there are curious differences. Shakespeare has the father of the boys "an old man," but not specifically a franklin, and he has increased the number of the sons from two to three. This is probably to emphasize the folklore character of the story, because as LeBeau begins his story Celia remarks, jestingly, "I could match this beginning with an old tale." There is a kind of parallel, because Sir Rowland de Boys of the play *has* three sons, and it is the youngest who is the least likely but who finally marries the princess. Moreover Shakespeare, softening the violence wherever he properly could, does not have the old man's sons killed outright, but has Charles break their ribs so that there is little hope of life left in them. Strangely enough, Shakespeare completely reverses the behavior of the father. In the novel he is the complete Stoic, not showing his feelings by the slightest change of expression; in Shakespeare it is reported that he makes such pitiful dole that all the beholders take his part with weeping.

In the source it is the Norman wrestler who is compared to Hercules; Shakespeare adapts this into Rosalind's wish for Orlando as he enters the ring: "Now Hercules be thy speed, young man" (I. ii. 210).

Lodge treats the bout itself in typical romantic fashion:

At last Rosader, calling to mind the beauty of his new mistress, the fame of his father's honors, and the disgrace that should fall to his house by his misfortune, roused himself and threw the Norman against the ground, falling upon his chest with so willing a weight that the Norman yielded nature her due and Rosader the victory.[6]

To Shakespeare, of course, the bout was a staging problem, and the only evidence remaining to show how he did it is the Stage Direction "Shout." Presumably the actors on the stage surround the wrestlers, cutting off the audience's view until the fall, when the crowd parts and we can see Charles lying on the stage. Charles is not dead, apparently, but when he is addressed by the Duke, LeBeau replies, "He cannot speak, my lord." This speechlessness Shakespeare develops into another parallel: Orlando is overthrown by Rosalind and cannot speak. When she gives him the chain from her neck he can only speak in an aside:

> Can I not say 'I thank you'? My better parts
> Are all thrown down, and that which here stands up
> Is but a quintain, a mere liveless block.
>
> (I. ii. 249-51)

The point is emphasized. Rosalind has started to go but comes back, asking if he called. The irony is sharp — he *couldn't* call. She makes the metaphor which is in Orlando's mind, too — falling in love is suffering a fall in wrestling.

> Sir, you have wrestled well, and overthrown
> More than your enemies.

He can make no reply to her; he is speechless like the overthrown Charles.

> What passion hangs these weights upon my tongue?
> I cannot speak to her, yet she urg'd conference.
> O poor Orlando, thou art overthrown!
> Or Charles or something weaker masters thee.

(It is not Charles, obviously. After the one short round of their match Orlando tells the Duke that he was not even well breathed.)

In the next scene the figure is continued. Rosalind has, like an overthrown wrestler, been silent, without a word to throw at a dog. Celia advises her to wrestle with her affections, and she replies that they take the part of a better wrestler than herself. But Celia predicts that she will "try in time, in despite of a fall." Here the jest is getting rather close to bawdy (like the joke of her husband's that Juliet's nurse was so fond of) so Celia proceeds by "turning these jests out of service." She does not forget the trope, however; she uses it again when she informs Rosalind of the identity of the unknown poet who adorns the trees of Arden with verses in praise of her. After some teasing, she tells her cousin that "It is young Orlando, that tripp'd up the wrestler's heels and your heart both in an instant" (III. ii. 223-25).

There is no metaphor of wrestling in Lodge; it is all Shakespeare's. He has taken the actuality, on the stage, and turned it into an image. We shall also encounter examples of the opposite, when he turns a figure of speech into dramatic actuality.

We noticed that Shakespeare made Orlando speechless, like a defeated wrestler, when he first falls in love with Rosalind. This is the dramatic-psychological effect. What was he transforming? The courtly-euphuistic style of Lodge. In *Rosalynde,* when Rosader receives the jewel from Rosalynde (he receives it by messenger, not from her own hands) there is no question of his being striken dumb by love. Instead, being unfurnished, as Lodge says, with a like jewel to send her, "yet that he might more than in his looks discover his affection, he stepped into a tent, and taking pen and paper wrote this fancy:"[7] This fancy is a ten-line sonnet, which he sends to her and which makes her blush, but with a sweet content. Her response, instead of the speechlessness of Shakespeare's heroine, is to utter a "passion," a set debate with herself, full of words and full of rhetoric, at the conclusion of which she picks up her lute and warbles out the ditty called Rosalynde's Madrigal:

> Love in my bosom like a bee
> Doth suck his sweet;
> Now with his wings he plays with me
> Now with his feet.
> Within mine eyes he makes his nest,
> His bed amidst my tender breast;
> My kisses are his daily feast,
> And yet he robs me of my rest.
> 　　Ah, wanton, will ye?[8]

78

Yet for all this, Shakespeare found a hint for his characterization of Rosalind in Lodge. Just before she fell in love, Lodge's heroine "accounted love a toy, and fancy a momentary passion, that as it was taken in with a gaze might be shaken off with a wink, and therefore feared not to dally in the flame." Moreover, after she has dressed up as Ganymede, she speaks in a scoffing way about women: "What mad cattle you women be, whose hearts sometimes are made of adamant that will touch with no impression and sometime of wax that is fit for every form. They delight to be courted, and then they glory to seem coy; and when they are most desired, then they freeze with disdain. And this fault is so common to the sex, that you see it painted out in the shepherd's passions, who found his mistress as froward as he was enamored." She explains later that she is only keeping decorum by speaking in the persona of Ganymede, but "put me but into a petticoat, and I will stand in defiance to the uttermost that women are courteous, constant, virtuous, and what not."[9] Some of the disguised girl's volatility, then, is indicated in Lodge, but Shakespeare greatly amplifies it, particularly as he has two new foils for her, Touchstone and Jaques.

The subject of Rosalind's disguise could be discussed at much greater length. An extremely perceptive note is given by Anne Righter: "In a sense, Rosalind's disguise, unlike those of the other heroines of earlier comedies, prefigures the complications of the final plays. As Ganymede, she pretends to be the Rosalind she really is for the benefit of the love-sick Orlando. Essentially, however, this manoeuvre is a little game, a fantasy with none of the solemn, almost magical qualities of Imogen's or Perdita's disguise."[10] In *Rosalynde* Ganymede scoffs at the extravagances of Ovidian poets. "I can smile at the sonnettos, canzones, madrigals, rounds and roundelays that these pensive patients pour out when their eyes are more full of wantonness than their hearts of passions."[11]

The famous speech in *As You Like It* in which Rosalind deflates the ancient myths about heroes who have died for love is partly developed from a hint in Lodge. "Daphne, that bonny wench, was not turned into a bay tree as the poets feign, but for her chastity her fame was immortal, resembling the laurel that is ever green."[12] This grows into

The poor world is almost six thousand years old, and in all this time there was not any man died in his own person, *videlicet,* in a love-cause. Troilus had his brains dash'd out with a Grecian club, yet he did what he could to die before, and he is one of the patterns of love. Leander, he would have liv'd many a fair year though Hero had turn'd nun, if it had not been for a hot midsummer night; for, good youth, he went but forth to wash him in the Hellespont, and being taken with the cramp was drown'd; and the foolish chroniclers of that age found it was — Hero of Sestos. But these are all lies: men have died from time to time and worms have eaten them, but not for love.

(IV. i. 93-108)

Here is a fusing of sources. It is clear that Shakespeare had read Marlowe's *Hero and Leander* before writing this play, because he quotes a line from it, "Whoever loved that loved not at first sight?" So the treatment of Daphne triggered the elaboration of Troilus and the evocation of the Hero and Leander story. Perhaps another passage in Lodge had an influence on the transformation. It is Phoebe's renunciation of her shepherd lover Montanus: "Wert thou, Montanus, as fair as Paris, as hardy as Hector, as constant as Troilus, as loving as Leander, Phoebe could not love because she cannot love at all; and therefore if thou pursue me with Phoebus, I must fly with Daphne."[13]

Shakespeare's shepherdesses do not talk classical mythology; this is the perquisite of his courtly, educated people. (Perdita in *The Winter's Tale* is really a princess, as the audience knows.) But in the artificial pastoral of Lodge there is no such sense of decorum. All the characters, of whatever rank or background, speak the same language. Lodge's romance is significantly subtitled "Euphues' Golden Legacy." But Shakespeare will pick up a phrase or idea from one character in Lodge and give it to another in his play. An example is from the same passage in which Phoebe rejects her lover; she says "Well, sir, if your market be made nowhere else, home again, for your mart is at the fairest." Shakespeare transfers this to Rosalind's mouth; it is said, not *by* Phoebe, but *to* her:

But mistress, know yourself, down on your knees
And thank heaven, fasting, for a good man's love;
For I must tell you friendly in your ear,
Sell when you can; you are not for all markets.

(III. v. 57-60)

It is an addition to the practical, common-sense aspect of Rosalind's character, a trait which is heightened by the contrast with Orlando's amorous extravagance and the whole tradition of romantic love reflected in the play.

The green world of Arden is one of Shakespeare's imaginative triumphs. It is not only the setting for the pastoral part (as opposed to the courtly part) of the play, but it is also, as C. L. Barber and Northrop Frye have pointed out, a therapeutic agent, a stage in a ritual renewal of life. In Frye's words, "The green world charges the comedies with a symbolism in which the comic resolution contains a suggestion of the old ritual pattern of the victory of summer over winter."[14]

Shakespeare's vision of pastoral was not new in *As You Like It,* though this is the first of his plays to develop the idea very fully. The pastoral life is contemplated by the King in *III Henry VI,* as he sits on a molehill while the battle is in progress:

O God! methinks it were a happy life
To be no better than a homely swain,
To sit upon a hill, as I do now,
To carve out dials quaintly, point by point,
Thereby to see the minutes how they run:
How many makes the hour full complete,
How many hours brings about the day,
How many days will finish up the year,
How many years a mortal man may live.
When this is known, then to divide the times:
So many hours must I tend my flock,
So many hours must I take my rest,
So many hours must I contemplate,
So many hours must I sport myself,

So many days my ewes have been with young,
So many weeks ere the poor fools will ean,
So many months ere I shall shear the fleece:
So minutes, hours, days, weeks, months, and years,
Pass'd over to the end they were created,
Would bring white hairs unto a quiet grave.
Ah! what a life were this! how sweet! how lovely!
Gives not the hawthorn bush a sweeter shade
To shepherds looking on their silly sheep
Than doth a rich embroider'd canopy
To kings that fear their subjects' treachery?
Oh yes, it doth; a thousandfold it doth.
And to conclude, the shepherd's homely curds,
His cold thin drink out of his leather bottle,
His wonted sleep under a fresh tree's shade,
All which secure and sweetly he enjoys,
Is far beyond a prince's delicates —
His viands sparkling in a golden cup,
His body couched in a curious bed,
When care, mistrust, and treason waits on him.   (II. v. 21-54)

The first we hear of the green world of Arden in *As You Like It* is in the report of court gossip given by Charles the wrestler to Oliver. He is asked what has become of the exiled Duke. "They say he is already in the forest of Arden, and a many merry men with him; and there they live like the old Robin Hood of England. They say many young gentlemen flock to him every day, and fleet the time carelessly, as they did in the golden world" (I. i. 114-19).

This identification of the pastoral Arden with the forest of Robin Hood and activities of the exiles with the pastimes prevalent in the golden age of innocence is not in Lodge's *Rosalynde*. But Shakespeare had already taken his hero into a forest, there to become the leader of a band of outlaws, in *The Two Gentlemen of Verona*. One of the outlaws exclaims, when he learns of Valentine's accomplishments, "By the bare scalp of Robin Hood's fat friar / This fellow were a king for our wild faction!" (IV. i. 36-37). And, in meditation, Valentine asserts the same values of the pastoral life as those dreamt of by King Henry VI:

How use doth breed a habit in a man!
This shadowy desert, unfrequented woods,
I better brook than flourishing peopled towns:
Here can I sit alone, unseen of any,
And to the nightingale's complaining notes
Tune my distresses and record my woes.

(V. iv. 1-6)

The first we see of Arden directly in Shakespeare's play is at the beginning of Act II. But we have been prepared for it immediately before, when Celia and Rosalind are preparing to run away to the forest and take the fool with them. Celia says

Now go [we in] content
To liberty, and not to banishment.   (I. iii. 137-38)

This is the emphasis of pastoral — liberty and content.

The exiled Duke's speech is more elaborate than that of King Henry or of Valentine. It is crucial to an understanding of the play:

Now, my co-mates and brothers in exile
Hath not old custom made this life more *sweet*
Than that of painted pomp? Are not these woods
More free from peril than the envious court?
Here feel we not the penalty of Adam,
The seasons' difference, as the icy *fang*
And churlish chiding of the *winter's* wind,
Which when it *bites* and blows upon my body
Even till I shrink with *cold,* I smile and say
"This is no flattery; these are counsellors
That feelingly persuade me what I am."
Sweet are the uses of adversity
Which, like the toad, ugly and *venomous,*
Wears yet a precious jewel in his head;
And this our life, exempt from public haunt,
Finds tongues in trees, books in the running brooks,
Sermons in stones, and good in everything.
I would not change it.   (II. i. 1-18)

The emphasis on the rigors of winter is not standard pastoral, nor is it a motif in Lodge. It is Shakespeare's emphasis and is not casual or accidental. The theme is reinforced by two songs, "Under the green-wood tree," of which the first line comes from a Robin Hood ballad, and Amiens' later song, "Blow, blow, thou winter wind." There is no enemy in the green world but winter and rough weather, it seems, but these rigors of climate are mild compared to the suffering we feel from human ingratitude, or benefits forgot.

This remarkable product of Shakespeare's imagination is related not so much to plays which he had written before but to something still to come. The theme, worked out partly comically here, as in Jaques' parody of "Under the greenwood tree," is to become a main tragic theme in *King Lear.* As Maynard Mack has pointed out, there are striking resemblances between the sunniest of Shakespeare's comedies and the darkest of his tragedies. Both plays contain (1) a displaced ruler, (2) good characters forced out of civilization into a natural environment, (3) a wind which is urged to blow because it is not so unkind as ingratitude, (4) a fool who knows he has been in a better place, but is loyal, (5) good and evil brothers, with the good brother leading an old man, and (6) a daughter of the displaced ruler united with her father before the play ends. We might say that this imaginative construction in *As You Like It* is the essential preparation for *King Lear* some six years later.[15]

The qualities of Arden are made the subject of comedy, too. There is an occasional bit of comedy in Lodge, as when a rustic character dresses in a costume which Elizabethan readers would recognize as absurd, but there is no comic evaluation of the pastoral world itself. Shakespeare introduces Touchstone and Jaques, his most important additions to the cast of characters provided by Lodge, largely for the purpose of providing commentary, from different points of view, on the values of Arden.

Touchstone is witty in Arden, but at court, under another name, he seems to have been a "Nature's natural, the cutter-off of Nature's wit," a dull fool who served as a whetstone for the wit of others (I. ii. 51-56). Whether Shakespeare changed his mind during the course of composition, because Kemp had given place to Armin as principal

84

comic actor, or whether this was mere carelessness, as in the case of the middle de Boys brother, Jaques, we will probably never know. But Touchstone in Arden is a character from court, who is condescending to the rustics, including the one he is to marry ("Bear yourself more seeming, Audrey") and his is the voice by which evaluation of the pastoral life is expressed. His first remark about Arden is that "When I was at home, I was in a better place." It is important to note, however, that he adds "but travellers must be content." He delights in showing off his philosophical skill in proving that one who has not been in court is damned, but he can balance very evenly the qualities of pastoral life when Corin asks his opinion of it. This kind of life is not for everybody, as Corin has realized when the project of buying a cottage, pasture and flock for Rosalind and Celia first comes up. Touchstone would say it is a matter of mood, so his paradoxes on it are essentially true though they sound contradictory. Fundamentally, of course, the forest is the real touchstone of people there; as the fool says, "You have spoken, whether wisely or no, let the forest judge" (III. ii. 121-22).

Jaques' satirical comments are usually directed at cultivated society, with its hypocrisies. He is the melancholy satirist, who invectively pierces through the body of the country, city, court. But he attacks the Robin Hood existence of the exiled Duke and his men as usurpation and tyranny over the deer and other denizens of the forest. Moreover, the stanza he composes to the idyllic "Under the greenwood tree" song condemns those who escape from the city to a pastoral scene:

> If it do come to pass
> That any man turn ass,
> Leaving his wealth and ease
> A stubborn will to please,
> Ducdame, ducdame, ducdame.
>
> (II. v. 52-56)

Renato Poggioli's analysis of *As You Like It* takes the bitterness of Jaques' rejection and the harshness of the weather in Arden to be an unexpected deviation from the pastoral scheme, but he thinks it provides "a happy paradox, inspiring the lovely songs of the play, which are at once charming pastorals of winter and lively idylls of the North."[16] Poggioli sees the play as moving on three levels: the exiled Duke and his companions, who are in Arden-Arcadia not from choice but from necessity; the shepherds, Corin, Sylvius, and Phebe, who are independent in a moral sense but not in a material sense, since they do not own their flocks and cannot practice the virtue of hospitality; and the churlish peasants Audrey and William. "Thus noblemen, shepherds and peasants stand respectively for poetry, literature, and reality; and the third group is set against the other two."

One might suppose from this that Poggioli reads Shakespeare's play as anti-pastoral, but this conclusion would be over-simplified in view of his comment on Touchstone's paradoxical answer to Corin's question of how he likes the shepherd's life in III. ii. 13-21. "Through the apparent nonsense of his witty clown Shakespeare seems to reply to three important questions. The first is whether he values or scorns the pastoral ideal. The second is whether this comedy is a pastoral play. The third is whether it reaffirms or denies the traditional poetics of the pastoral. The equivocal answer the clown gives to all three on behalf of the poet amounts to an echo of the comedy's title: as you like it."

We have been watching Shakespeare's imagination in the act of transforming what he found in the euphuistic romance of Lodge; we have considered the structure, the plot, the characters, the setting and its meaning, the commentary. But we have not considered, in enough detail, the words. The great pioneer in this kind of study was Walter Whiter, whose book *Specimen of a Commentary,* published in 1794, is devoted to *As You Like It,* or rather, to an illustration of Whiter's method, based upon Locke's theory of the association of ideas, as applied to *As You Like It.* "It is extremely curious," writes Whiter, "that our poet has caught many words and even turns of expression belonging to the novel from which the play is taken; though he has applied them in a mode generally different, and often very remote from the original."[17]

His first example comes from a passage early in the novel, after the dreary business of the legacy of Sir John of Bordeaux' legacy to his sons, at the beginning of the characterization of Saladyne and Rosader, the point at which Shakespeare may be supposed to have begun to take an interest in the story: "As he [Rosader] was thus ruminating his melancholy passions, in came Saladine with his men, and seeing his brother in a brown study, and to forget his wonted *reverence,* thought to *shake* him out of his dumps thus."

In the play, after Orlando's first expository speech to Adam about the cruelty of his older brother, Oliver enters, and Orlando tells the old servant to "Go apart, Adam, and thou shalt hear how he will *shake* me up." The dialogue for the next few lines merely recapitulates the expository speech, but finally Orlando says "I have as much of my father in me as you, albeit I confess your coming before me is nearer to his *reverence.*" Such an example may be merely "curious," as Whiter calls it, but there are more elaborate examples of word association which may not go back to Lodge but instead to some other association of ideas, or words, in Shakespeare's mind like the famous dog-candy-flattery-heels complex, which Whiter was the first to discover.

This famous image cluster plays a part in the Duke's opening speech in Act II, as C. H. Hobday has pointed out.[18] The cluster is a complex one, and includes the terms *sweet* or *candy* (as a verb); *poison* or *venom; winter, ice,* or *hail; cold; melt* or *thaw; sun; brook* or *stream; drop; tears* and *stone,* as well as *dog* and *fawning.* The Duke's first speech, quoted above, contains *sweet,* (twice), *icy, winter, cold, flattery, venomous, brooks, stones, pomp, court,* and *tongues. The dog* appears in *fang* and *bites.* Not much later, the report of the first Lord on the musings of the melancholy Jaques on the wounded deer, contains *brook* (twice), *tears* (twice) and *stream.* The most compressed form of this image cluster occurs in *Timon* in the lines

> Will the *cold brook,*
> *Candied* with *ice,* caudle thy morning taste?
>
> (IV. iii. 225-26)

The word "candy" meant "to form into crystal," as in the following quotation from Sylvester's DuBartas, 1598:

> Th' excessive cold of the mid-aire *candies* it
> (a dropping shower) all in bals of *Y cy-stone.*

Another illustration of the persistent life of this image complex is a passage of dialogue in *Antony and Cleopatra:*

> *Antony:* To *flatter* Caesar, would you mingle eyes
> With one that ties his points?
> *Cleopatra:*   Not know me yet?
> *Antony: Cold*-hearted toward me?
> *Cleopatra:*   Ah dear, if I be so,
> From my *cold* heart let heaven engender *hail,*
> And *poison* it in the source, and the first *stone*
> Drop in my neck; as it determines, so
> *Dissolve* my life! The next Caesarion [smite],
> Till by degrees the memory of my womb,
> Together with my brave Egyptians all,
> By {*discandying*} of this pelleted storm,
> Lie graveless, till the flies and gnats of Nile
> Have buried them for prey!
>
> (III. xiii. 156-67)

Hobday's commentary continues: "In Cleopatra's speech a number of ideas associated by Shakespeare with flattery but with no logical connection with one another are integrated into the image of the hailstorm; the stones of *As You Like It* become a hailstone, Richard II's waterdrops a verb, and the ideas of *candy* and *melt* are fused into *discandying.* We do not normally associate Egypt with hailstones; when writing this passage Shakespeare, who made considerable use of Biblical imagery in *Antony and Cleopatra,* evidently had in mind the hardening of Pharaoh's heart, the plagues of hail, flies, gnats, and the death of the first-born in the story of the plagues of Egypt" (p. 13).

I might add that it is only a short time after the Duke's speech in *As You Like It,* when Jaques, making his exit, says he will go sleep, if he can; if not, he will rail against all the first-born of Egypt. The association noticed in *Antony and Cleopatra* already existed in Shakespeare's mind when he wrote *As You Like It.* Jonas Barish, in commenting on the logical patterns in Shakespeare's prose, says about this speech, "It is worth noticing here, as with most of Shakespeare's logical schemes, that though the pattern itself is highly formulaic, the completion of it is anything but predictable. 'Ile go sleepe if I can' may prompt us to suspect an antithesis; 'if I cannot' confirms the suspicion. But who could have foreseen the bizarre outcome, 'Ile raile against all the first borne of Egypt'?"[19] I suppose no one could have predicted it, since literary criticism is not a predictive science but an interpretive art, but we have been able to trace, through Shakespeare's associations and memory, fragments which enable us to understand the speech more clearly.

My colleague Dr. Jenijoy LaBelle points out to me that Psalm 78:51 contains the line "And smote all the firstborn in Egypt" and that in the Geneva Bible (1560 edition) the page on which that verse occurs has a note at the top of the page reading MAN'S INGRATITUDE. In the next scene but one after this, Amiens sings his song about Man's Ingratitude. This exact phrase occurs nowhere else in Shakespeare.

The topic, however, is central in the plays, not only in the tragedies, especially *King Lear,* but in the comedies as well. In *Twelfth Night* Viola declares

> I hate ingratitude more in a man
> Than lying, vainness, babbling, drunkenness,
> Or any taint of vice whose strong corruption
> Inhabits our frail blood ...
>
> (III. iv. 354-57)

In Act II, when Jaques has given his elaborate praise of the fool he met in the forest, he concludes with the wish that he too shall have a motley coat. Jaques replies:

> It is my only *suit,*
> Provided that you *weed* your better judgments
> Of all opinion that grows *rank* in them
> That I am wise. (II. vii. 44-47)

"Suit" and "weed" are both words for clothes, but "suit" also means accommodate, and "weed" also means a plant. Toward the end of

Jaques' pronouncement of what he would do as fool-satirist and what his defense would be, occur the lines

> Or what is he of basest function
> That says his *bravery* is not on my cost,
> Thinking I meant him, but therein *suits*
> His folly to the mettle of my speech? (II. vii. 79-82)

In *Coriolanus,* one of the tribunes, urging the people to turn against the hero, says

> Besides, forget not
> With what contempt he wore the humble *weed:*
> How in his *suit* he scorned you.
>
> (II. iii. 220-22)

A "weed," the plant, is often rank in Shakespeare, because of its smell (there are several examples in *Hamlet*), but the association does not require that every link in the chain be present for it to work. So, in a quibbling between Rosalind and Orlando, we find

> *Orlando:* Who could be out, being before his beloved mistress?
> *Rosalind:* Marry, that should you, if I were your mistress, or I should think my honesty *ranker* than my wit.
> *Orlando:* What, of my *suit?*
> *Rosalind:* Not out of your apparel, and yet out of your *suit.*
>
> (IV. i. 81-85)

Whiter goes on to say that "the reader, I hope, will not imagine that I refine too much, when I inform him that the word *services* is to be referred to the same association; and that it was suggested to the poet by another signification which *suit* sometimes bears of *livery,* the peculiar dress by which the servants and retainers of one family were distinguished from those of another."[20] So, he thinks, when Rosalind gives the chain to Orlando, saying "Wear this for me, one out of *suits* with fortune," she is declaring that she no longer wears Fortune's livery, an interpretation which Steevens, who holds no doctrine of association, agrees with and which Kittredge allows as possible. There is certainly much in *As You Like It* about service, and there is much about the clothes one is garbed in. Furness remarks that "it is not necessary that we should agree with Whiter in order to admire his ingenuity. That his theory is incapable of downright proof must be confessed, and yet who can gainsay it?"

Professor Bullough, in his excellent account of the sources of *As You Like It*, says that in general Shakespeare looked to his sources for incidents, plots, and personages, but that he also used them for themes —"not fixed ideas such as made Spenser an allegorist and Ben Jonson a dramatist of Humours — but general motifs to be manipulated in the process of re-creation." The theme he found in Lodge, Bullough continues, is the general one of the opposition between Fortune and the Good Life, between Nature and Artifice, between the manners of the Court and those of the Country.[21]

What needs further attention is the way in which Shakespeare developed aspects of this theme (or series of themes), often from the slenderest of hints. There is not much discussion of the difference between courtly and country manners in Lodge, for the good reason that the shepherds in his romance are as courtly (or euphuistic) as the courtiers. Corydon, in delivering his praise of country life to Aliena, says "Care cannot harbor in our cottages, nor do our homely couches know broken slumbers. As we exceed not in diet, so we have enough to satisfy; and, mistress, I have so much Latin, *satis est quod sufficit.*" If old Corydon knows some Latin, it is not surprising that Montanus (the original of Shakespeare's Silvius) knows the myth of Narcissus and is capable, when his passions are aroused, of composing a sonnet in French. There is, however, one small passage in which the manners of court and country are contrasted. It is spoken by Aliena (who is really courtly herself, under the disguise) to Saladyne:

> But, sir, our country amours are not like your courtly fancies, nor is our wooing like your suing; for poor shepherds never plain them till love pain them, where the courtier's eyes is full of passions, when his heart is most free from affection. They court to discover their eloquence, we woo to ease our sorrows.

From such a mild challenge to the sincerity of a professed lover Shakespeare, it seems, developed the marvellously comic dialogue between Touchstone and Corin. In this argument, though Corin gives up before the superior courtly wit of Touchstone, yet his sense of values earns him the title of natural philosopher, and his statement of his life and condition is the ultimate in humble pride:

> Sir, I am a true laborer; I earn that I eat, get that I wear, owe no man hate, envy no man's happiness, glad of other men's good, content with my harm; and the greatest of my pride is to see my ewes graze and my lambs suck.
>
> (III. ii. 73-77)

Another theme of some importance in Shakespeare's play is the subject of time. It is a natural enough theme for pastoral, because, as Ralegh's answer to Marlowe's "Passionate Shepherd" and many other passages show, the most idyllic pastoral environment has one hostile element in it — time. Yet Shakespeare was not increasing the pastoral element he found in Lodge, but decreasing it. However, a dozen passages in *As You Like It* deal with time, and in such a way as to make it a major theme of the play. Charles describes the followers of the banished Duke fleeting the time carelessly, as they did in the golden world. This is hearsay; the Duke at the end of the play speaks of the "shrewd days and nights" they have spent together. Touchstone's debut before his most admiring critic, Jaques, was a disquisition on time, considered hour by hour; Jaques' own contribution, later on in the same great scene, is the satirical Seven Ages of Man speech, which is in effect a discussion of time. Touchstone drew a dial from his poke, and he was apparently well provided, for we are explicitly told that there is no clock i' the forest (III. ii. 301). The relative speed of the passing of time is the subject of Ganymede's showy display of his wit to Orlando on first meeting in the forest. Then of course, time is important to lovers, so Rosalind can discourse wittily and somewhat bitterly on dividing up an hour into smaller parts (IV. i. 44-49). She is scornful of the sentimentality of the expectation of infinite time when she advises against saying "forever and a day (IV. i. 146).

Emphasis on time is reiterated in the arranged conclusion, for the wedding and the unraveling of all the mystery is staged for *tomorrow*. Finally, there is the question of value, so pervasively asked throughout this play — what does it mean to keep time or to waste it? An innocent song ("It was a lover and his lass") is the occasion. The pages insist they kept time while they sang, but Touchstone — should it not have been Jaques? — says he counts it but time lost to hear such a foolish song.

Of course Shakespeare was not confined to Lodge's *Rosalynde* when he was writing his play, but it is curious to see how little interest there is in time in the novel. One gets an occasional remark like that of Ganymede's on Rosader's first visit to the cottage, "therefore we shepherds say, 'tis time to go to dinner; for the sun and our stomachs are shepherds' dials." That is all. The continued and profound interest in time is all Shakespeare's.

The subject of what Shakespeare did to Lodge's *Rosalynde* has been treated by many critics. It is perhaps not yet exhausted. Helen Gardner remarks that "Shakespeare added virtually nothing to the plot of Lodge's novel. There is no comedy in which, in one sense, he invents so little."[24] According to Harold Jenkins, "It is in the defectiveness of its action that *As You Like It* differs from the rest of the major comedies — in its dearth not only of big theatrical scenes but of events linked together by the logical intricacies of cause and effect."[25]

Helen Gardner thinks that "story was not Shakespeare's concern in this play; its soul is not to be looked for there. If you were to go to *'As You Like It'* for the story you would, in Johnson's phrase, 'hang yourself'" (p. 20). Dr. Johnson himself, however, would not agree. He declared that "of this play the fable is wild and pleasing."[26] Marco Mincoff, like others, wonders why Shakespeare chose Lodge's novel at all. "Here we have, in *As You Like It,* that combination of the theme of love's foolishness with the clash between appearance and reality that lies at the bottom of most of Shakespeare's riper comedies and for which Lodge's novel, though it offered him ample opportunities to develop it, gave him nothing directly."[27] It was the comic possibilities inherent in the disguised heroine which interested him most, Mincoff thinks. "It is not only the fact that all Shakespeare's real invention and reorganization of plot and content is concentrated on the comedy of courtship that shows us where the chief interest of the story lay for him, and that guying of pastoral was mainly a by-product thrown in for good measure and demanding very little brainwork on his part. The fact that the result is so much the mixture as before confirms that interpretation."

He subdued the violence, the melodrama and the theatrical scenes available to him in his source; he made the play *less* pastoral than the novel, if by pastoral we mean the traditional Arcadian pastoral; his major invented characters, Touchstone and Jaques, are commentators rather than characters essential to the plot. In fact, his Rosalind spends most of her time commenting rather than doing, and she comments on a very wide range of subjects.

We have suggested that Shakespeare's borrowings from Lodge were not confined to characters and plot. One critic, surveying pastoral romance and finding it largely a matter of the hero's observation of himself in two contexts, an actual and an ideal one — believes that the important device is "conscious artifice, the deliberate playing of a role through a mask." "And," continues Walter R. Davis, "it is Lodge's *Rosalynde* that uses histrionics in the interests of ethical clarification more fully than any other work of Elizabethan prose fiction, pastoral or otherwise,"[28]

It is certainly true that Shakespeare, though he did not choose to exploit theatrical scenes available to him in the novel, did *dramatize* whatever he took, and that dramatization is largely dialogue. The wit combats of Rosalind and Orlando, of Touchstone and the rustics, of Jaques and the world at large — these are the stuff of the play. And, as to what it means, Helen Gardner, who calls it Shakespeare's "most Mozartian comedy," may well sum it up: "The discovery of truth by feigning, and of what is wisdom and what folly by debate, is the centre of *As You Like It*."[29]

Chapter 6

THE WINTER'S TALE AND PANDOSTO

There is a whole generation of critics growing up for whom A Winter's Tale *and* The Tempest *are as important as* King Lear *or* Hamlet, *not more, but not less.*

A. Bartlett Giamatti

When Shakespeare turned to Greene's *Pandosto* for material, he may have thought wryly of the author, now long dead, who had attacked Shakespeare when he was just emerging as a playwright: "An upstart crow, beautified with our feathers." He now had feathers far more beautiful than any Greene or his fellow university wits could display. He would take this romance about jealousy and the triumph of time and make of it something new and popular for the stage.[1] But perhaps a more recent memory inspired him even more. His younger colleague, John Fletcher, had written in 1608 a play called *The Faithful Shepherdess.* It was a failure. Fletcher explained, in the published quarto of the play, the reason why. He had been trying to write tragicomedy and the audience, he said, expected something else. The people expected, he said, "a play of country hired shepherds in gray cloaks, with curtailed dogs in strings," in other words, realistic English low-life characters (like the Shepherd and the Clown and Autolycus). Furthermore they wanted the traditional elements of folk festival, so, says Fletcher, "missing Whitsun-ales, cream, wassail and morris dances, they began to be angry." Shakespeare, in Act IV, scene iv of *The Winter's Tale,* gave the audience what it wanted and vainly expected to

95

get in *The Faithful Shepherdess*. It is one of the longest and most varied scenes he ever wrote. It contains not only the familiar, recognizable and very funny rustic characters, but also a Whitsun-ale masquerading, with two dances, several ballads, and a catch. There is nothing in *Pandosto* that compares in any way with Act IV, scene iv of *The Winter's Tale*. The meeting of Dorastus (Florizel) and Fawnia (Perdita) may have given some faint hint for the sheepshearing festival, but no more:

> It happened not long after this that there was a meeting of all the farmers' daughters in Sicily, whither Fawnia was also bidden as the mistress of the feast. Who, having attired herself in her best garments, went among the rest of her companions to the merry meeting, there spending the day in such homely pastimes as shepherds use.
>
> As the evening grew on and their sports ceased, each taking their leave of the other, Fawnia, desiring one of her companions to bear her company, went home by the flock to see if they were well folded. And as they returned it fortuned that Dorastus (who all that day had been hawking and killed store of game) encountered by the way these two maids. And casting his eye suddenly on Fawnia, he was half afraid, fearing that with Actaeon he had seen Diana. For he thought such exquisite perfection could not be found in any mortal creature.[2]

This sounds more like Ferdinand than like Florizel. Still, we do not know, for Shakespeare chose to show us Florizel and Perdita already in love; he leaps over the firstlings of their relationship except for a reminiscence:

> *Florizel:*   I bless the time
> When my good falcon made her flight across
> Thy father's ground.

(IV. iv. 14-16)

Pandosto did indeed affect the writing of *The Tempest* as well as *The Winter's Tale*. As Walter Davis remarks, "we can see human purposes operating effectively in the beautiful dialectical process (repeated by Ferdinand and Miranda in *The Tempest* III. i) by which Dorastus descends from his pride of place, Fawnia gives up a little of humility's security, and they both reach the middle ground of content where each is the other's servant."[3]

For the tedious debates, with each other and with themselves, which Greene's hero and heroine indulge in, Shakespeare substitutes the poetry of impassioned, though somewhat fearful, love. Yet even then he can pick up a detail from the alien atmosphere of *Pandosto*. In the romance Fawnia has grown, in a couple of paragraphs, from an infant who has learned to call the old shepherd and his wife "Dad" and "Mom," to a sixteen-year-old of great beauty:

> But the people, thinking she was daughter to the shepherd Porrus, rested only amazed at her beauty and wit. Yea, she won such favor and commendations in every man's eye, as her beauty was not only praised in the country but also spoken of in court. Yet such was her submiss modesty that, although her praise daily increased, her mind was no whit puffed up with pride, but humbled herself as became a country maid and the daughter of a poor shepherd. Every day she went forth with her sheep to the field, keeping them with such care and diligence as all men thought she was very painful, defending her face from the heat of the sun with no other veil but with a garland made of boughs and flowers. Which attire became her so gallantly as she seemed to be the goddess Flora herself for beauty.[4]

When Perdita first appears in Act IV, her appearance having been prepared for by the Chorus and by the conversation between Polixenes and Camillo which takes note of rumors about a shepherd's daughter "of most rare note," she is in festive costume, and Florizel comments:

> These your unusual weeds to each part of you
> Do give a life; no shepherdess, but Flora,
> Peering in April's front.

> (IV. iv. 1-3)

It is of the first importance to realize the meaning of Perdita's "unusual weeds." She is in costume for the festivities, a costume suggesting the goddess Flora, "most goddess-like prank'd up." She feels uneasy in her "borrowed flaunts," and suspects she would swoon if she saw herself in a mirror. For, as she knows, one's costume affects one's behavior; when she goes farther than she would usually go, in her natural innocence, in speaking of her lover buried alive in her arms, she almost repents:

> Methinks I play as I have seen them do
> In Whitsun pastorals. Sure this robe of mine
> Does change my disposition.

(IV. iv. 133-35)

She is abashed also that the royal Florizel has obscured himself with a swain's wearing, and trembles prophetically to think of being discovered by his father. Florizel cites the example of the ancient gods, Jupiter, Neptune, Apollo, disguising themselves in the pursuit of love, but makes the distinction that his disguise is more innocent than theirs

> since my desires
> Run not before mine honor, nor my lusts
> Burn hotter than my faith.

(IV. iv. 33-35)

Perdita and Florizel are in costume, but they are not disguised; everybody recognizes them. The purpose is not deception; it is to contrast the festive merriment of the feast, with its traditional aura of sexual laxity, with the innocence and purity of the lovers. In *As You Like It* Shakespeare had used disguise for deception and had got his contrasting views of love by juxtaposing Rosalind-Orlando with Audrey-Touchstone. The technique in *The Winter's Tale* is simpler, more delicate, more refined.

In some respects it is unfair to compare Shakespeare's handling of his sources in *As You Like It* and *The Winter's Tale* because *Pandosto* is not the same thing as *Rosalynde*. For one thing it is shorter; *Rosalynde* is about two and a half times as long. (The plays are roughly the same length; *As You Like It* has 21,305 words; *The Winter's Tale* has 24,543). In writing *The Winter's Tale* Shakespeare was not forced to compress, as he was in *As You Like It;* he omits some of his source, but he amplifies a great deal more. Furthermore, the themes are different. Shakespeare is no longer interested in the conflict between Fortune and Nature, and this fact is of some critical interest. Fortune causes everything in *Pandosto;* it is subordinate in *The Winter's Tale.* This is true not only in general, but also in specific detail. Let us look at the passage which Kenneth Muir says is "the only substantial passage in the novel which Shakespeare borrows with comparatively little alteration."[5] It is the accused queen's defense at her second trial. Greene's Bellaria says, "If the divine powers be privy to human actions (as no doubt they are) I hope my patience shall make fortune blush and my unspotted life shall stain spitefully discredit."[6] Shakespeare's Hermione:

> But thus, if pow'rs divine
> Behold our human actions (as they do)
> I doubt not then but innocence shall make
> False accusation blush, and tyranny
> Tremble at patience. You, my lord, best know
> ([Who] least will seem to do so) my past life
> Hath been as continent, as chaste, as true,
> As I am now unhappy; which is more
> Than history can pattern, though devis'd
> And play'd to take spectators . . .

> (III. ii. 28-37)

Whereas *fortune* was made to blush in the source, *false accusation* is the culprit in *The Winter's Tale.* The conflict is a dramatic one, with the trial made into a play, to which the gods are audience, and the characters morality-types — Innocence and Patience on the one side, confronted by False Accusation and Tyranny on the other. This is merely the climactic scene; the whole first half of the play is the incredible contrast between her pure, blameless past life and her present misery, which outdoes anything history can summon up, *though divis'd / And play'd to take spectators.*

This same speech of Bellaria's Shakespeare combined with another, from her first trial, in the lines concluding Hermione's defense:

99

> if I shall be condemn'd
> Upon surmises (all proofs sleeping else
> But what your jealousies awake), I tell you
> 'Tis rigor and not law. Your honors all
> I do refer me to the oracle:
> Apollo be my judge! (III. ii. 111-16)

He makes Hermione stand throughout, though Greene has Bellaria fall to her knees; Bellaria in prison wrings her hands and gushes forth streams of tears; Hermione is a Stoic who says to her women

> Do not weep, good fools,
> There is no cause: when you shall know your mistress
> Has deserv'd prison, then abound in tears
> As I come out. (II. i. 118-21)

As Fitzroy Pyle remarks, concerning the way in which Shakespeare's imagination was stimulated by details in *Pandosto,* "The effect of a stimulus is unpredictable, however. It may set the imagination to work but does not determine how it will work."[7]

Another reason why the comparison between the handling of sources in *As You Like It* and in *The Winter's Tale* is complicated is that in the meantime Shakespeare had written other plays and the writing of these plays affected his imagination and therefore his treatment. Of special importance are *Much Ado about Nothing, Pericles,* and, surprisingly, *Macbeth. Much Ado* may have been written before *As You Like It* or at about the same time; its relationship to *The Winter's Tale* logically arises from similarities in plot. As summarized by Ernest Schanzer, they are these:

> In both plays the husband (or bridegroom) publicly accuses his wife (or bride) of unchastity; she falls into a swoon and is believed to be dead by all who are present; but she recovers and is secretly hidden away while her husband (or bridegroom) continues to believe her to be dead. He discovers her innocence, repents of his actions, devises an epitaph setting forth the cause of her death, and vows to visit the tomb as an act of penance.[8]

Some details from the *source* of *Much Ado,* unused in that play, lingered in Shakespeare's mind for use in *The Winter's Tale.* One is that the repentant slanderer promises that when he does marry again it will be to a wife chosen for him by someone dear to the supposedly dead woman.

One further hint Shakespeare may have derived from the *novella* (Bandello's 20th novel). Describing the slandered woman lying in her swoon, Bandello remarks that she resembled a marble statue rather than a live woman. This may have suggested the idea of making Hermione pose as her own statue, a not uncommon motif in narrative and dramatic romance.[9]

The resemblances between *Pericles,* the first of the romances, and *The Winter's Tale* are also important if we are trying to see how Shakespeare's imagination worked in handling his material. In both plays a queen is supposed dead and appears alive again after a number of years — the time it takes her daughter to grow up from an infant to a young woman. In *Pericles* Shakespeare utilized to the utmost the pathos of the recovery of a lost daughter, so in *The Winter's Tale* the reunion with Perdita is minimized and all the emphasis, theatrical and poetic, is placed upon the restoration of Hermione. The influence of the predecessor play upon the *ending* of *The Winter's Tale* is particularly significant because it is the ending of *Pandosto* that Shakespeare has most radically changed. Pandosto's wife really dies, and is not brought back to life; the old king, not recognizing his daughter, tries to seduce and threatens to rape her. The conclusion is wholly unlike the "precious winners all" of *The Winter's Tale:*

> Pandosto, calling to mind how first he betrayed his friend Egistus; how his jealousy was the cause of Bellaria's death; that contrary to the law of nature, he had lusted after his own daughter — moved with these desperate thoughts, he fell in a melancholy fit and, to close up the comedy with a tragical stratagem, he slew himself.[10]

That *The Winter's Tale* is not, like its source *Pandosto,* in any important way a treatment of jealousy is of course to be explained by the fact that Shakespeare had already explored that subject thoroughly in

Othello. Leontes' affliction is not the green-eyed monster which grows by what it feeds on; it is a sudden seizure, a perturbation of mind, what Cicero called *Affecio*.[11] The interest in the play is not focused upon how Leontes was persuaded to entertain the awful and mistaken distrust of his wife and friend; the important thing is its consequences. Greene's novel even gives slightly more color of probability to the suspicion than Shakespeare's play does, for in the novel

> Bellaria (who in her time was the flower of courtesy), willing to show how unfeignedly she loved her husband by his friend's entertainment, used him likewise so familiarly that her countenance bewrayed how her mind was affected towards him, oftentimes coming herself into his bedchamber to see that nothing should be amiss to mislike him.[12]

Shakespeare changed all this, because he had fully portrayed the growth of jealousy in *Othello* and had no need to dramatize it in another play.

Dr. Jenijoy LaBelle points out the interesting fact that though Leontes is quite unlike Othello, he has some traits in common with Iago, and there are similarities in the language they use. They are both voyeurs, watching a woman true to her husband and loyal to his best friend:

> *Iago: (Aside)* He takes her by the *palm* .... Ay, *smile* upon her do .... it had been better you had not *kissed* your three *fingers* so oft, which now again you are so apt to play the sir in .... Yet again your *fingers* to your *lips?*
>
> (II. i. 167-76)

> *Didst thou not see her paddle* with the *palm* of his hand? *Didst not mark that?*
>
> (II. i. 253-55)

> *Leontes:* (Aside) But to be *paddling palms* and pinching *fingers* As *now* they are, and making practiced *smiles* ... *Didst note it? ... Didst perceive it? ... Kissing* with inside *lip?*
>
> (I. ii. 115-213, 216, 286)

Fitzroy Pyle maintains that Leontes is his own Iago, and that this recollection may account for the fact that the lady who waits on Hermione in prison is named Emilia, like Iago's wife, "but," he adds, "this is a trifle."[13]

But if Leontes is wholly unlike Othello, despite the similarity of plot situation, he curiously enough has some traits in common with another of Shakespeare's tragic heroes, Macbeth. When it is discovered that Polixenes and Camillo have fled Leontes' court, the king of Sicilia delivers a remarkable soliloquy:

> How blest am I
> In my just censure! in my true opinion!
> Alack, for lesser knowledge! how accurs'd
> In being so blest! There may be in the cup
> A spider steep'd, and one may drink, depart,
> And yet partake no venom (for his knowledge
> Is not infected), but if one present
> Th' abhorr'd ingredient to his eye, make known
> How he hath drunk, he cracks his gorge, his sides,
> With violent hefts. I have drunk, and seen the spider.
>
> (II. i. 36-45)

The corresponding passage in *Pandosto* (though it occurs before the departure of the originals of Polixenes and Camillo) has a very different, and much less "psychological" style:

> In the meantime, Pandosto's mind was so far charged with jealousy that he did no longer doubt, but was assured (as he thought) that his friend Egistus had entered a wrong point in his tables and so had played him false play.[14]

Othello expressed a similar view about the happiness of the ignorant cuckold when he says

> What sense had I of her stolen hours of lust?
> I saw't not, thought it not, it harm'd not me.
> I slept the next night well, fed well, was free
>   and merry;

I found not Cassio's kisses on her lips.
He that is robb'd, not wanting what is stol'n,

. . . .

Let him not know't, and he's not robb'd at all.
I had been happy if the general camp,
Pioners and all, had tasted her sweet body,
So I had nothing known.

(III. iii. 338-47)

The rhetoric and the passion here are saved for the "Othello's occupa-tion's gone" aria which follows immediately.

In Leontes' soliloquy there is a quality much more like Macbeth than like Othello. It is the Scottish thane who speaks of poisoned chalices and a mind full of scorpions, not the general of Venice. Leontes, like Macbeth, is interested in how the mind works, how it attaches itself to unrealities, and then, at times, to realities as well.

Macbeth, when he is "rapt," troubled, absorbed and has to be re-called to reality by his companions, just like Leontes here, says in soliloquy

why do I yield to that suggestion
Whose horrid image doth unfix my hair
And make my seated heart knock at my ribs,
Against the use of nature? Present fears
Are less than horrible imaginings:
My thought, whose murther yet is but fantastical,
Shakes so my single state of man that function
Is smother'd in surmise, and nothing is
But what is not.

(I. iii. 134-42)

"More than any other of Shakespeare's plays," writes Ernest Schanzer, "it {The Winter's Tale} resembles *Macbeth* in the nature and use of its imagery, a kinship which derives from an affinity of themes. This is above all true of the first half, which shares with *Macbeth* the con-trast of images of planting and growth with those of uprooting and blight, and of images of health and physic with those of sickness and infection."[15] Dr. Jenijoy LaBelle comments that both men feel claustrophobic and contracted:

> *Leontes:* [Camillo] has discover'd my design, and I
> Remain a pinch'd thing.
>
> (II. i. 50-51)
>
> *Macbeth:* ... now I am cabin'd, cribb'd, confin'd, bound in
> To saucy doubts and fears.
>
> (III. iv. 24-25)

Another small detail may owe something to *Macbeth*. In *Pandosto* the king suffers from sleeplessness very early in his experience of jealousy:

> These and such like doubtful thoughts, a long time smothering in his stomach, began at last to kindle in his mind a secret mistrust which, increased by suspicion, grew at last to a flaming jealousy that so tormented him as he could take no rest.[16]

But in *The Winter's Tale* Leontes' sleeplessness comes upon him after Hermione is in prison, in II. iii, where the scene begins with a soliloquy that might have come from *Macbeth*:

> Nor night, nor day, no rest, It is but weakness
> To bear the matter thus — mere weakness.

As Ernest Schanzer has well said, "Like Macbeth, Leontes creates a wintry landscape of death and desolation around him."[17]

This atmosphere does not pervade Leontes' court, however. Mamillius does start to tell a tale — a sad tale's best for winter — about a man living by a churchyard, whom some supersensitive critics have taken to symbolize Leontes himself. But there is much playfulness in the atmosphere of the court. Hermione's dialogue is full of it, before she is accused, and the relationship between the ill-fated Antigonus and his dominating wife Paulina is one more appropriate to comedy than to tragedy. Sicilia is not a place where light thickens and the crow makes wing to the rooky wood; it is a place where ladies chatter and tease the young prince (as does his father), where, though it is winter, spring cannot be far behind.

In fact, it is curious how many images in the first part, centered in the court, anticipate the feeling of the second, or summer part of the play; images which remind us that the court is not everything; there is also the pastoral world:

> Nine changes of the wat'ry star hath been
> *The shepherd's note* since we have left our throne
> Without a burthen . . .
>
> (I. ii. 1-3)

> We were as *twinn'd lambs* that did frisk i' th' sun,
> And bleat the one at th' other
>
> (I. ii. 67-68)

Miss Mahood thinks that these images in the first half of the play which have echoes in the second half "help to bridge the 'great gap' of time and place over which we pass later to the shepherd kingdom of Bohemia."[18] I would doubt whether such a subtle effect could work on the stage, but I think it tells us something about the nature of Shakespeare's imagination.

The theater itself is of course one of Shakespeare's favorite images, and one could, if he chose, make something of the appearance of this image in both the first and second parts of *The Winter's Tale*. When Leontes dismisses his son, Mamillius, at the beginning of his soliloquy on cuckolds, he says

> Go play, boy, play. Thy mother plays, and I
> Play too, but so disgrac'd a part, whose issue
> Will hiss me to my grave: contempt and clamor
> Will be my knell.
>
> (I. ii. 187-90)

The word *play* is used in three senses: to sport, to do anything for pleasure (Schmidt's meaning 1) ; to wanton or dally (Schmidt's meaning 4) ; and to act on the stage (Schmidt's meaning 7).[19] Miss Mahood fancies another — to manipulate a fish, in view of Leontes' aside a few lines earlier, "I am angling now, Though you perceive me not how I give line." This meaning of the word *play* is not recorded in the Oxford Dictionary, however, earlier than Richardson's *Pamela*. Leontes, as the actor, will play "so disgrac'd a part" that the issue or result, his known cuckoldry, will pursue him to his grave, as the hisses of the audience pursue the actor on his exit. "Grac'd" had a special association with acting in Shakespeare's mind, apparently, as in the passage

> As in a theater the eyes of men,
> After a well-graced actor leaves the stage,
> Are idly bent on him that enters next . . .
>
> (*Richard II* V. ii. 23-25)

In the famous flower scene of the fourth act, Perdita again uses the word *play* in different senses, when she wishes she had flowers to strew on Florizel and he asks if she means like a corpse:

> No, like a bank, for love to lie and *play* on:
> Not like a corse; or if — not to be buried,
> But quick and in mine arms. Come, take your flow'rs:
> Methinks I *play* as I have seen them do
> In Whitsun pastorals. Sure this robe of mine
> Does change my disposition.
>
> (IV. iv. 130-35)

If the figure of acting on the stage was the equivalent for Leontes of suffering the ignominy of being a known cuckold, it permits his chaste and modest daughter to assume for a moment the pleasures of love. It is one of the most charming of the many touches that characterize Perdita. Hermione, in her defense, compares her story to a play

> which is more
> Than history can pattern, though devis'd
> And play'd to take spectators.
>
> (III. ii. 34-37)

Some critics find the statue scene a scene of play acting, but this is to look at it with modern eyes. There is no trace of theatrical imagery in the scene.[20] Instead, it is thick with references to magic. The attitude of the beholders, on the stage and off, is supposed to be an attitude of awe and wonder, not of mere theatrical effect. Shakespeare would wait until *The Tempest* before equating magic and the stage.

Shakespeare declined to repeat himself, though of course he would reuse a motif for a different purpose. In *As You Like It* he had treated the relative merits of court and country in a comical way; he saw no need to do it again in *The Winter's Tale*, though his source gave him sufficient occasion. Dorastus asks Fawnia what are the pleasures of a shepherd's life that counterbalance its drudging labors. She replies:

> Sir, what richer state than content, or what sweeter life than quiet? We shepherds are not born to honor nor beholding unto beauty. The less care we have to fear fame or fortune. We count our attire brave enough if warm enough, and our food dainty if to suffice nature. Our greatest enemy is the wolf, our only care in safekeeping our flock. Instead of courtly ditties, we spend the days with country songs. Our amorous conceits are homely thoughts, delighting as much to talk of Pan and his country pranks as ladies to tell of Venus and her wanton toys. Our toil is in shifting the folds and looking to the lamb's easy labors, oft singing and telling tales (homely pleasures). Our greatest wealth, not to covet; our honor, not to climb; our quiet, not to care. Envy looketh not so low as shepherds. Shepherds gaze not so high as ambition. We are rich in that we are poor with content, and proud only in this: that we have no cause to be proud.[21]

Shakespeare's Bohemia is much more realistically English. It is not the Forest of Arden, where such considerations were relevant. The shepherd who is Perdita's foster-father is quite prosperous in a worldly way, as anyone can discover who will do the clown's little problem which he could not solve without counters; "every 'leven wether tods; every tod yields pound and odd shilling; fifteen hundred shorn, what comes the wool to?" (IV. iii. 32-34). The sheepshearing festival, with its Whitsun elements and its attendant rogue Autolycus, is not a conventional Arcadia. It is more removed from it than the Forest of Arden is. Even the edges of the picture are filled with homely, realistic detail. The wife of the old shepherd, who appears in *Pandosto* as a shrew who suspects that the foundling is a bastard of her husband's, appears in Shakespeare only as a memory,[22] and not a shrew at all, but the compleat country hostess:

> Fie, daughter, when my old wife liv'd, upon
> This day she was both pantler, butler, cook,
> Both dame and servant; welcom'd all, serv'd all;
> Would sing her song and dance her turn; now here
> At upper end o' th' table, now i' th' middle;
> On his shoulder, and his; her face o' fire
> With labor, and the thing she took to quench it
> She would to each one sip.

(IV. iv. 55-62)

And when, at the end of that magnificent long scene, Autolycus must get rid of the shepherd and clown so he can deliver a soliloquy, he says to them

> Walk before toward the sea-side, go on the right hand,
> I will but look upon the hedge and follow you.

(IV. iv. 824-26)

Autolycus, though he seems original and spontaneous, has a long and respectable ancestry. He is descended from the vice of medieval morality plays, from the clever servant of classical comedy, from various beggars, peddlers, thieves, and rogues of popular drama. In John Bale's *The Three Laws of Nature* (1538) Infidelitas, the vice, sings "Broom, buy broom!" In George Wapull's *The Tide Tarryeth No Man* (1576) two characters named Corage and Profite sing about living without working. In *The Marriage of Wit and Science* (1568) Snatch and Catch sing of thievery. Nichol Newfangle, the vice in Ulpian Fulwell's *Like Will to Like* (1568) sings a line and shows his wares as a peddler. In Robert Wilson's *Three Ladies of London* (1581) three beggars sing in praise of begging, wenching, and tumbling in the grass. And in *The Pedlar's Prophecy* (1561) a peddler sings with others in a part song.[23]

Like Falstaff, Autolycus is superior to all of his kind. He is more rogue than minstrel, but his merriment is the means by which the winter part of the play is transformed into the spring part. Jenijoy

LaBelle comments that his opening song establishes this, and also that "he had changed his wonted livery as winter does in spring, as Perdita does for the festival, and as Hermione does from stone to flesh." With respect to the other characters he is the epitome of deceit. He is "a man of masks, and he is so in a play wherein Providence itself wears a mask." [24] He was littered under Mercury and therefore has a knavish and thieving disposition. If, as seems most likely, Shakespeare got the idea of him from Golding's Ovid, he was in fact named for Mercury's son by Chione:

> Now when shee full her tyme had gon, shee bare by Mercurye
> A sonne that hyght Awtolychus, who provde a wyly pye,
> And such a fellow as in theft and filching had no peere.[25]

But he is a philosopher of his calling, not unworthy to be classed with Falstaff and P. T. Barnum: "Every lane's end, every shop, church, session, hanging, yields a careful man work." The pious commentators are shocked at his saying "For the life to come, I sleep out the thought of it." Frank Kermode says that "Autolycus, with his courtly pretences, is the blackest rogue available."[26] But this is surely too severe. He is a rogue all right, but he is enchanting. He enjoys the irony of his help- ing to bring about the happy ending, though there was actually no functional need for him in the plot. In this respect he serves somewhat as Dogberry does in *Much Ado about Nothing*. A stage tradition has him picking his benefactor's pocket again at the end of the play, as he does at the beginning, but there is no warrant for this in the text. Fitzroy Pyle unaccountably approves of it, and he even more strangely thinks that "a tall fellow of your hands" means "nimble-fingered."[27]

Shakespeare's romanticism is centripetal rather than centrifugal; it seeks familiar Warwickshire on its most imaginative flights rather than the exotic lands of Othello's travels. The transformation of Greene's *Pandosto* in the second half of *The Winter's Tale* illustrates this. It is useless to quarrel about whether it is pastoral or not. Greg argued it was not, and Greenlaw countered that it is "the most exquis- ite and satisfying pastoral in Elizabethan literature."[28] Perhaps Mary Lascelles has put the matter to rest by saying *"The Winter's Tale* transcends the models in which it is framed by obtaining their ultimate purpose."[29]

If the sheepshearing feast provides the longest and richest scene in the play, where Shakespeare's imagination may be seen at its most liberated and characteristic level, the statue scene is the one which has provided the commentators most difficulty, though the general testimony is that it is effective on the stage. In writing it Shakespeare totally abandoned his source, because in Greene's novel the queen does actually die and the king finally commits suicide. It was a ludicrous plot device with which Greene had closed up his comedy; he calls it "a tragical strategem" himself. Once Shakespeare abandoned that catastrophe, and the reason for it, the king's incestuous passion for his unrecognized daughter, the happy recognition-reunion ending became possible. Leontes' fidelity to his lost wife justifies her restoration to him. It is not a resurrection, nor is the Alcestis myth relevant. What is relevant is the restoration-reunion in *Pericles,* but there the emphasis was put upon the recognition and reunion of father and daughter. In *The Winter's Tale* that part of it is done by report, and the more dramatic scene is left for the reunion of husband and wife. Adrien Bonjour has shown how carefully Shakespeare prepares for the statue scene:

> Before the characters in the play do realize it, the spectator, who has thus been gradually prepared to guess it, knows the truth. When presently a music sounds and, under the spell of the incantation, Hermione actually comes down from her pedestal, he enjoys the scene all the more that his imagination had just anticipated it. The way in which the progression has been effected from the first slight hints to the point where the anticipation is likely to take place, focuses our attention on what is going to happen in such a manner that we finally partake, in some way, of the "miracle" itself; and this allows us to enjoy the effect produced on the characters of the play much better than if we had received at the same time with them the shock of the *complete* surprise. On the other hand, the surprise loses none of its flavour for us since there is always a margin between an intimation, or even an anticipation, and its full and vivid realization.[30]

E. A. J. Honigmann thinks that the statue scene was in Shakespeare's mind from the start because of comments on living to see something take place (I. i. 44 ff); people almost dead being revived (IV. iv. 783 ff); and references to "breaking the grave" (V. i. 42) and to "marble" persons (V. ii. 90).[31]

Further evidence is the way in which Shakespeare develops Paulina, who is not in Greene's *Pandosto*. She is made into the second most important character in the play, measured by the number of lines spoken. And if Shakespeare had first intended to have Hermione really die and not brought back to life, it is difficult to see why he would have invented Paulina at all. There were constraints on the number of boy actresses available to play female parts.[32]

The second of these images is of some interest on its own account. It is the answer Autolycus gives to the clown as to what punishment shall be meted out to the shepherd's son (the clown himself), the narrator pretending complete ignorance of the identity of the victim and his listener:

> He has a son, who shall be flay'd alive; then 'nointed over with honey, set on the head of a wasp's nest; then stand till he be three quarters and a dram dead; then recover'd again with aqua-vitae or some other hot infusion; then, raw as he is (and in the hottest day prognostication proclaims), shall he be set against a brick-wall, the sun looking with a southward eye upon him, where he is to behold him, with flies blown to death. But what talk we of these traitorly rascals, whose miseries are to be smil'd at, their offenses being so capital?
>
> (IV. iv. 783-93)

This bit Shakespeare got, in simpler form, not from *Pandosto,* but from the ninth tale of the second day in Boccaccio's *Decameron,* which he had used as a source for his most recent play, *Cymbeline.* He did not use it in *Cymbeline,* for his villain was let off without any severe punishment, but his memory saved it and used it as a purely comic threat in *The Winter's Tale.* There are other examples of Shakespeare's thrift in the use of his sources.

Some of them merely involve the transfer of a word or idea from one context to another, but this is perhaps the most typical example of the working of the Shakespearian imagination. In *Pandosto* the prototype of Polixenes makes his escape in one sentence:

> For Egistus, fearing that delay might breed danger and willing that the grass should not be cut from under his feet, taking *bag and baggage* with the help of Franion, conveyed himself and his men out of a *postern* gate so secretly and speedily that without any suspicion they got to the seashore, where, with many a bitter curse, taking their leave of Bohemia, they went aboard.[33]

In *The Winter's Tale* Leontes is soliloquizing on the universality of cuckoldry:

> Physic for't there's none.
> It is a bawdy planet, that will strike
> Where 'tis predominant; and 'tis pow'rful — think it —
> From east, west, north, and south. Be it concluded,
> No barricado for a belly. Know't,
> It will let in and out the enemy,
> *With bag and baggage.* Many thousand on's
> Have the disease, and feel 't not.
>
> (I. ii. 200-07)

The transfer of context seems to have arisen from Shakespeare's associations with the word *baggage,* which can be well illustrated from one of the brothel scenes in *Pericles*:

> *Pander:* Thou sayest true, there's two unwholesome, a' conscience. The poor Transylvanian is dead that lay with the little *baggage.*[34]

The other word, *postern,* has no associations. It is used literally when Leontes asks, after the flight of Polixenes and Camillo,

> How came the posterns
> So easily open?
>
> (II. i. 52-53)

Our interest in Shakespeare's imagination takes us usually into images and figurative language, discovering when we can the origin of the figure, its associations, and how it gets to be a part of the language of the play. Shakespeare's mind most characteristically worked in images — such examples as

> And many a man there is (even at this present,
> Now, while a speak this) holds his wife by th' arm,
> That little thinks she has been sluic'd in's absence
> And his pond fished by his next neighbor — by
> Sir Smile, his neighbor.
>
> (I. ii. 192-96)

or

> if I mistake
> In those foundations which I build upon,
> The centre is not big enough to bear
> A schoolboy's top
>
> (II. i. 100-03)

or

> Stars, stars,
> And all eyes else, dead coals!
>
> (V. i. 67-68)

all come from Leontes, but the language of other characters would afford still greater variety.[35]

We have seen how figures may be transferred from one context to another; each new context provides a new point of view on the figure and the subject of the figure. Shakespeare's imagination is profoundly transformational. He may write in a genre and comment on that genre, as he does in *As You Like It*. He may enlarge an image, in his various treatments of it, so much that it becomes almost a world view; the most obvious instance is his image of the world as a stage and men and women as players. What someone does becomes a figure, as when

114

Othello puts out the light. But we now have a chance to see Shakespeare doing the opposite — taking one of his own images and making out of it a theatrical action.

The first half of the play, the winter half, ends with a fantastic scene. Antigonus and the mariner have touched upon the seacoast of Bohemia, where Antigonus deposits the infant Perdita after narrating a dream in which the child's dead mother appeared to him. There is a storm, the mariners perish and Antigonus is pursued and eaten by a bear. The witnesses are two rustics, a shepherd and his son, called in the play the Clown. Tillyard sees this scene as not only the conclusion to the tortured world of Leontes and Hermione, but also the finest exhibition of the planes of reality which he considers to be so important in the play.[36] The stage direction, "Exit, pursued by a bear," has been denounced as absurd, as unprepared for, (though forty-five lines earlier the mariner has warned Antigonus that "this place is famous for the creatures of prey that keep upon't") and as a concession to the spectacular theatricality popular at the Jacobean court. It is pointed out that the very popular *Mucedorus,* when revived in 1610, had a bear in it, and the learned editors have debated at length whether it was a tame bear, of which there was at least one in London, or an actor in a bear's skin, with the effect intentionally comic. However that may be, this extraordinary stage business seems to have had its origin, as Wilson Knight pointed out, in an image in *King Lear:*

> Thou think'st 'tis much that this contentious storm
> Invades us to the skin; so 'tis to thee;
> But where the greater malady is fix'd,
> The lesser is scarce felt. Thou'dst shun a bear,
> But if [thy] flight lay toward the roaring sea,
> Thou'dst meet the bear i' th' mouth.[37]

We have said that Shakespeare was not interested in the discussion about the gifts of fortune and the gifts of nature in *The Winter's Tale,* as he was in *As You Like It.* But that is not to say that he had lost his interest in nature. Far from it. In fact, though I dissent from much in Wilson Knight's interpretation of *The Winter's Tale,* I agree with his statement, "Nature rules our play." The key passage is the dialogue between Polixenes and Perdita in IV. iv. 70-108. Perdita is herself a child of nature; though of royal blood, she has been brought up far from courts and polite society. Like Guiderius and Arviragus in *Cymbeline,* she excels in the simple life, but suggests something above it. Polixenes himself says of her

> Nothing she does, or seems,
> But smacks of something greater than herself,
> Too noble for this place.
>
> (IV. iv. 157-59)

She is the exemplar of, and the spokesman for, the beauty of "great creating nature," and she will have nothing to do with flowers that have been adapted by human skills. They are the carnations and streaked gillyvors that seem artificial and resemble painted women. Polixenes gives her an answer that is traditional, as Harold S. Wilson has shown:[38] the art which mends nature comes from nature itself and should not therefore be disparaged. Shakespeare very cleverly makes Polixenes expound his doctrine so earnestly that he unconsciously undermines the doctrine he presently upholds about the unsuitability of marrying "a gentler scion to the wildest stock, / And make conceive a bark of baser kind / By bud of nobler race." But the irony is double, for if Polixenes only knew it, the shepherd lass is as noble as himself or his son; she may seem only a queen of curds and cream, but she is the putative heir to the throne of Sicilia. Polixenes' arguments have been called "a devastating comment on the primitivism of Montaigne" by A. O. Lovejoy.[39] It seems however, that Shakespeare, though he knew Montaigne and was to use his essay on the cannibals explicitly in *The Tempest,* depended rather more upon a passage in Puttenham's *Arte of English Poesie:*

> In another respect arte is not only an aide and coadjutor to nature in all of her actions but an alterer of them, and in some sort a surmounter of her skill, so as by meanes of it her owne effects shall appeare more beautifull or straunge and miraculous, as in both cases

116

before remembered.... And the Gardiner by his arte will not onely make an herbe, or flowr, or fruite, come forth in his season without impediment, but also will embellish the same in vertue, shape, odour and taste, that nature of her selfe would neuer haue done, as to make a single gilliflowre, or marigold, or daisie, double.... any of which things nature could not doe without mans help and arte. These actions also are most singular when they be most artificiall.[40]

The summer atmosphere of this part of the play is created, not only by the incomparable lines in praise of flowers which Shakespeare puts into Perdita's mouth, but by philosophical discussion, with its ironies, about what is natural, about nature and art.

Some attention must now be paid to the question of Grace as a theme in *The Winter's Tale,* since several influential critics have constructed theories on this which enlarge into a whole reading of the play. Two passages are crucial:

> My last good deed was to entreat his stay:
> What was my first? It has an elder sister,
> Or I mistake you. O, would her name were Grace!
>
> (I. ii. 97-99)

and

> Do not weep, good fools;
> . . . .
> this action I now go on
> Is for my better grace.
>
> (II. i. 118-22)

F. C. Tinkler thought that "the keynote of the play is Grace and Graciousness, terms which occur most frequently in the speeches of Hermione and Polixenes before the estrangement and after the reconciliation."[41] M. D. H. Parker, in her reading, takes every occurence of the word "grace" in a Christian sense, though Schmidt's lexicon distinguishes eleven meanings of the noun in Shakespeare. She also maintains that "Whatever the image, the shepherdess Perdita, 'grown in grace' and needing no 'instructions,' stands in the play for both grace *and* nature, and for the one precisely because for the other."[42] Derek Traversi also finds a heavy emphasis upon grace, and he believes that Shakespeare's conception of it has grown: "Shakespeare seems to reinforce the Christian associations already acquired in *Macbeth* with a deeply personal intuition of natural fertility, fulfilled in the intimate unity of the family."[43] Northrop Frye agrees that Hermione is associated with grace, "But such grace is not Christian or theological grace, which is superior to the order of nature, but a secular analogy of Christian grace which is identical with nature: the grace that Spenser celebrates in the sixth book of *The Faerie Queene.*"[44]

First, let us see what Shakespeare did with his source in the matter of Hermione's imprisonment, for there is nothing in *Pandosto* to give a basis for Hermione's playful use of the name Grace in the first quotation. Green thus describes Bellaria's imprisonment:

> The guard, unwilling to lay hands on such a virtuous princess, and yet fearing the king's fury, went very sorrowfully to fulfill their charge. Coming to the queen's lodging, they found her playing with her young son Garinter, unto whom, with tears doing the message, Bellaria, astonished at such a hard censure and finding her clear conscience a sure advocate to plead in her case, went to the prison most willingly. Where, with sighs and tears, she passed away the time till she might come to her trial.[45]

Emphasis on grace as a motif in *The Winter's Tale* is especially congenial to those critics who wish to Christianize or allegorize the late plays. S. L. Bethell says, in the conclusion of his interpretation of *The Winter's Tale,* "Natural and supernatural, humanism and asceticism, the life-affirming and the life-denying, are seen to be mutually necessary and interdependent in a world where sin interferes with the pattern of natural goodness and grace must reintegrate our fallen nature."[46] The allegorists go further. F. David Hoeniger proclaims that "Only if we approach *The Winter's Tale* as an allegory can we do justice to its greatness."[47] And J. A. Bryant, Jr., explains that Hermione is indeed Grace and also represents Christ; Leontes is the Jew; Mamillius is the Jewish church; and Paulina is, of course, St. Paul.[48] The word "grace" (without discriminating its meanings) appears as many times in *Macbeth, Pericles,* and *Cymbeline* as in *The Winter's Tale,* and the relative frequency of occurrence is about the same as in *Hamlet* but not so great as in *Pericles, Macbeth,* or *Lear.*

There has been much ado about the theme of time in *The Winter's Tale.* It arises naturally enough from the structure of the play, and the chorus, time itself, which introduces Act IV. There are other references, some apparently insistent. Polixenes has visited Leontes for nine months at the beginning of the play. The old shepherd makes his first entrance with the wish that there were no age between ten and three-and-twenty, or that youth would sleep out the rest, for there is nothing in between but getting wenches with child, wronging the anciently, stealing, fighting. Autolycus says "for the life to come, I sleep out the thought of it" (IV. iii. 30), and Florizel, when he is about to flee Bohemia, asks Camillo to quiet his father's anger and "let myself and fortune / Tug for the time to come" (IV. iv. 496-97). Moreover, the play is full of contrasts of the generations, which is an exemplification of time. *Pandosto* has as its subtitle "The Triumph of Time," but this means only that time brings all to light, that truth is the daughter of time, and such standard platitudes.

Yet in *The Winter's Tale* there is nothing like the emphasis on time, or the meaning of it, that we find in *As You Like It.* The general view of critics is that in the later plays Shakespeare was looking at life with a greater serenity, with a greater awareness of the wonder of reconciliation and fulfilment, of the joy of reunion when the lost are found, of acceptance of the strange doctrine that eventually crabbed age and youth can live together. It is to be expected that a generally-held view will be attacked, and this one has been opposed by Inga-Stina Ewbank, in an essay called "The Triumph of Time in 'The Winter's Tale.'"[49] Her argument is that although time has disappeared from the verbal imagery of *The Winter's Tale,* it is all the more intensely present as a controlling and shaping figure behind the dramatic technique and structure. Her arguments are ingenious; she considers Leontes a man who is unwilling to trust Time the revealer; she emphasizes the adaptations Shakespeare made in the time scheme of *Pandosto;* she takes the statue scene to be a ritual and revelation of the Triumph of Time motif. She admits that it would be wrong to think of *The Winter's Tale* as a treatise on time, but "through its action, its structure and its poetry, it communicates a constant awareness of the powers of time." I believe it is a special aspect of time, not the iconographic one which she mentions, which dominates the world of Shakespeare's imagination. It is well expressed by Ernest Schanzer, "As we watch, twice over in the play's symbolic pattern, the progression from summer to winter, with the return of spring and summer at the end, the affinity between human affairs and the cycle of the seasons, which is close to the imaginative core of *The Winter's Tale,* is borne in upon us."[50]

It has been shown that Shakespeare, in dramatizing Lodge's *Rosalynde,* reduced the pastoral element in his source. He naturalized it somewhat, too, by evoking the atmosphere of Robin Hood and his merry men in Sherwood Forest to surround the banished Duke and his retinue in Arden, and by introducing shepherds as real as Corin and William. In *The Winter's Tale* he curiously enough made the play more like the Greek romances than the novel he was dramatizing. And of all Elizabethan fiction, as Wolff points out,[51] *Pandosto* exhibits with greatest fullness the influence of the Greek romances. But Shakespeare goes further: his play, unlike the novel, has a happy ending; it has a wonderful and spectacular scene at the end; it includes a dream vision (Antigonus') and a shipwreck, and an attack by a wild beast. These are all common motifs in the Greek romances.

In a sense, then, the difference between Shakespeare's artistic style in the later period from his style at the time he wrote *As You Like It* is that he formalizes more. He underlines or fortifies the convention he is working in. But he does this in the part of the play which derives from *Pandosto.* Most of Act IV is independent of Greene's romance, and it is here that Shakespeare makes his most realistic, earthy pictures — the shopping list for the sheepshearers' feast, the cozening tricks of Autolycus, the broadside ballads, the portrait of the late wife of the shepherd as the compleat country hostess.

Chapter 7

A MIDSUMMER NIGHT'S DREAM
AND THE TEMPEST

The dream's here still; even when I wake, it is
Without me, as within me; not imagin'd, felt.

Cymbeline

Though external evidence is lacking to show whether *Romeo and Juliet* was written before or after *A Midsummer Night's Dream*, the two plays both date from 1594-1595, and there are several connections between them which suggest that Shakespeare's imagination was perhaps simultaneously attracted to several themes which interpenetrate the two plays.

Romeo, at the opening of the tragedy, is a doting lover. His passion for Rosaline, who never appears in the play, is a kind of midsummer madness:

> Love is a smoke raised with the fume of sighs,
> Being purg'd, a fire sparkling in lovers' eyes,
> Being vex'd, a sea nourished with loving tears.
> What is it else? a madness most discreet,
> A choking gall and a preserving sweet.

(I. ii. 190-94)

But he also has a foreboding of tragedy:

> For my mind misgives
> Some consequence yet hanging in the stars
> Shall bitterly begin his fearful date
> With this night's revels, and expire the term
> Of a despised life clos'd in my breast
> By some vile forfeit of untimely death.   (I. iv. 106-11)

This mood was induced, in part, by a dream he had last night, and his mention of this dream leads to Mercutio's famous Queen Mab speech, which exhibits for the first time Shakespeare's distinctive Warwickshire fairy lore. *A Midsummer Night's Dream* is of course about dreaming, and fairies play an important part in the plot, but in *Romeo and Juliet* the fairy lore is extraneous, not only to the plot but indeed to the character of Mercutio who delivers the speech:

> O then I see Queen Mab hath been with you.
> She is the fairies' midwife, and she comes
> In shape no bigger than an agot-stone
> On the forefinger of an alderman,
> Drawn with a team of little atomies
> Athwart men's noses as they lie asleep.
>
> . . . .
>
> Her waggon spokes made of long spinners' legs,
> The cover of the wings of grasshoppers,
> Her traces of the smallest spider's web,
> Her collars of the moonshine's wat'ry beams,
> Her whip of cricket's bone, the lash of film,
> Her waggoner a small gray-coated gnat,
> Not half so big as a round little worm
> Pricked from the lazy finger of a [maid]
>
> . . . .
>
> And in this state she gallops night by night
> Through lovers' brains, and then they dream of love ...

and so on, through the various classes of men, whose dreams, stimulated by Mab's nocturnal rides, merely reveal their already conditioned characters. But Mab is a practical joker, too:

> This is that very Mab
> That plaits the manes of horses in the night,
> And bakes the [elf] locks in foul sluttish hairs,
> Which, once untangled, much misfortune bodes.
> This is the hag, when maids lie on their backs,
> That presses them and learns them first to bear,
> Making them women of good carriage. (I. iv. 53-94)

I take it that *A Midsummer Night's Dream* is slightly later than *Romeo and Juliet,* and that Shakespeare's mind while composing his tragedy was already turning to the fairy lore which would provide matter for his comedy, and he found himself unable to resist the elaboration of the activities of the Fairies' midwife. She is not a midwife in the sense that she brings fairies into the fairy world, but in the sense that she delivers human beings of their nightly offspring, their dreams.

The light-and-darkness imagery of *Romeo and Juliet* has often been noticed; I think a particular example of that imagery — of lightning at night — lingered in the playwright's memory and rose to the surface again in another context. Juliet says, after Romeo has attempted to swear by the moon, or by himself, that he is true,

> Well, do not swear. Although I joy in thee,
> I have no joy in this contract tonight,
> It is too rash, too unadvis'd, too sudden,
> Too like the lightning, which doth cease to be
> Ere one can say it lightens. (II. ii. 116-20)

In *A Midsummer Night's Dream,* Hermia and Lysander discourse on the theme "The course of true love never did run smooth," and Lysander says,

> Or, if there were a sympathy in choice,
> War, death, or sickness did lay siege to it
> Making it momentany as a sound,
> Swift as a shadow, short as any dream,
> Brief as the lightning in the collied night,
> That, in a spleen, unfolds both heaven and earth;
> And ere a man hath power to say "Behold!"
> The jaws of darkness do devour it up:
> So quick bright things come to confusion. (I. i. 141-49)

Another link between the two plays is the relationship between the tedious brief scene of Pyramus and Thisbe and the romantic tragedy of Romeo and Juliet. In both stories the lover mistakenly thinks his mistress is dead and kills himself; she finds him dead and joins him in suicide. The Pyramus and Thisbe story, distanced as it is by the grossly amateurish production of the rude mechanicals, and still more by the supercilious jests of the court party, may be viewed as a kind of parody of the Romeo and Juliet plot.[1]

If the fairy part of *A Midsummer Night's Dream* grew out of the Queen Mab speech in *Romeo and Juliet,* we have other links to explore, this time with a play written much later — *The Tempest*. It is commonly said that *A Midsummer Night's Dream* is Shakespeare's most imaginative play before *The Tempest*. This is not merely because in Puck and Ariel we have attendant spirits, or because we have the elaborate landscape of moonlit woods and banks to compare with the strange sights and sounds of a magic island. There is in both plays the greatest possible contrast of characters: Bottom-Titania and Caliban-Ariel. In both plays there is a presiding mage, Oberon and Prospero. They have as counterparts rude mechanicals and drunken servants. In both plays there is a monster whose identity is a puzzle. In both plays there is much ado about dreams and illusions, though all of the comedies have some of this motif.

A pretty use of it is in the Induction to *The Taming of the Shrew,* when Christophy Sly, the drunken tinker, is put to bed by a lord and persuaded by his servants that he is indeed himself a lord, that he has had a disease for fifteen years which keeps him asleep and dreaming that he is no lord but a common tinker at odds with the village alewife and Cicely Hacket, her maid. Sly soon accepts the persuasive arguments that he is a lord, but he is puzzled at what a lord calls his wife — Alice Madam or Joan Madam — and he still prefers a pot of the smallest ale to a cup of sack, which he declares he never drank in his life. The question Sly first asks when he finds himself attended by solicitous servants is whether he is dreaming, or has been dreaming up to now. The strolling players then perform for him the play about Kate and Petruchio, the first "comonty" he ever saw, except Christmas gambols and tumbling tricks.

The dilemma of which is dream and which is reality lies at the base of Shakespeare's comedy, from *A Midsummer Night's Dream* to *The Tempest*. Actual experience can seem like a dream from which one has awakened, as Perdita says in *The Winter's Tale,* Prince Hal in *Henry IV Part II,* and Cleopatra.[2] And very often the dream-reality dilemma is associated with some reference to acting or the theater, as it is in *The Taming of the Shrew.*

In *A Midsummer Night's Dream,* Bottom, the would-be actor of many parts, is cast during rehearsal in a role he had hardly thought of, that of an ass. His fellow mechanicals are frightened away by the apparition of Bottom with an ass's head on his shoulders, but Bottom, aware of their fear, goes about to sing a song to show he is not afraid. The song only wakens the sleeping Queen of the Fairies, who falls in love with him.

Bottom's greatness as a comic character has been well described by John Palmer.[3] His essential trait is hard to define, but Palmer says the French have a word for it, *débrouillard,* equal to all occasions and at home wherever he may be. This is not cleverness or ingenuity on Bottom's part—he is, in some sense, an ass—but is a kind of imperturbability that comes from proceeding steadily on the assumptions already made.

Shakespeare has an earlier comic character who has some of this quality — Launce in *The Two Gentlemen of Verona.* Launce rests on the assumption that his dog, Crab, has the same emotions, and should have the same behavior, as a person. To illustrate his disappointment in Crab, he dramatizes a scene — the scene of his parting from his family. His left shoe represents his mother, his right shoe his father; his staff is his sister and his hat is Nan, the maid. They all cry at Launce's departure, but not Crab. "He is a stone, a very pebble stone, and has no more pity in him than a dog." This is hilarious, but Shakespeare did not hesitate to use the same device in *King Lear,* when the aged king in the storm dramatizes the trial of his daughters by using a couple of joint-stools. On the milkmaid he is in love with, Launce comments, "She hath more qualities than a water-spaniel — which is much in a bare Christian." Finally he tells how he saved his dog from a whipping, and sadly reproaches him for not following the model of behavior that Launce has furnished him:

Did I not bid thee still mark me and do as I do? When didst thou see me heave up my leg and make water against a gentle-woman's farthingale? Didst thou ever see me do such a trick?

(IV. iv. 37-39)

Bottom, because of his transformation, has certain unrecognized assumptions which create the very center of the comic situation. He recognizes Titania's aristocracy and comments that reason and love keep little company together nowadays. When she says he is as wise as beautiful, he denies it but says, practically, that if he had enough wit to get out of this wood it would be enough to serve his turn. He treats the fairies courteously, calling them "your worships" and "Master" and "Monsieur." The French title may reflect a vague realization of their foreignness to his world, but he accepts their services to scratch him: "I must to the barber's, monsieur, for methinks I am marvail's hairy about the face; and I am such a tender ass, if my hair do but tickle me, I must scratch." He has a reasonable good ear in music, favoring the tongs and bones, and when he is hungry he has a great desire for a bottle of hay. "Good hay, sweet hay, hath no fellow."

When he awakes from his nap, his ass's head gone and the fairies all vanished, he thinks that all that has happened since the rehearsal has been a dream. But it has been so marvelous that no one can explain it; only a broadside ballad composed by Peter Quince the carpenter can do it justice:

I have had a most rare vision. I have had a dream, past the wit of man to say what dream it was. Man is but an ass if he go about [t'] expound this dream. Methought I was — there is no man can tell what. Methought I was, and methought I had — but man is but [a patch'd] fool, if he will offer to say what methought I had. The eye of man hath not heard, the ear of man hath not seen, man's hand is not able to taste, his tongue to conceive, nor his heart to report, what my dream was. I will get Peter Quince to write a ballet of this dream. It shall be call'd Bottom's Dream, because it hath no bottom.

(IV. i. 203-16)

He is quoting, as his addled mind remembers it, a passage from I Corinthians ii, 9-10. In the Geneva New Testament, 1557, the passage reads: "But we preache it as it is written, Things which eye hath not sene, and eare hath not heard, nether haue entred into mans mynde, which thinges God hath prepared for them that loue hym. But God hath opened them vnto vs by his Sprite, for the Spirite searcheth all thinges, yea, the *botome* of Goddes secretes."[4]

A Midsummer Night's Dream and *The Tempest* are related in that in both plays much of the dramatic interest comes from the fact that the characters, or some of them, are not sure whether what they are seeing — or hearing — is reality or illusion. In the *Dream* the central source of illusion is love. Choice of the beloved is arbitrary, "swift as a shadow, short as any dream" according to Lysander (I. i. 144), and the lover of either sex is frequently described as *doting,* or *erring.* Helena says "And as he errs, doting on Hermia's eyes, / So I, admiring of his qualities" (I. i. 230-31). Titania is so deceived by a love charm that she regards the ass-headed Bottom as an angel (III. i. 129). When one recovers from *doting,* he thinks that his past experience, though real, is but a dream.

> When they next wake, all this derision
> Shall seem a dream and fruitless vision,
>
> (III. ii. 370-71)

says Oberon, and when he is straightening out all the mixups, he declares that they will all return to Athens

> And think no more of this night's accidents
> But as the fierce vexation of a dream.
>
> (IV. i. 68-69)

The lovers themselves comment on the dilemma of sleep or waking:

> *Demetrius:* These things seem small and undistinguishable,
> Like far-off mountains turned into clouds.
> *Hermia:* Methinks I see these things with parted eye,
> When everything seems double.

127

Helena: So methinks:
And I have found Demetrius like a jewel,
Mine own, and not mine own.
Demetrius: Are you sure
That we are awake? It seems to me
That yet we sleep, we dream. Do you not think
The Duke was here, and bid us follow him?
Hermia: Yea, and my father.
Helena: And Hippolyta.
Lysander: And he did bid us follow to the temple.
Demetrius: Why then, we are awake. Let's follow him,
And by the way let's recount our dreams.

(IV. i. 187-99)

The competition between dream and reality is involved in one of the great hyperboles in *Antony and Cleopatra.* The queen says to Dolabella, who is vainly trying to interrupt her to deliver a message from Caesar, that she has dreamt there was an Emperor Antony, whose legs bestrid the ocean and whose reared arm crested the world, in whose livery walked crowns and crownets and from whose pockets realms and islands dropped like plates.

Think you there was or might be such a man
As this I dreamt of?
Dolabella: Gentle madam, no.
Cleopatra: You lie up to the hearing of the gods!
But if there be, nor ever were one such,
It's past the size of dreaming. Nature wants stuff
To vie strange forms with fancy; yet t'imagine
An Antony were nature's piece 'gainst fancy,
Condemning shadows quite.[5]

If reality upon waking can seem like a dream, then one thinks of the illusion produced by the stage, by acting. There is a multiple vision here, as when Peter Quince, the manager and director of *Pyramus and Thisbe,* says of his versatile star Bottom, "You have not a man in all Athens able to discharge Pyramus but he."[6] And the illusion is complex, as when Peter Quince points to his Elizabethan stage and says "This *green plot* shall be our *stage,* this *hawthorn brake* our *tiring house,* and we will do it in action as we will do it before the Duke" (III. i. 2-6).

The actions of the tangled-up lovers are, from the point of view of Robin Goodfellow, a "fond pageant" or foolish crude dramatic performance; he is as superior to them as the courtiers of Theseus are to the rude mechanicals as actors: "Lord, what fools these mortals be!"[7] Of course the elaborate concerns about theatrical illusion on the part of Peter Quince and his colleagues provide a comic variation on the whole serious subject of illusion and reality.

Shakespeare commented at unusual length, for him, on the subject of imagination. And in doing so he gave his Duke Theseus an ambiguous or inconsistent role. Theseus appears to be very distrustful of the accounts of lovers as to what actually happened to them:

> *Hippolyta:* 'Tis strange, my Theseus, that these lovers speak of.
> *Theseus:* More strange than true. I never may believe
> These antique fables not these fairy toys.
> Lovers and madmen have such seething brains,
>
> . . . .
>
> One sees more devils than vast hell can hold;
> That is the madman. The lover, all as frantic,
> Sees Helen's beauty in a brow of Egypt.
>
> . . . .
>
> Such tricks hath strong imagination,
> That if it would but apprehend some joy,
> It comprehends some bringer of that joy;
> Or in the night, imagining some fear
> How easy is a bush suppos'd a bear!   (V. i. 1-22)

There is nothing new here about the relationship between lovers and madmen. Shakespeare would use it again in *As You Like It,* when his swaggering Rosalind, in disguise, of course, says,

> Love is merely a madness, and I tell you deserves as well a dark house and a whip as madmen do; and the reason why they are not so punished and cured is, that the lunacy is so ordinary that the whippers are in love too.
>
> (III. iii. 420-24)

In the previous scene Rosalind has informed the audience that she will speak to Orlando like a saucy lackey, and play the knave with him (III. ii. 313-15).

Having put lovers and madmen in the same basket, and having treated the subject of reality and illusion in terms of the theater and life, Shakespeare had a second thought — that the poet, like the lover and the madman, uses his imagination to go beyond reason. So he inserted the lines:

> Such shaping fantasies, that apprehend
> More than cool reason ever comprehends.
> The lunatic, the lover, and the poet
> Are of imagination all compact.
>
> . . . .
>
> The poet's eye, in a fine frenzy rolling,
> Doth glance from heaven to earth, from earth to heaven;
> And as imagination bodies forth
> The forms of things unknown, the poet's pen
> Turns them to shapes, and gives to airy nothing
> A local habitation and a name.[8]

What is this "airy nothing"? It takes us back to *Romeo and Juliet:*

> *Romeo:*   Peace, peace, Mercutio, peace!
> Thou talk'st of nothing.
> *Mercutio:*   True, I talk of dreams,
> Which are the children of an idle brain,
> Begot of nothing but vain fantasy,
> Which is as thin of substance as the air.

(I. iv. 95-99)

Though Theseus is skeptical about the tales told by lovers, and accuses them of being, like madmen and poets, of imagination all compact, he is a defender of the imagination as a quality necessary in a member of the audience. Hippolyta, that practical Amazon, sees no point in watching the performance by the rude mechanicals, who, according to Philostrate, can do nothing in this kind. But Theseus replies to her

The kinder we, to give them thanks for nothing.
Our sport shall be to take what they mistake;
And what poor duty cannot do, noble respect
Takes it in might, not merit. (V. i. 89-92)

This might be put down as mere magnanimity on the part of a ruler, for he goes on to tell about how great clerks attempting to give him a speech of welcome, have been so struck by stage fright that they have broken off, yet he has picked a welcome out of their tongue-tied simplicity. But during the performance, when Hippolyta says "This is the silliest stuff that ever I heard," Theseus replies, "The best in this kind are but shadows; and the worst are no worse, if imagination amend them" (V. i. 215-16). Actors are *shadows*, then, pale imitations of reality, who must be supported by the imagination of the audience if they are to be taken seriously. That the term "shadows" is meant seriously is shown by the opening lines of the epilogue, spoken by Robin Goodfellow:

If we shadows have offended,
Think but this, and all is mended —
That you have but slumbered here
While these visions did appear. (V. i. 430-34)

A Midsummer Night's Dream is pure comedy, full of pleasant mirth. It has the mixed-up lovers, a conventional cross-eyed Cupid situation familiar in romances like Montemayor's *Diana* and Sidney's *Arcadia;* the audience knows all along that this mixup will be solved. It is an illustration of the country proverb which Robin Goodfellow quotes to remind us:

And the country proverb known,
That every man should take his own,
In your waking shall be shown:
Jack shall have Jill,
Naught shall go ill,
The man shall have his mare again, and all shall be well.
(III. ii. 458-63)

131

Besides, it has the rich character comedy of Bottom, which almost outgrows its occasion; the performance at the Duke's wedding; and that which fits with such marvellous appropriateness into the fairy element — Oberon's plot against Titania. It has also the nostalgic, legendary, dignified matter of Theseus' conquest of the Amazon and his marriage to her. These elements are blended together in the most skilfull way. Moonshine illuminates it all.

Even so, though it is recognized that the play has the pleasant and happy atmosphere appropriate to a wedding for which it may have been commissioned and almost certainly at which it was performed, there are those among the critics who will have it that this is a most serious work. Bottom's transformation Frank Kermode traces back to Apuleius' *Golden Ass:*

> Apuleius, after his transformation, might not speak of the initiation he underwent; but he was vouchsafed a vision of the goddess Isis. St. Paul was initiated into the religion he had persecuted by Ananias in Damascus. What they have in common is transformation, and an experience of divine love. Bottom has known the love of the triple goddess in a vision. . . . To Pico, to Cornelius Agrippa, to Bruno, who distinguish the nine kinds of fruitful love-blindness, this exaltation of the blindness of love was both Christian and Orphic; Orpheus said that love was eyeless; St. Paul and David that God dwelt in darkness and beyond knowledge. Bottom is there to tell us that the blindness of love, the dominance of the mind over the eye, can be interpreted as a means to grace as well as to irrational animalism; that the two aspects are, perhaps, inseparable.[9]

He goes on to say that "unless we see that these mature comedies are thematically serious we shall never get them right. And it might even be added that *A Midsummer Night's Dream* is more serious in this way than *Cymbeline,* because the patterns of sight and blindness, wood and city, phantasma and vision, grow into a large and complex statement, or an emblematic presentation, not to be resolved into its component parts, of love, vulgar and celestial." David P. Young pleads for productions of the play which do not treat it as a kind of Elizabethan *Peter Pan,* and he says "Frank Kermode's suggestion that the play is Shakespeare's best comedy is less astounding today than it would have been twenty years ago."[10] Peter F. Fisher says that Puck's marching jingle

> Up and down, up and down,
> I will lead them up and down.
> I am fear'd in field and town.
> Goblin, lead them up and down.

reminds him of Heraclitus' "The unlike is joined together, and from difference results the most beautiful harmony, and all things take place by strife."[11] In the last act, he finds that reason and order occupy the seat of honor and power; passionate desire has come within rational control, and "the world of imagination and fantasy remains as the undercurrent which ends the play." James E. Robinson, in a recent study, considers that the marriage (!) of Bottom and Titania translates the comprehension of the relation of nature and experience into comic myth. In the play as a whole, he thinks, "society has been elevated by participation in ritual into the comic myths of communion with nature and its gods."[12]

After describing the Oberon tradition from Huon of Bordeaux through Greene's *James IV* and Jonson's *Masque of Oberon,* Paul A. Olson says "In this tradition, Shakespeare's king of shadows is also a delicate figure for grace. He is the play's Prospero."[13] Other critics have noticed the similarity. Of course Oberon is not the protagonist of the *Dream,* as Prospero is of *The Tempest,* and he has no social responsibility as the returning Duke of Milan does. Yet there are interesting correspondences, as Fitzroy Pyle points out:

> Oberon is not, like Prospero, human, but they are both princes who have at their command beings not dissimilar in nature, through whom in very similar ways they control events. In fairy comedy man does not need power over airy spirits: it is fun that their actions should be unpredictable for it is axiomatic that they can do no lasting harm. But in the world of tragicomedy such power, if available, should be under beneficent control, for there man stands in danger from man. From this point of view *The Tempest* can be seen as the tragi-comic correlative of *A Midsummer Night's Dream.*[14]

Other commentators have insisted that *The Tempest* is not a fairy-tale like *A Midsummer Night's Dream,* but that Prospero is a magus like Dr. John Dee, or perhaps Dr. Simon Forman.[15] There are those who see Prospero as central in the play, and interpret the plot as a kind of purging of Prospero's soul. The climax, for such critics, is of course the passage in which Prospero, stimulated by Ariel's suggestion, decides upon mercy for his enemies:

> Though with their high wrongs I am strook to th' quick,
> Yet, with my nobler reason, 'gainst my fury
> Do I take part. The rarer action is
> In virtue than in vengeance. They being penitent,
> The sole drift of my purpose doth extend
> Not a frown further. Go release them, Ariel.
> My charms I'll break, their senses I'll restore,
> And they shall be themselves.
>
> (V. i. 25-32)

A recent book on *The Tempest* sees Shakespeare as using Prospero as his mouthpiece for saying a farewell to the long tradition of magic in Europe.[16] It has often been noticed that Prospero is a rather testy character, and the obvious reason is overlooked — that Prospero has no enemies strong enough to constitute a real obstacle to his will, so he must "artificially," so to speak, create difficulties. Madeleine Doran, in her judicious and profound book *Endeavors of Art,* (Madison, 1954), finds *The Tempest* to be a structural triumph and a play which deals primarily with discovery:

> The great structural triumph is in *The Tempest,* which is all discovery; the complication within the play — the shipwreck and its consequences of conspiracy among nobility and servants alike — is only a mirror of that earlier complication of conspiracy and is the cause of his now having his enemies in his power. The action of the play is Prospero's discovery to his enemies, their discovery of themselves, the lovers' discovery of a new world of wonder, and Prospero's own discovery of an ethic of forgiveness and renunciation of power.

In one voyage
Did Claribel her husband find at Tunis,
And Ferdinand, her brother, found a wife
Where he himself was lost; Prospero his dukedom
In a poor isle, and all of us ourselves,
When no man was his own.

Structure and idea are one.[17]

A recent critic has, however, labeled this the "sentimental" reading of the play. The "hard-nosed" reading, which he favors, is not the most popular, though it can claim the adherence of W. H. Auden and Clifford Leech. The "hard-nosed" approach concerns itself with problems such as these:

1. Prospero's language in describing the usurpation to Miranda encourages us to believe that he is partly responsible for what happened, yet he never seems to take this into account.
2. Gonzalo was Antonio's accomplice.
3. Gonzalo is a bit of a fool.
4. Gonzalo's final speech (just quoted) should be the end of any romance but is followed by 113 lines.
5. Why was Ariel punished by being stuck in a tree?

and so on. And what conclusions come from these difficult questions? Why, that Prospero "had renounced the dukedom in his mind before handing it over to Antonio." "Sycorax is the nightmare which complements his wish-fulfillment." "Though Sycorax is motivated by pure evil, and Prospero's motives by contrast seem very good, both are equally antisocial, both have withdrawn into themselves, have proved unfit for, or inadequate to, social and political existence." And Caliban — is he the savage and deformed slave described in the folio? Not at all. "*We* see in him all man's possibilities in their undeveloped form, and this means that we see longing for brightness and beauty as no less real, no less rooted and persistent, than the tendency to darkness and evil. This is not what Prospero sees. Caliban is his epitome of human degradation."[18] This has, perhaps, its closest affinities with the analysis of *Macbeth* given to the astonished lady in a secluded spot near the putting green by James Thurber.[19]

The Tempest is a play in which nobody in the cast, except Prospero, and perhaps Ariel, knows whether what he sees and hears is natural or supernatural, whether it is reality or an illusion. The shipwreck itself is ambiguous. It is a "direful spectacle of the wrack" which Miranda sees and which she pities so. But actually, it seems, nothing unfortunate happened to those she heard and saw,

> No, not so much perdition as an hair
> Betid to any creature in the vessel
> Which thou heard'st cry, which thou saw'st sink.
>
> (I. ii. 30-32)

Ferdinand, who walks about the island led by Ariel's music, cannot be sure whether he is awake or not: "My spirits, as in a dream, are all bound up."

Prospero's attendants are actors, and they put on all kinds of theatrical performances, from the "urchin-shows" which fright Caliban to the "living drollery" which involves a dance and a banquet brought in to the King of Naples and his companions; it persuades them that the phoenix legend and travelers' tales are all true.[20] The performances are usually musical in *The Tempest,* and they sometimes represent pure pleasure, even for Caliban:

> Be not afeard. The isle is full of noises,
> Sounds, and sweet airs, that give delight and hurt not.
> Sometimes a thousand twangling instruments
> Will hum about mine ears, and sometime voices,
> That, if I then had wak'd after long sleep,
> Will make me sleep again; and then, in dreaming,
> The clouds methought would open, and show riches
> Ready to drop upon me, that when I wak'd,
> I cried to dream again.
>
> (III. ii. 135-43)

Ferdinand, when he becomes accustomed to the island and to the mysterious ways of his prospective father-in-law, has to assume that the actors in the masque are probably spirits. He is assured by Prospero that they are, but that their dissolution into thin air is no greater than the dissolution of everything else — what we call reality:

> These our actors,
> (As I foretold you) were all spirits, and
> Are melted into air, into thin air.
> And, like the baseless fabric of this vision,
> The cloud-capp'd tow'rs, the gorgeous palaces,
> The solemn temples, the great globe itself,
> Yea, all which it inherit, shall dissolve,
> And, like this insubstantial pageant faded,
> Leave not a rack behind. We are such stuff
> As dreams are made on; and our little life
> Is rounded with a sleep.
>
> (IV. i. 148-58)

It is Shakespeare's most philosophical statement. Its eloquence is start-ling, coming where it does in the play. But it is not the conclusion. Much remains to be revealed, not to the young lovers but to their confused and still enquiring elders. Alonso doesn't know whether Prospero is real or not (V. i. 112-19) nor does Gonzalo. Alonso thinks that Ferdinand and Miranda, discovered playing chess, may be a vision (V. i. 75).

The continuation of this dilemma after its most important expres-sion in the great speech has something, I think, to do with the epilogue, spoken by Prospero:

> Now my charms are all o'erthrown,
> And what strength I have's mine own,
> Which is most faint. Now 'tis true,
> I must be here confin'd by you,
> Or sent to Naples. Let me not,
> Since I have my dukedom got,
> And pardon'd the deceiver, dwell
> In this bare island by your spell;
> But release me from my bands
> With the help of your good hands:
> Gentle breath of yours my sails
> Must fill, or else my project fails,

Which was to please. Now I want
Spirits to enforce, Art to enchant,
And my ending is despair,
Unless I be reliev'd by prayer,
Which pierces so, that it assaults
Mercy itself, and frees all faults.
As you from crimes would pardon'd be,
Let your indulgence set me free.

Anyone who has struggled through the tangles of the allegorical and Christian interpreters of this epilogue must be grateful for the lucid exposition of it given by Frank Kermode:

> The most immediate and commonplace play on the idea of the magician-without-magic has reference to the actor-without-part. I am now outside the tale you have just followed; just as I surrendered my powers in that tale, so I now stand before you stripped of imaginary glamour. One might say that the success of my enterprise as an actor is parallel to the happy outcome of my stage-plot. I behaved well in my fictitious character (and I hope, acted well also); my fictitious reward is to return to Italy. To complete the parallel, you might release me from the bonds of failure as a performer.... I implore you to exercise mercy towards me, as you would have mercy procure forgiveness for your own trespasses.[21]

This epilogue has the same function of distancing as the epilogue to *As You Like It.* There the actor who has played Rosalind appears first as a lady, the fictional heroine of the play. Then, after some quibbling of exactly the same sort we find in the epilogue to *The Tempest,* there is a change from the role of Rosalind to an admission that it is a boy actor: "If I were a woman, I would kiss as many of you as had beards that pleased me . . ." And the plea is not for mercy, but for favor. Prospero asks for mercy, not because this is a Christian play, but because mercy is what he has shown to Antonio and Sebastian and what he accordingly deserves. Theodore Spencer, refuting W. C. Curry and Middleton Murry, puts the matter well: "But the prayer is obviously merely a prayer to the audience. It is conventional for an actor to step half out of character in an epilogue, and that is what Prospero is doing here. His 'prayer' consists of the last two lines, and has no metaphysical connotations."[22]

The matter of dreaming and reality in the two plays has been succinctly summarized by Robert Ellrodt: "Pour le poète du *Songe d'une Nuit d'Eté,* le songe même était réalité: pour l'auteur de la *Tempête,* la réalité même n'est qu'un songe."[23]

Prospero's magic needs to be properly understood. To a modern audience the appeal to the imagination to help may be felt to be necessary because nobody believes in magic any more, but this was not the case with Shakespeare's contemporaries. Take Sir Walter Ralegh, for example. He was interested in magic in the same way he was interested in chemistry and medicine. Magic is "the wisdom of nature," Ralegh wrote, "The third kind of magic containeth the whole philosophy of nature; not the brabblings of the Aristotelians, but that which bringeth to light the inmost virtues, and draweth them out of nature's hidden bosom to human use." He defined magic as "the investigation of those virtues and hidden properties which God hath given to his creatures, and how fitly to apply things that work to things that suffer."[24]

The play is saturated with references to magic; it is displayed frequently but even more it is talked about. Every scene in the play, except the first, of course, has at least one mention of it, and the first scene, the storm, is a demonstration of it, though we in the audience do not know it at the time. Modern audiences tend to overlook or underemphasize the magic. Dr. Johnson, who disliked magic, was well aware of its importance in *The Tempest.* "In this he differs from nineteenth and twentieth century critics," says Robert H. West, "who incline to view the magic as comprehensive analogy or symbol that parallels or stands for some such abstraction as government, art, or science. In *The Tempest,* as Johnson saw, magic as standing in and for itself — has as much reality as Prospero's dukedom does, and of course far more prominence. Dukedoms and magic alike have largely gone out of being."[25]

Equally important in *The Tempest* is that imaginative creation of a land of romantic adventure which might include some traits gleaned from the tales of travelers to the new world. The line between fiction and geographical reporting was not clearly drawn, and Spenser could use this vagueness to defend the fiction of his Faerie Land:

> But let that man with better sence aduize,
>   That of the world least part to us is red:
>   And dayly how through hardy enterprize,
>   Many great regions are discouered,
>   Which to late age were neuer mentioned.
>   Whoeuer heard of th' Indian *Peru?*
>   Or who in venturous vessel measured
>   The *Amazons* huge riuer now found trew?
> Or fruitfullest *Virginia* who did euer vew?
>
> Yet all these were, when no man did them know;
>   Yet haue from wisest ages hidden beene:
>   And later times things more unknowne shall show.
>   Why then should witlesse man so much misweene
>   That nothing is, but that which he hath seene?
>
> *(FQ* II, Proem, 2-3)

To talk of Peru, the Amazon, and fruitfulest Virginia, is to talk of the accounts of voyages of discovery, and we are on firm ground in supposing that Shakespeare read them, for, as Malone pointed out in the eighteenth century, *The Tempest* is in part based on some accounts of the shipwreck of Sir George Somers in Bermuda. But it also seems clear that Shakespeare had read Richard Eden's *History of Travaile* (1557) because he takes the name of Caliban's, or rather Sycorax's, god, Setebos, from it.[26] What his imagination could do with the material provided by Eden may perhaps be illustrated from some passages usually neglected.

In Eden's relation of Magellan's encounter with the giants of Patagonia one gets an introduction to a world not unlike that on Prospero's island. In the first part of the narrative there is an island, one of the Canaries, where a cloud appears daily at noon over a certain tree and discharges enough water into it to serve the whole island. Magellan, like Somers, experienced the strange fire called corposant. Some ignorant folk, says Eden, think these strange fires are spirits — as indeed

Ariel was — but actually "they are but naturall thynges, proceedyng of naturall causes, and engendred of certayne exhalations."[27] There are two kinds, it seems, true fire which is seen on the mast, is hot enough to melt brass, and "is a token of drownyng, forasmuch as this chaunceth only in great tempestes." The false fires leaping from cable to cable "with a certayne fluttering noyse lyke byrdes, are a token of securitie, and of the tempest overpassed."[28]

When Magellan's crew came upon the Patagonian giants, they captured some of them by a ruse — loading their arms with presents and then shackling their legs — "when they sawe howe they were deceiued, they roared lyke bulles, & cryed vpon theyr great deuill Setebos, to helpe them."[29] One of Magellan's ships deserted at the straits and returned to Spain, carrying in it a captured Patagonian giant who died on the way. (A dead Indian, exhibited in England, would bring in money according to Trinculo, II. ii. 34). Eden tells us that another Indian, more fortunate, was shown a cross and was terrified. "He sodaynely cryed Setebos, and declared by signes, that if they made any more crosses, Setebos would enter into his bodie, and make him brust. But when in fine he sawe no hurte to come thereof, he tooke the crosse, and imbrased and kyssed it oftentymes, desirying that he myght be a Christian before his death: He was therefore baptysed, and named Paule." Caliban's conversion is not so spectacular as Paul's, but he does reproach himself for worshipping false gods, and promises to be wise hereafter and seek for grace.

As the reading of the Bermuda accounts may have turned Shakespeare to the reading, or rereading, of Eden, so he could encounter something in Eden which would send him back to his favorite Montaigne. It is a description of a primitive ideal commonwealth:

> The inhabitauntes of these ilandes haue ben euer so used to lyue at libertie, in play and pastyme, that they can hardly away with the yoke of seruitude, which they attempt to shake of by all meanes they may.
>
> And surely yf they had receiued our religion I woulde thynke theyr lyfe most happie of all men, yf they myght therewith enjoy theyr auncient libertie. A fewe things content them, hauyng no delyte in suche superfluities, for the whiche in other places men take infinite

paynes, and commit manye vnlawfull actes, and yet are neuer satisfied, whereas manye haue to muche, and none yenough. But among these simple soules, a few clothes serue the naked: weightes and measures are not needeful to such as can not skyl of craft and deceyte, and haue not the vse of pestiferous money, the seede of innumerable mis-cheeues: so that yf we shall not be ashamed to confesse the trueth, they seeme to liue in that golden worlde of the which olde writers speake so muche, wherein men lyued symplye and innocentlye with-out enforcement of lawes, without quarrellyng, iudges, and libelles, content only to satisfie nature, without further vexation for know-ledge of thynges to come.[30]

Perhaps travelers' tales coincide with the landscape of the romances because the travelers themselves were prepared by the romances for what they found in the new world. As J. H. Parry says about the Spanish explorers:

> The *Orlando Furioso* of Ariosto was quickly translated and widely read in Spanish. Epics and romances of all kinds enjoyed a great vogue in Spain in the early sixteenth century. Bernal Díaz, writing of his first breathtaking sight of the city of Mexico, remarked quite natur-ally that it put him in mind of the Amadis romances.[31]

As if there were not enough that was suggestive of *The Tempest* in Eden's account of Magellan's voyage, we should note that there was a conspiracy to bring about the death of the general, but the leaders were caught and hanged and quartered. The guilty conspirators against Prospero suffered from conscience and from displays of Ariel's tricks, but they were perhaps not very far from the explorers who were assaulted by bats:

> These battes haue oftentymes assalted men in the night in theyr sleepe, and so bytten them with theyr venemous teeth, that they haue ben therby almost dryuen to madnes, in so much that they haue been compelled to flee from such places, as from rauenous harpies.[32]

Ariel appears as a harpy in the banquet scene, and the strangers to the island are driven nearly mad (III. iii. 53-110). The Spanish explorers use dogs against the savages, as Prospero and Ariel do against Stephano, Trinculo, and Caliban.[33] Finally, there is most unexpectedly a suggestion of beautiful music in this primitive environment, though it is made by natural means. The Europeans frightened the natives with a volley of ordnance which terrified them, but when they were treated well they approach nearer "and heard the noyse of the fluites, shawlmes, and drummes, they were wonderfully astonied at the sweet harmonie thereof."[34]

Shakespeare's imagination, at the time he wrote *The Tempest,* would appear to have been stimulated by the accounts of travel and exploration in the new world. The magic island over which Prospero ruled owed something to the accounts of Magellan's voyages. This is not after all very surprising, since the telescope and the microscope influenced the imagination of writers in the seventeenth century, as Marjorie Nicolson has demonstrated.[35]

In *A Midsummer Night's Dream* Shakespeare had already combined a fairy world, the world of night and moonlight, with classical mythology and the daytime figures of Theseus the conqueror, kinsman of Hercules, and his Amazon bride Hippolyta. In *The Tempest* the vision was enlarged with spirits and magic. Iris and Ceres and Juno are there, to bestow blessings on a wedding, but they are spirits who perform a masque at Prospero's bidding. The beauty of their ceremonious performance is a far cry from the effects of magic on the stage in such early plays as Greene's *Friar Bacon and Friar Bungay* or Marlowe's *Doctor Faustus.*

Finally, as Dryden was the first to see, Shakespeare not only described things which existed in popular belief, like the fairies — as such, they might be considered part of "Nature" and accordingly the poet was imitating nature or holding the mirror up to it. He went further when he depicted Caliban, "a species of himself, begotten by an incubus on a witch," and yet an identifiable person, with his own tastes and peculiarities, and indeed "with a language as hobgoblin as his person." Speculating on how Shakespeare could contrive such a character led Dryden to add a new word to our critical vocabulary. "He seems there to have *created* a person which was not in Nature, a boldness which, at first sight, would appear intolerable."[36] Shakespeare was bold in contriving a character not found in nature or in common popular belief, which is part of nature. Dryden may seem even bolder in using the word *create,* generally heretofore applied only to the Deity, to signify what a poet or dramatist does, but the imaginative triumphs of *The Tempest* justify his boldness.

Chapter 8

SCENERY AND "LANDSCAPE"

But if there be, nor ever were one such,
It's past the size of dreaming. Nature wants stuff
To vie strange forms with fancy . . .

Antony and Cleopatra

The term "landscape" will be used here to signify that world which is described in visual terms but not shown visually on the stage.[1] It is brought into the dialogue for various purposes, for characterization, for elevating an event which takes place offstage to an importance as great as it might have if it were presented visually to the audience, or even, at times, for ironic or symbolic effects. An example is the elaborate description of the disturbed seasons in *A Midsummer Night's Dream*. Titania is accusing Oberon of disturbing her troupe with his brawls:

> Therefore the winds, piping to us in vain,
> As in revenge, have suck'd up from the sea
> Contagious fogs, which, falling in the land,
> Have every pelting river made so proud
> That they have overborne their continents.
> The ox hath therefore stretch'd his yoke in vain,
> The plowman lost his sweat, and the green corn
> Hath rotted ere his youth attain'd a beard.
> The fold stands empty in the drowned field,
> And crows are fatted with the murrion flock.
> The nine men's morris is fill'd up with mud,

And the quaint mazes in the wanton green,
For lack of tread, are undistinguishable.
The human mortals want their winter here,
No night is now with hymn or carol blest,
Therefore the moon, the governess of floods,
Pale in her anger, washes all the air,
That rheumatic diseases do abound.
And thorough this distemperature we see
The seasons alter. Hoary-headed frosts
Fall in the fresh lap of the crimson rose,
And on old Hiems' thin and icy crown
An odorous chaplet of sweet summer buds
Is, as in mockery, set. The spring, the summer,
The childing autumn, angry winter, change
Their wonted liveries, and the mazed world,
By their increase, now knows not which is which.
And this same progeny of evils comes
From our debate, from our dissension.   (II. i. 88-116)

This passage contributes little or nothing to the plot of the play; it is not obviously useful in characterizing either Titania or Oberon; yet it is very detailed and elaborate. Some scholars think it is a topical allusion and refers to the very bad summer of 1594, though why Shakespeare should be interested in recording unusual weather to an audience which knew about it as well as he does not seem obvious. One film producer, not realizing the difference between this described, imaginary landscape and the visible scenery on the stage, photographed the greater part of the play in rain and mud, so Hermia and Lysander, Helena and Demetrius, were sopping, bedraggled victims of the weather rather more than the comic exemplars of temporarily misdirected love. The audience at that movie had good reason to agree with Puck when he said "Lord, what fools these mortals be!" since clearly they didn't have sense enough to go in out of the rain. The passage serves to make a connection which the play emphasizes over and over again between the imaginary world of the fairies and the actual world of fields and crops and rude mechanicals. The exotic and the homely embrace — Titania and Bottom.

Another example is the passage in *Macbeth* in which Duncan and Banquo comment on the atmosphere outside Macbeth's castle:

> *Duncan:* This castle hath a pleasant seat, the air
> Nimbly and sweetly recommends itself
> Unto our gentle senses.
> *Banquo:*　　　　　This guest of summer,
> The temple-haunting martlet, does approve
> By his loved mansionry that the heaven's breath
> Smells wooingly here. No jutty, frieze,
> Buttress, nor coign of vantage but this bird
> Hath made his pendent bed and procreant cradle.
> Where they most breed and haunt, I have observ'd
> The air is delicate.　　　　　　　　　　(I. vi. 1-10)

Here the description augments the actual stage. The audience is asked to supply with its imagination what the limitations of the stage cannot supply, though doubtless the film producer who made the rainy *Midsummer Night's Dream* would search everywhere until he found a castle swarming with martlets. But the passage has a more significant function; it is deeply ironic. The bird is described as "the guest of summer," and royal Duncan is a *guest* at this castle, and as Macbeth makes explicit, there are deep moral obligations in hospitality. It is "the temple-haunting martlet," and the castle is a "temple" in that it is to harbor the sanctified person of a king. When Macduff announces the discovery of Duncan's murder he uses a figure which might by itself be considered stilted but which has a terrible irony in connection with the passage in this scene:

> *Macduff:* Confusion now hath made his masterpiece.
> Most sacrilegious murder hath broke ope
> The Lord's anointed temple, and stole thence
> The life o' the building.　　　　　　　　(II. iii. 71-74)

The "heaven's breath" that smells wooingly outside the castle is to give way to the stench of hell inside and the smell of blood which all the perfumes of Arabia will not sweeten. The symbolic bird also changes. Instead of the temple-haunting martlet it is the raven:

> The raven himself is hoarse
> That croaks the fatal entrance of Duncan
> Under my battlements.
>
> (I. v. 39-41)

Another example of description closely related to the stage itself is that of the apothecary shop in *Romeo and Juliet.* The audience sees only the door to it, from which the apothecary enters the stage, but the interior, just beyond that door, is described in elaborate detail:

> I do remember an apothecary,
> And hereabouts he dwells, which late I noted
> In tatter'd weeds, with overwhelming brows,
> Culling of simples. Meager were his looks,
> Sharp misery had worn him to the bones.
> And in his needy shop a tortoise hung,
> An alligator stuff'd and other skins
> Of ill-shaped fishes; and about his shelves
> A beggarly account of empty boxes,
> Green earthen pots, bladders, and musty seeds,
> Remnants of packthread and old cakes of roses,
> Were thinly scatter'd to make up a show.
>
> . . . .
>
> As I remember, this should be the house
> Being holiday, the beggar's shop is shut.
>
> (V. i. 37-56)

Still a different use of "landscape" in this sense is illustrated in the passage in which the Queen describes the death of Ophelia. It is dramatically absurd, or at least its pretext is, when Laertes, on hearing that his sister is drowned, says, "Oh where?". Someone might have said, as Banquo says in *Macbeth,* "Too cruel anywhere." But the scene is vividly conveyed:

> There is a willow grows aslant a brook
> That shows his hoar leaves in the glassy stream.

148

There with fantastic garlands did she come
Of crowflowers, nettles, daisies, and long purples
That liberal shepherds give a grosser name,
But our cold maids do dead-men's fingers call them.
There on the pendent boughs her coronet weeds
Clambering to hang, an envious sliver broke,
When down her weedy trophies and herself
Fell in the weeping brook. Her clothes spread wide,
And mermaid-like awhile they bore her up —
Which time she chanted snatches of old tunes,
As one incapable of her own distress,
Or like a creature native and indued
Unto that element. But long it could not be
Till that her garments, heavy with their drink,
Pulled the poor wretch from her melodious lay
To muddy death.   (IV. vii. 167-84)

This passage has been much commented on, with respect to its inherent improbability; anyone with leisure to observe all the Queen reports could presumably have rescued Ophelia. Many have noticed the strange accuracy of the color of the under side of willow leaves and the reminiscent or symbolic suggestion of the indecent names given to a flower by "liberal shepherds" contrasted to the innocent name given them by "cold maids" like Ophelia (except that she knew some songs which perhaps liberal shepherds liked to sing).

Its justification, if it needs one, is surely to be seen from its context — it comes in the midst of the sinister plotting between Claudius and Laertes on how to get rid of Hamlet, and it also marks, with pathos and beauty, the end of Ophelia's story. Not quite the end — it prepares for the Queen's epitaph in the next scene,

Sweets to the sweet, farewell!
I hop'd thou shouldst have been my Hamlet's wife.
I thought thy bride bed to have deck'd, sweet maid,
And not have strew'd thy grave.   (V. i. 243-46)

As Dr. Johnson remarked, "the gratification which would arise from the destruction of an usurper and a murderer is abated by the untimely death of Ophelia, the young, the beautiful, the harmless, and the pious."[2]

If one considers the "landscape" and the scenery in *Timon of Athens* one must bear in mind that it is probably an unfinished play, probably abandoned in favor of *Coriolanus*.[3] But it has some important connections with the romances, even if it is not, as Clifford Leech thinks, the germ of them.[4] The first important piece of "landscape" in *Timon* is conventional and emblematic; it is the description of Fortune's Hill, given by the poet but described by the painter as the subject of a thousand moral paintings (I. i. 63-92). This is significant in itself, and it to some extent accounts for the impression of the play which is well expressed by Bullough: "So the play is not a tragedy like *Lear* or *Coriolanus*, but a Jacobean morality play in which the characters are little more than embodiments of ethical attitudes."[5]

> *Poet:*   Sir,
> I have upon a high and pleasant hill
> Feigned Fortune to be thron'd. The base o' th' mount
> Is rank'd with all deserts, all kind of natures,
> That labor on the bosom of this sphere
> To propagate their states. Amongst them all,
> Whose eyes are on this sovereign lady fix'd,
> One I do personate of Lord Timon's frame,
> Whom Fortune with her ivory hand wafts to her,
> Whose present grace to present slaves and servants
> Translates his rivals.
> *Painter:*   'Tis conceived to scope.
> This throne, this Fortune, and this hill, methinks,
> With one man beckon'd from the rest below,
> Bowing his head against the steepy mount
> To climb his happiness, would be well express'd
> In our condition.
> *Poet:*   Nay, sir, but hear me on:
> All those which were his fellows but of late —
> Some better than his value — on the moment
> Follow his strides, his lobbies fill with tendance,
> Rain sacrificial whisperings in his ear,
> Make sacred even his stirrup, and through him

Drink the free air.
Painter: Ay, marry, what of these?
Poet: When Fortune in her shift and change of mood
Spurns down her late beloved, all his dependants
Which labored after him to the mountain's top
Even on their knees and [hands], let him [slip] down,
Not one accompanying his declining foot.
Painter: 'Tis common:
A thousand moral paintings I can show
That shall demonstrate these quick blows of Fortune's
More pregnantly than words.

In this instance the "landscape" said almost all there was to say, and the play lacked matter. There are suggestions of a world offstage throughout the play, but nothing as substantial as the emblem of Fortune's Hill. Horses and hounds, the gifts of senators (II. ii. 180 ff.) and hunting, the sport of noblemen, are referred to, and of course war and the camp in the scenes focused on Alcibiades (III. v). Most notable is Apemantus' speech about the woods. Quintessentially Shakespearian, it concentrates themes about the harshness of nature compared to the comforts of court, which is the subject of much philosophizing in *As You Like It,* and the folly of submitting oneself as a poor, bare, unaccommodated animal to the fury of the elements, a great theme in *Lear:*

Apemantus: Thou hast cast away thyself, being like thyself,
A madman so long, now a fool. What, think'st
That the bleak air, thy boisterous chamberlain,
Will put thy shirt on warm? Will these moist trees,
That have outliv'd the eagle, page thy heels
And skip when thou point'st out? Will the cold brook,
Candied with ice, caudle thy morning taste
To cure thy o'ernight's surfeit? Call the creatures
Whose naked natures live in all the spite
Of wreakful heaven, whose bare unhoused trunks,
To the conflicting elements expos'd,
Answer mere nature; bid them flatter thee.   (IV. iii. 220-31)

The "landscape" is sometimes brought near to the themes of the play, as when Timon describes the woods to the bandits:

All: We are not thieves, but men that much do want.
Timon: Your greatest want is, you want much of meat.
Why should you want? Behold, the earth hath roots;
Within this mile break forth a hundred springs;
The oaks bear mast, the briers scarlet heps;
The bounteous huswife Nature on each bush
Lays her full mess before you. Want? Why want?
First Bandit: We cannot live on grass, on berries, water,
As beasts and birds and fishes.
Timon: Nor on the beasts themselves, the birds and fishes;
You must eat men.   (IV. iii. 416-25)

The two passages on the site for Timon's tomb, one of which I believe Shakespeare would have canceled had he finished the play, of course extend the "landscape," giving it that mysterious and inconclusive air which leads some readers and editors idly to speculate on whether Timon committed suicide or not, and who buried him.

On the whole, there is more scenery than "landscape" in *Timon;* in other words, the attention of the audience is drawn to what takes place on the stage rather than to described scenes which take place off. There is the banquet in I. ii, the very visualization of Timon's extravagance and generosity. Its counterpart is of course the banquet of warm water — and perhaps stones, too, the evidence is not quite clear — in III. vi. Courtly splendor is exhibited in the masque introduced by Cupid at I. ii. 126. There is a scene in which the wooden structure of the stage becomes Athens seen from outside, and cursed in IV. i, an effect which Shakespeare was to use more strongly when he came to dramatize the life of Coriolanus. And finally, the hard, concrete image of the ironic last half of the play is presented to our eyes when we see Timon on the stage digging for roots and instead finding gold.

The "landscape" of *King Lear* is very rich. It includes suggestions of an early, primitive world, long before the Christian era, when one could speak of "waterish Burgundy" and fair France, with its vines, but could think of England as a country

> With shadowy forests and with champains rich'd,
> With plenteous rivers and wide-skirted meads.   (I. i. 64-65)

Edgar, having heard himself proclaimed, escaped capture by the happy hollow of a tree (II. iii. 2-3) but near Gloucester's castle "for many miles about / There's scarce a bush" (II. iv. 303-04). This is of course functional: the attack of the elements on the defenseless Lear must seem as cruel as possible. The greatest "landscape" anywhere in Shakespeare is the storm. It is conveyed principally by Lear's words, for though the storm is real and is physical, it is also mental and conveys the old king's spiritual suffering. The notorious argument about the actability of *Lear* (an argument which should have been settled by Granville-Barker's preface) would have been unnecessary if it had been realized that the storm is "landscape," not scenery, and a modern producer who relies too heavily on sound and lighting effects is doing irreparable damage to the play. Maynard Mack aptly quotes Coleridge on the great storm scene III. iv:

> O what a world's convention of agonies is here! All external nature in a storm, all moral nature convulsed, — the real madness of Lear, the feigned madness of Edgar, the babbling of the Fool, the desperate fidelity of Kent. Surely such a scene was never conceived before or since! Take it but as a picture for the eye only, it is more terrific than any which a Michel Angelo, inspired by a Dante, could have conceived, and which none but a Michel Angelo could have executed.[6]

The famous description of Dover cliff is also "landscape," and perhaps it is the clearest example of all of the deliberate use of "landscape" for dramatic purposes:

> *Edgar:* Come on, sir; here's the place; stand still. How fearful
> And dizzy 'tis to cast one's eyes so low!
> The crows and choughs that wing the midway air
> Show scarce so gross as beetles. Half way down
> Hangs one that gathers sampire, dreadful trade!
> Methinks he seems no bigger than his head.
> The fishermen, that [walk] upon the beach
> Appear like mice; and yond tall anchoring bark·
> Diminish'd to her cock; her cock, a buoy
> Almost too small for sight. The murmuring surge,

That on th' unnumb'red idle pebble chafes,
Cannot be heard so high. I'll look no more,
Lest my brain turn, and the deficient sight
Topple down headlong.

(IV. vi. 11-24)

Then, of course, the imaginary cliff is described again, as if from below:

> *Edgar:* Hadst thou been aught but gossamer, feathers, air,
> So many fathoms down precipitating,
> Thou'dst shivered like an egg; but thou dost breathe,
> Hast heavy substance, bleed'st not, speak'st, art sound,
> Ten masts at each make not the altitude
> Which thou hast perpendicularly fell:
> Thy life's a miracle. Speak yet again.
> *Gloucester:* But have I fall'n or no?
> *Edgar:* From the dread summit of this chalky bourn.
> Look up a-height; the shrill-gorged lark so far
> Cannot be seen or heard: do but look up.
>
> . . . .
>
> Upon the crown o' th' cliff what thing was that
> Which parted from you?
> *Gloucester:* A poor unfortunate beggar.
> *Edgar:* As I stood here below methought his eyes
> Were two full moons; he had a thousand noses,
> Horns whelk'd and wav'd like the enridged sea;
> It was some fiend; therefore, thou happy father,
> Think that the clearest Gods, who make them honors
> Of men's impossibilities, have preserv'd thee.

Kenneth Muir has shown that the hint for much of this "landscape" came from Holinshed, and that the description of the fiend owes something to the account of the fight between Corineus and Gogmagog which comes just two pages before the King Lear account in the chronicle.[7]

In contrast to the landscape, the scenery of *King Lear* is exceptionally simple.[8] As Granville Barker pointed out and W. W. Greg has emphasized, the staging requirements for the play are such that it could be done on a stage simpler than that at the Globe. It does not require a balcony or an inner stage or "disclosure space," apparently. Greg even thought that there were signs that need for the curtained recess was being avoided by the order to have the stocks brought forth. The stocks, a chair for Lear and for the blinding of Gloucester, two joint-stools for the trial scene: these are all the properties that seem absolutely required. (When Lear goes to sleep at the end of III. vi he says "Draw the curtains" but I think he is under the illusion that he is in his bed at home.)

Much of the action, though not dependent upon properties or elaborate staging, is incredibly specific and vivid. I would instance only Lear's tearing off of his royal robes in III. iv. 103-08 and the reminiscent and pathetic moment just before his death:

> Thou'lt come no more,
> Never, never, never, never, never!
> Pray you, undo this button; thank you, sir.
>
> (V. iii. 308-10)

The blinding of Gloucester and the awakening of Lear are scenes which are superbly "present" and related to their own time and place. The major sources of *King Lear* are the old play *King Leir,* which is far more Christian in atmosphere than Shakespeare's — indicating that Shakespeare toned down this element in that source; Sidney's *Arcadia,* which produced the Gloucester subplot but also affected the main plot of the play; and Holinshed's Chronicle. Sidney's *Arcadia* presents a pagan society.[9] And Holinshed, in the pre-Christian part of his history, is particularly concerned to present a pagan world. Accordingly, the "landscape" and the scenery of Shakespeare's *King Lear* are both non-Christian.[10]

Examination of landscape and scenery in *Pericles* is not simple, because the play itself exists in a peculiar condition. It is not evident that the first two acts are by Shakespeare; only a few phrases suggest his pen. Moreover the structure is very uncharacteristic of Shakespeare. The plot is a mere sequence of episodes, revealed in a stylized way by the presenter, old Gower, with dumb shows and a narrative, rather than dramatic, technique. Gower represented to contemporary audiences an "old" poet, no longer considered great, but highly moral and indisputably quaint. It may be that the popular tale of Apollonius of Tyre was thus "excused" to sophisticated audiences. Certainly Gower provides some distancing: who can be seriously critical of an action which is introduced with the lines

> And he, good prince, having all lost,
> By waves from coast to coast is toss'd.
> All perishen of man, of pelf,
> Ne aught escapend but himself;
> Till Fortune, tir'd with doing bad,
> Threw him ashore, to give him glad.
> And here he comes. What shall be next,
> Pardon old Gower, — this 'longs the text.
>
> (Chorus before Act II, 33-40)

There is no "landscape" except that of romance, and Gower's summary of the shipwreck is feeble for any purpose of visualizing it. George Wilkins, capitalizing upon the popularity of the play by turning out a prose narrative, *The Painfull Adventures of Pericles Prince of Tyre,* saw what was needed and supplied it:

> At last, Fortune having brought him heere, where she might make him the fittest Tennis-ball for her sport: euen as sodainely as thought this was the alteration, the heauens beganne to thunder, and the skies shone with flashes of fire: day now had no other shew but only name, for darknes was on the whole face of the waters, hills of seas were about him one sometimes tossing him euen to the face of heauen, while another sought to sincke him to the roofe of hell, some cryed, others laboured, hee onely prayed: at last, two rauenous billowes meeting, the one, with intent to stoppe vp all clamour, and the other, to wash away all labour, his vessels no longer able to wrestle with the tempest, were all split. In briefe, he was shipwrackt, his good friends and subiectes all were lost, nothing left to helpe him but distresse, and nothing to complaine vnto but his misery. O calamity! there might you haue heard the windes whistling, the raine dashing, the sea roaring, the cables cracking, the tacklings breaking, the ship tear-

ing, the men miserably crying out to saue their liues: there might you haue seene the sea searching the ship, the boardes fleeting, the goodes swimming, the treasure sincking, and the poore soules shifting to saue themselues, but all in vaine, for partly by the violence of the tempest, and partly thorow that dismall darkenesse, which vnfortunately was come vpon them, they were all drowned, gentle *Pericles* only excepted . . .[11]

When Shakespeare required "landscape" for a shipwreck, he could provide it, as he did in the comic-grotesque way of the clown's description in *The Winter's Tale* III. iii. 88-101. Or he could achieve the effect by a combination of scenery-staging and "landscape," as he did in *The Tempest* I. i and I. ii — the "landscape" being Miranda's and Ariel's description of the storm in the second scene. In fact, he does some of it in the Shakespearian part of *Pericles* itself, when he has Marina re-create the storm in which she was born:

> *Marina:* When I was born, the wind was north.
> *Leonine:*   Was't so?
> *Marina:* My father, as nurse says, did never fear,
> But cried "Good seamen!" to the sailors, galling
> His kingly hands haling ropes,
> And, clasping to the mast, endur'd a sea
> That almost burst the deck.
> *Leonine:* When was this?
> *Marina:* When I was born.
> Never was waves nor wind more violent;
> And from the ladder-tackle washes off
> A canvas-climber. "Ha!" says one, "wolt out?"
> And with a dropping industry they skip
> From [stem] to stern. The boatswain whistles, and
> The master calls, and trebles their confusion.[12]

The dramatic function of this "landscape" is to prepare the audience, by arousing its sympathy — by whatever far-fetched means — for Marina, who is about to be killed, we suppose, by Leonine, who has promised to do it.

Another piece of "landscape" is the dialogue between Marina and Boult:

Marina: What canst thou wish thine enemy to be?
Boult: Why, I could wish him to be my master, or rather, my mistress.
Marina: Neither of these are so bad as thou art,
Since they do better thee in their command.
Thou hold'st a place for which the pained'st fiend
Of hell would not in reputation change;
Thou art the damned door-keeper to every
Custrel that comes inquiring for his Tib.
To the choleric fisting of every rogue
Thy ear is liable; thy food is such
As hath been belch'd on by infected lungs.
Boult: What would you have me do? Go to the wars, would you? where a man may serve seven years for the loss of a leg, and not have money enough in the end to buy him a wooden one?
Marina: Do anything but this thou doest. Empty
Old receptacles, or common shores, of filth;
Serve by indenture to the common hangman:
Any of these ways are yet better than this;
For what thou professest, a baboon, could he speak.
Would own a name too dear.

(IV. vi. 158-79)

This passage may seem too immediately relevant to the action to be called "landscape," but it has reverberations that go far beyond the dramatic necessities of the occasion. Marina has to prevail over Boult, to be sure; that is what the plot calls for. But Boult's citing of the crippled veteran brings in a pathos which is related to feelings about poor soldiers in *Henry IV Part I,* and the relationship between pandering and serving the common hangman is reminiscent of the comical business between Abhorson and Pompey in *Measure for Measure* IV. ii.

That the last three acts of *Pericles* are Shakespearian needs no proof. They are frequently suggestive of passages in the later romances; if one may trace, as I have tried to do, the continuity of the romances with the earlier tragedies on the one hand and the earlier comedies on the other, one can find in *Pericles* first approximations of passages in the later plays.

The storm at the beginning of Act III is a good example:

> *1 Sailor:* Slack the bolins there! — Thou wilt not, wilt
> thou? Blow, and split thyself.
> *2 Sailor:* But sea-room, and the brine and cloudy billow
> kiss the moon, I care not.
>
> (III. i. 43-46)

The forthright address to the storm prefigures the boatswain's defiance in *The Tempest,* I. i. 7: "Blow till thou burst thy wind, if room enough."

A comparison of Shakespeare's shipwreck scene in *The Tempest* with another Elizabethan treatment, by Thomas Heywood, was made by George F. Reynolds. He remarked that both playwrights use the same means to produce effects: nautical language, "a tempestuous noise of thunder and lightning," "cries within," "enter mariners wet." "One might say that a great difference between Heywood and Shakespeare is that Shakespeare never taxes our imagination quite so much, never has so great a distance between the theatrical fact and the imagined situation. But after all it is not so much more difficult to imagine the front stage as first one ship and then another than it is to imagine it a ship at all. Really, Shakespeare asks quite as much of us as Heywood but helps us more to conceive it. What makes *The Tempest* storm scene memorable is its convincing humanity: the voluble boatswain with his 'What cares these roarers for the name of king,' and his impatience; the quiet humor of Gonzalo; the hysterical anger of Antonio and Sebastian; and above all the vivid phrasing."[13]

The "humanizing" of the storm through showing its emotional effects on various kinds of people Shakespeare had already accomplished in *Pericles.* In addition to the storm, the imagery of a drowned person buried at sea is continuous in the two plays:

> nor have I time
> To give thee hallow'd to thy grave, but straight
> Must cast thee, scarcely coffin'd, in [the ooze],
>
> (*Pericles* III. i. 58-60)

which becomes "My son i' th' ooze is bedded" in *Tempest* III. iii. 100.

159

(The first of these was noticed by Malone; the emendation in the *Pericles* passage, "ooze" for "oare" was made by Steevens.)

The flower passage when Marina goes to honor the grave of her nurse Lychorida is the forerunner of beautiful passages in *Cymbeline* and *The Winter's Tale:*

> *Marina:* No, I will rob Tellus of her weed
> To strow thy green with flowers. The yellows, blues,
> The purple violets, and marigolds,
> Shall as a carpet hang upon thy grave,
> While summer days doth last. Ay me! poor maid,
> Born in a tempest when my mother died,
> This world to me is a lasting storm,
> Whirring me from my friends.
>
> *(Pericles IV. i. 13-20)*

> *Arviragus:*   With fairest flowers,
> Whilst summer lasts and I live here, Fidele,
> I'll sweeten thy sad grave. Thou shalt not lack
> The flower that's like thy face, pale primrose, nor
> The azur'd harebell, like thy veins; no, nor
> The leaf of eglantine, whom not to slander,
> Outsweet'ned not thy breath. The raddock would
> With charitable bill (O bill, sore shaming
> Those rich-left heirs that let their fathers lie
> Without a monument!) bring thee all this,
> Yea, and furr'd moss besides. When flow'rs are none,
> To winter-ground thy corse.
>
> *(Cymbeline IV. ii. 218-29)*

So Perdita, in the superb flower speech in IV. iv, talks about flowers of the various seasons, and even, in a mistaken meaning, she is thought to refer to the body of a dead loved one.

Still, more is done with scenery than with landscape in *Pericles.* This is largely because of the device of Gower, the chorus, and the dumb shows which he explains. He points to the ominous heads of the unsuccessful suitors in the prologue to Act I. He asks the audience to imagine the stage a ship in Act II and again in Act V. He apologizes for the time lapse, and he occasionally introduces characters or identifies the locality,

> Making, to take our imagination
> From bourn to bourn, region to region.

(IV. iv. 3-4)

Two different statues, one of Pericles and one of Marina, are properties in the dumb-shows. It is possible that the extraordinary popularity of *Pericles,* "mouldy tale" though Jonson declared it to be, owed something to its combination of naiveté with spectacle.

There is a marked difference between the choruses prefixed to the first two acts and the choruses of the later, or Shakespearian part. Ernest Schanzer compares the choruses introducing Act II and Act III and concludes:

"We still have archaisms (y-slacked, eyne) but the verse is incomparably more vivid, vigorous, and accomplished. Moreover, into these Shakespearian choruses enters an element not found in those of Acts I and II, but familiar to us from the choruses in *Henry V:* the audience is repeatedly asked to use its imagination to eke out what is being presented on the stage (e.g. 'And time that is so briefly spent / With your fine fancies quaintly eche'; 'In your supposing once more put your sight; / Of heavy Pericles think this his bark')."[14]

If *Pericles* is an artless and naive play suited to an older fashion and perhaps to a less sophisticated audience, *Cymbeline,* which is Shakespeare's alone, is clearly a play of greater substance. The critics divide on its merits; sometimes it is not even included in the anthologies of "Shakespeare's Major Plays." Yet it has a defender in Granville Barker, the most knowledgeable man of the theater ever to write significantly about Shakespeare, and his theory of it requires attention. What strikes us as artless in *Cymbeline,* says Barker, is designed to call attention to its artlessness. Thus, at the most theatrical moment of the play, when Jachimo confesses his injury to Imogen and to Posthumus, he interrupts himself with "Whereupon — Methinks I see him now!" and Posthumus, stepping forward, says "Ay, so thou dost, Italian fiend!" He then proceeds to give a passionate speech, as uncontrolled as that of the youthful Romeo, blaming himself entirely and inviting every punishment and degradation to be inflicted upon him, and concludes with

O Imogen!
My queen, my life, my wife, O Imogen,
Imogen, Imogen!

He is restrained by the page, who is of course Imogen in disguise,

Peace, my lord, hear, hear —

and he knocks her down with the angry question

Shall's have a play of this?

(V. v. 225-28)

This deliberate artlessness has had several explanations. One is that Shakespeare simply chose to be irresponsible and knew he would be detected so he flaunted it. "The world of tragedy can be redeemed as it could not in earlier Shakespearian tragedy, the play seems to say, simply because the playwright can deny its tragic inevitability by his power over the plot. This is, to be sure, an odd and perhaps a disappointing theme; yet it seems to be the sum of what Shakespeare has to say in both *Pericles* and *Cymbeline*.[15] Another view is that *Cymbeline* is "experimental romance," that the playwright was handling untractable material, and that he employed here, as nowhere else, an impressionistic technique based upon the "recognition that life itself is not a coherent pattern leading by orderly degrees to prosperity, as in comedy, or to destruction, as in tragedy, but a confused set of experiences, good and evil, grave and gay, momentous and trivial."[16] A third view maintains that the peculiarities of the play do not come from its experimental nature, or from Shakespeare's irresponsibility or senility, but from "a rather late use of Elizabethan theatrical conventions." Barbara Mowat thinks that Shakespeare was deliberately using something like Brecht's *Verfremdungseffekt*. She notes that up until *Cymbeline* he had been cutting down on the number of soliloquies, but here he is prodigal, using 24 soliloquies, countless asides, doggerel exit tags and the like. "He controlled audience concern over the characters by reminding us over and over that we are in a theater watching a play." His purpose in all this? "In *Cymbeline* Shakespeare uses presentational conventions, deliberately made artificial, in order to provide just that distancing needed for his Romance story."[17]

Cymbeline is made of two different kinds of materials, and this may account for some of the critical dilemmas the play has presented to the critics. It is not merely a matter of the plot material containing two stories, the story of what happened to Imogen and the story of what happened to her brothers. These can be fused together, in the style of romance, though the structure will of course be loose. It is rather a matter of the difference in "landscape" between the two parts.

The wager story — the misdeeming of Imogen and the eventual rectifying of the mistake — is from Boccaccio and a German derivative, *Frederick of Jennen.* It is a tale of a bet on a wife's chastity. It comes out of the contemporary world, or the world of fiction where time and place are unimportant. Jachimo is a Renaissance Italian, though not a villain of the Iago sort. He is a sportsman; he will stoop to deceitful tricks, but he very notably repents. There is a very marked strain of commercial imagery in the play, which I think indicates a clear derivation from *Frederick of Jennen,* where the wagerers and their friends are all merchants.

The other part of the play is the historical part, the elements of which come from Holinshed's account of the reign of Kymbeline, like Lear a pre-Christian king in primitive Britain. Much of the "landscape" here is vague, as it is in *Lear,* but it is clearly different from the "landscape" of Renaissance Italy. In court, to be sure, the princess' bedroom has tapestries of silk and silver, showing Cleopatra in all her glory when she first met Mark Antony on the river Cydnus; the chimneypiece is chaste Diana bathing; the ceiling displays golden cherubim, and the andirons are blind Cupids. But Cymbeline's Britain is a country where youths have to be sent to Rome to be taught chivalry and be knighted; it is a country where everything away from court is wild, where lost princes hunt in the most primitive manner, where a questing prince has his head cut off, where an old man and two boys in a narrow lane can defeat a Roman army. There is a good deal that comes from the account of Brute in Holinshed's Book II, Chapter I, which colors the Cymbeline plot. Brute by accident while hunting slew his father, and, for fear of his grandfather (whose name was Silvius Posthumus) fled the country and eventually arrived in Britain. (His wife was named Innogen, which a contemporary playgoer took to be the name of Shakespeare's heroine.) [18]

The scenery of *Cymbeline,* as distinct from the "landscape," is elaborate. The bedroom scene must be played in an enclosed space. The direction is "Enter Imogen in her bed"; the bed is not thrust out, and there are several important properties in the room — the chest containing Jachimo, a book, a burning taper, and a clock which strikes. Some of the court scenes are ceremonial, such as III. i, in which Cymbeline, the Queen, Cloten and Lords enter at one door and Caius Lucius and attendants at another. The enclosed space would also serve as Belarius' cave in III. iii; III. vi; III. vii; and IV. ii. Two scenes of spectacle in the last act have very full stage directions. In V. ii, "Enter Lucius, Jachimo, and the Roman army at one door: and the Briton army at another: Leonatus Posthumus following like a poor soldier. They march over, and go out. Then enter again, in skirmish, Jachimo and Posthumus: he vanquisheth and disarmeth Jachimo, and then leaves him." This is very like the old-fashioned dumb shows which Shakespeare and his collaborator used in *Pericles.* A similar situation exists at the end of V. iii, where the stage direction looks like either a dumb show or a note for a scene that was not written: "Enter Cymbeline, Belarius, Guiderius, Arviragus, Pisanio, and Roman captives. The Captains present Posthumus to Cymbeline, who delivers him over to a gaoler."

The most spectacular scene is V. iv, in which Posthumus is chained to one of the stage posts, like a horse tethered in a field; he delivers a soliloquy and then sleeps. The stage direction then introduces the much discussed vision scene: "Solemn music. Enter (as in an apparition) Sicilius Leonatus, father to Posthumus, an old man, attired like a warrior, leading in his hand an ancient matron (his wife, and mother to Posthumus) with music before them. Then, after other music, follow, the two young Leonati (brothers to Posthumus) with wounds as

164

they died in the wars. They circle Posthumus round as he lies sleeping." Then, in response to their plea, "Jupiter descends in thunder and lightning, sitting upon an eagle; he throws a thunderbolt. The ghosts fall on their knees." Granville Barker thought he descended only to the upper stage, and this suggestion is endorsed by Nosworthy, but Jupiter has to descend far enough to deliver to the ghosts the tablet which they lay upon Posthumus' breast before they fade, and it is not clear that this could be done from the balcony or upper stage. It is more notable that Jupiter ascends on the eagle again. This business has been identified as a clear sign that *Cymbeline,* in the text of it we have, was produced at the Blackfriars rather than the Globe. Bernard Beckerman points out that "It is pertinent that a dream scene, very similar to the one in *Cymbeline,* occurs in *Pericles* (V. i), one of the last plays to be produced before the King's Men took over Blackfriars. Instead of Jupiter, Diana appears but does not descend. Nor did the god Hymen in the last scene of *As You Like It.* Could it have been that the company lacked means for flying actors until it moved to Blackfriars? . . . For the Globe, at least so far as the plays demonstrate, no machinery for flying existed."[19] This has some bearing on the date of the play, also. Burbage recovered Blackfriars in August, 1608, but the King's Men didn't play there until late 1609 or early 1610. The theaters were closed during 1608 and up to December, 1609, though the King's Men acted at court during those years.[20] Finally, the conclusion of the play, which has led to some rather extravagant interpretations, may safely be described by Granville Barker as dissolving in pageantry.

In *Cymbeline* we have the retreat into the green world, to a kind of Arcadia, which resumes the pastoral pattern of *As You Like It* and is repeated, in a general way, in *The Winter's Tale* and *The Tempest.* The mountains of Wales may not seem to be Arcadian, but noble outlaws live in a cave there, are hospitable to needy strangers but capable of executing a bully and buffoon. Imogen yearns wistfully for a pastoral life before she ever leaves the court:

> Would I were
> A neat-herd's daughter, and my Leonatus
> Our neighbor shepherd's son!   (I. i. 148-49)

Shakespeare's pastoral atmosphere in the late plays was modified in certain important ways from the pastoralism of *As You Like It,* but that it is true pastoral is, I think, beyond question.

The Winter's Tale, in so far as it is a play about Leontes and Perdita, is modeled on *Pericles;* in both the father is central in Acts I, II, III, and V, but is missing in Act IV, which is his daughter's. In so far as *The Winter's Tale* is a play about a wrongly suspected wife who is supposed dead turns out to be alive and is vindicated, it goes back to *Cymbeline* and beyond that to *Much Ado.*[21] The structure of the play is firm and clear, and despite the striking differences between the two halves of the play, there are links which bind them together.

One of these links is the pastoral imagery which at times penetrates the court atmosphere at Sicilia. The account of the boyhood of Leontes and Polixenes, for example, is pastoral:

> We were as twinn'd lambs that did frisk i' th' sun,
> And bleat the one at th' other. What we chang'd
> Was innocence for innocence; we knew not
> The doctrine of ill-doing, nor dream'd
> That any did.

(I. ii. 67-71)

Its bearing on the business of the play is subtle. The innocence portrayed contrasts strongly with the evil that will possess Leontes' mind shortly.

There is a curious bit of "landscape" in the tale Mamillius starts to tell. It is a sad tale, best for winter. It involves sprites and goblins. The hero is a man who lives by a churchyard, and some of the more fanciful critics have taken this mysterious figure from the "landscape" to stand for Leontes. The little episode is perhaps a premonition and preparation for the death of Mamillius himself (II. i. 25-30).

The relationship between *The Winter's Tale* and its source *Pandosto* has been described, but there is an extraordinary bit of "landscape" in the account of the old shepherd's dead wife, whom he cites as a model to his adopted daughter Perdita. In the source the old shepherd's wife is still alive and she is a shrew, but Shakespeare changed it all:

166

Fie, daughter, when my old wife liv'd, upon
This day she was both pantler, butler, cook,
Both dame and servant; welcomed all, serv'd all;
Would sing her song and dance her turn; now here
At upper end o' th' table, now i' th' middle;
On his shoulder, and his; her face o' fire
With labor, and the thing she took to quench it
She would to each one sip.   (IV. iv. 55-62)

This picture has for its immediate justification the calling forth of Perdita to assume the center of the stage, which she does as she distributes her flowers; it shows that in her native modesty she has to be urged to come forward.

The oracle on which so much in the plot depends is also "landscape." It is described by the two envoys, Cleomenes and Dion. In some twenty lines they convey the beauty of the isle, the clarity and sweetness of the climate, the majesty and reverence of the sacrifices and the holy ceremonies, the deafening voice of the oracle, the "rare, pleasant, speedy" character of their whole mission. The impression is very strong that the answer of the oracle, though now sealed up and secret, will be favorable to Hermione, with whom at least Cleomenes sympathizes.

The events of the shipwreck and of the eating of Antigonus are of course reported, and Shakespeare has them done in a comical manner that has been called grotesque. But III. iii presents some interesting problems, and he had to solve them all at once. The dream of Antigonus, reported as he leaves the infant Perdita, raises critical problems because he clearly believes that Hermione is dead and he also believes that the baby is the offspring of Polixenes. The theatrical "Exit, pursued by a bear" has also caused critical problems. The strange world of the seacoast of Bohemia, where creatures of prey inhabit, and there are fierce storms which do not disturb hunters but bother the shepherds because they drive some of their sheep into dangerous territory, is almost all "landscape"; the bear is scenery. Finally, in the great pastoral scenes IV. iii and iv, there are many details of cony-catching in the background of Autolycus, plus the surprising news that he once served Prince Florizel but was whipped from court for some of his virtues.

The Winter's Tale notoriously has a chorus, Time, who separates the two parts of the play and invites the audience to pretend that it has slept during the interval of fifteen or sixteen years between Acts III and IV. The staging of *The Winter's Tale* is straightforward and generally unlocalized, with three very important exceptions. The first is the bear scene. The second is the very elaborate festival scene iv of Act IV. Here we continue the ballads of Autolycus, begun in the scene before. In addition we have a dance of shepherds and shepherdesses (line 167) a three-part song (line 297) a dance of twelve satyrs, and a change of costume on stage (line 620).

The reconciliation scene, which was so powerfully handled in *Pericles,* is here reported (V. ii) no doubt in order to save theatrical effect for the scene which is to follow, but also to permit the more highly comic treatment of the resolution of the tangled plot than Shakespeare had ventured upon in *Pericles* or *Cymbeline.* Finally, the statue scene, which is as theatrical as might be, provides plenty of suspense and an accompaniment of music.

What you will believe is one of the main themes of *The Winter's Tale;* it is a subject which occupies the dramatist's attention in *A Midsummer Night's Dream* and *Hamlet* also. The errors of belief in Leontes are dramatized in the first part. The plea of Paulina just before she makes Hermione move is a climax: "It is required / You do awake your faith" (V. iii. 94-95). And even the conversion of that sceptic Antigonus involves belief:

> I have heard (but not believ'd) the spirits o' the dead
> May walk again
>
> . . . .
>
> Affrighted much,
> I did in time collect myself and thought
> This was so, and no slumber. Dreams are toys,
> Yet for this once, yea, superstitiously,
> I will be squar'd by this.   (III. iii. 16-41)

There are two ways of inculcating belief on the stage. One is by "landscape" and the other is by setting. "Landscape" is easier, but perhaps not so powerful. If we are Thomases who believe because we see, we may be less blessed than those who can believe without seeing, but we are more firmly convinced.

We have observed how an Arcadia could be transformed by the picture of newly discovered countries, and this combination is largely responsible for the "landscape" of *The Tempest*. But there is much more to it than that. The island is pervaded by magic, it has a past, and its atmosphere is deliberately mysterious in part. Malone, who was the first to recognize the relationship of the Bermuda pamphlets to *The Tempest,* also saw the value of mystery:

> I may add, that our poet himself also, in some measure, contributed to lead the most sedulous inquirer astray, by very properly making the scene of his piece an island at a considerable distance from Bermuda, in order to give the magical part of his drama a certain mysterious dignity which Bermuda itself, then the general topic of conversation, could not have had. Without having read Tacitus, he well knew that OMNE IGNOTUM PRO MAGNIFICO EST; that an unknown island would give a larger scope to his imagination, and make a greater impression on theatrical spectators, than one of which the more enlightened part of his audience had recently read a minute and circumstantial account.[22]

The island has a past. It is related to Ariel, who already knows it, by Prospero, on the excuse that he must repeat it once a month because Ariel keeps forgetting:

> *Prospero:*   I must
> Once a month recount what thou hast been,
> Which thou forget'st. This damn'd witch Sycorax
> For mischiefs manifold, and sorceries terrible
> To enter human hearing, from Argier,
> Thou know'st, was banish'd; for one thing she did
> They would not take her life. Is not this true?
> *Ariel:* Ay, sir.
> *Prospero:* This blue-ey'd hag was hither brought with child,
> And here was left by th' sailors. Thou, my slave,
> As thou report'st thyself, was then her servant;
> And, for thou wast a spirit too delicate
> To act her earthy and abhorr'd commands,

169

Refusing her grand hests, she did confine thee,
By help of her more potent ministers,
And in her most unmitigable rage,
Into a cloven pine, within which rift
Imprison'd, thou didst painfully remain
A dozen years; within which space she died,
And left thee there, where thou didst vent thy groans
As fast as mill-wheels strike. Then was this island
(Save for the son that [she] did litter here,
A freckled whelp, hag-born) not honored with
A human shape.
Ariel: Yes — Caliban her son.
Prospero: Dull thing, I say so; he, that Caliban,
Whom now I keep in service. Thou best know'st
What torment I did find thee in; thy groans
Did make wolves howl, and penetrate the breasts
Of ever-angry bears. It was a torment
To lay upon the damn'd, which Sycorax
Could not again undo. It was mine art,
When I arriv'd and heard thee, that made gape
The pine, and let thee out.   (I. ii. 261-93)

It is indeed mysterious. We do not know whether the mill-wheels which strike so fast are a mere memory from Prospero's past in Milan (presumably they are) and we do not know whether the island actually contains wolves and ever-angry bears (though none certainly make their appearance in the play). They are a part of the wild, mysterious atmosphere of *The Tempest*.

Although Ariel, a spirit, is Prospero's servant, and Prospero seems supreme on the island, so that everything that happens on the island may be attributed to him, yet there is a kind of beauty, and music especially, not directly attributed to the magician. The island is in some sense a *locus amoenus,* at least in Caliban's description:

Be not afeard. The isle is full of noises,
Sounds, and sweet airs, that give delight and hurt not.
Sometimes a thousand twangling instruments
Will hum about mine ears, and sometime voices,

That, if I had been wak'd after long sleep,
Will make me sleep again; and then, in dreaming,
The clouds methought would open, and show riches
Ready to drop upon me, that when I waked,
I cried to dream again.   (III. i. 133-41)

The Tempest is Shakespeare's greatest achievement in what I have called "landscape." This is why it has been a favorite of romantic critics, ever since the blossoming of Shakespeare appreciation in the eighteenth century. Joseph Warton, for example, wrote in 1753:

"Of all the plays of Shakespeare, *The Tempest* is the most striking instance of his creative power. He has there given the reins to his boundless imagination, and has created the romantic, the wonderful, and the wild, to the most pleasing extravagance."[23]

I have said that the storm in *The Winter's Tale* is "landscape," while the bear is scenery. The storm in *The Tempest* is more complex. Functionally, the storm in the earlier play is a conclusion to the "winter" or tragic half of the play, grotesquely mingled, in the clown's account, with the destruction of Antigonus by the bear. In *The Tempest* the storm is the first of the demonstrations of Prospero's "Art" and the means by which Miranda is introduced to the outside world. As scenery, the storm occurs in Act I scene i, and much of the violence of the weather is conveyed by the violence of the language used on board the ship. But it is the later scenes that the storm becomes landscape. Miranda first gives description of it:

> If by your Art, my dearest father, you have
> Put the wild waters in this roar, allay them.
> The sky, it seems, would pour down stinking pitch
> But that the sea, mounting to th' welkin's cheek
> Dashes the fire out.
>
>   (I. ii. 1-5)

Then, much later in the same scene, is the evidence brought not by a spectator, like Miranda, but by an agent in the storm, Ariel, as he reports to Prospero:

I boarded the king's ship; now on the beak,
Now in the waist, the deck, in every cabin,
I flam'd amazement. Sometime I'ld divide,
And burn in many places; on the topmast,
The yards and boresprit, would I flame distinctly,
Then meet and join. Jove's lightning, the precursors
O' th' dreadful thunder-claps, more momentary
And sight-outrunning were not; the fire and cracks
Of sulphurous roaring the most mighty Neptune
Seem to besiege, and make his bold waves tremble,
Yea, his dread trident shake

. . . .

          All but mariners
Plung'd in the foaming brine, and quit the vessel;
Then all afire with me, the King's son, Ferdinand,
With hair up-staring (then like reeds, not hair),
Was the first man that leapt; cried, "Hell is empty,
And all the devils are here!"

                      (I. ii. 196-215)

The third witness is not an observer from shore, not the spirit who perpetrated the storm, but one of its victims, Francisco. He is trying to comfort the king with the possibility that his son did not drown:

          Sir, he may live
I saw him beat the surges under him
And ride upon their backs. He trod the water,
Whose enmity he flung aside, and breasted
The surge most swoll'n that met him. His bold head
'Bove the contentious waves he kept, and oared
Himself with his good arms in lusty stroke
To th' shore, that o'er his wave-worn basis bowed,
As stooping to relieve him I not doubt
He came alive to land.

                      (II. i. 114-23)

Now, the fact that Ariel is able to undo all that he did in the storm has made some critics say there are two storms in the play — that the violent one was an illusion. But which is the dream and which is waking reality is a constant theme in the late plays, and it is never better done than in the tempest of *The Tempest*. The Boatswain is not sure which is dream:

> *Boatswain:* The best news is, that we have safely found
> Our king and company; the next, our ship —
> Which, but three glasses since, we gave out split —
> Is tight and yare, and bravely rigg'd as when
> We first put out to sea.
> *Ariel: {Aside to Pros.}* Sir, all this service
> Have I done since I went.
> *Prospero: {Aside to Ariel.}* My tricksy spirit!
> *Alonso:* These are not natural events; they strengthen
> From strange to stranger. Say, how came you hither?
> *Boatswain:* If I did think, sir, I were well awake,
> I'ld strive to tell you. We were dead of sleep
> And (how we know not) all clapp'd under hatches,
> Where, but even now, with strange and several noises
> Of roaring, shrieking, howling, jingling chains,
> And moe diversity of sounds, all horrible,
> Where we, in all our trim, freshly beheld
> Our royal, good, and gallant ship; our master
> Cap'ring to eye her. On a trice, so please you,
> Even in a dream, were we divided from them,
> And were brought moping hither.[24]

Ariel's performances offstage are of course part of the "landscape." His conduct of the storm has already been discussed. Aside from this, his activities are largely musical, as when he conducted Ferdinand from his landing place to an odd angle of the isle:

> *Ferdinand:*   Sitting on a bank,
> Weeping again the King my father's wrack,
> This music crept by me upon the waters,
> Allaying both their fury and my passion
> With its sweet air; thence I have follow'd it,
> Or it hath drawn me rather.
>   (I. ii. 390-95)

This offstage music is beautifully integrated into what I have called scenery when Ariel introduces his music on the stage, as in "Come unto these yellow sands" and "Full fadom five," but also when he plays, invisibly, the tune of the comedians' catch on his tabor and pipe. The climactic "shows" are of course scenery, and they are quite elaborate, but their success probably depends upon their relationship to the "landscape" of magic which has already been established. The banquet presented by strange shapes in III. iii is introduced by a solemn and strange music and is ended by thunder and lightning when Ariel returns as a harpy and the banquet vanishes. The vision of the goddesses who celebrate the union of Miranda and Ferdinand with their blessing is introduced by soft music and concludes with a dance of reapers and nymphs (IV. i. 60-138). Finally, the hunting scene in which spirits "in the shape of dogs and hounds," urged on by Prospero and Ariel in their pursuit of Caliban, Stephano, and Trinculo, bring to the stage on a more familiar or comic level the scenic effects which have a larger connotation and relate to the whole "landscape" of the island.[25]

The difference between scenery and "landscape" is the difference between what you see on the stage and what you can only see in the imagination, the difference between this cockpit and the vasty fields of France, the ability to "sit and see, / Minding true things by what their mockeries be." But what happens when the things we see melt into air, into thin air? This is the subject of Prospero's great speech at IV. i. 148 ff. In it we are shown that all the pompous great external world, too, shall fade and become no more substantial than what we see in imagination or a dream. Here, in one of Shakespeare's most profound and most eloquent utterances, is the fusion of scenery and "landscape."

Chapter 9
LANGUAGE AND STYLE

Art is the miracle of the romances; Shakespeare's art makes itself known, declaring its own identity in the face of the world, and it is through the wonder of art that the romances approach meanings close to a single reality.

Geoffrey Bush

The language of the romances is distinctive, and the versification so free and flexible that Shakespeare critics generally agree about the dating of these plays; they show a kind of bemused wonder that Dryden could have supposed that *Pericles* was one of Shakespeare's first dramatic efforts. Take, for example, two passages in which a husband supposes his wife has been unfaithful to him. The first is Posthumus in *Cymbeline:*

> O, all the devils!
> This yellow Jachimo in an hour — was't not? —
> Or less — at first? Perchance he spoke not, but,
> Like a full-acorn'd boar, a German [one],
> Cried "O!" and mounted; found no opposition
> But what he look'd for should oppose and she
> Should from encounter guard. Could I find out
> The woman's part in me, for there's no motion
> That tends to vice in man, but I affirm
> It is the woman's part: be it lying, note it,
> The woman's; flattering, hers; deceiving, hers;
> Lust and rank thoughts, hers, hers; revenges, hers;
> Ambitions, covetings, change of prides, disdain,
> Nice longing, slanders, mutability,

All faults that name, nay, that hell knows,
Why, hers, in part or all; but rather all;
For even to vice
They are not constant, but are changing still:
One vice but of a minute old, for one
Not half so old as that. I'll write against them,
Detest them, curse them; yet 'tis greater skill
In a true hate, to pray they have their will:
The very devils can not plague them better.

(II. v. 13-35)

The other is Leontes in *The Winter's Tale:*

You have mistook, my lady,
Polixenes for Leontes. O thou thing!
Which I'll not call a creature of thy place,
Lest barbarism (making me the precedent)
Should a like language use to all degrees,
And mannerly distinguishment leave out
Betwixt the prince and beggar. I have said
She's an adultress, I have said with whom:
More — she's a traitor, and Camillo is
A federary with her, and one that knows
What she should shame to know herself
But with her most vild principal — that she's
A bed-swerver, even as bad as those
That vulgars give bold'st titles; ay, and privy
To this their late escape.

(II. i. 81-95)

To be sure, the situations are somewhat different. Posthumus is speaking a soliloquy and Leontes is accusing his queen before the whole court. Yet both are self-conscious, rhetorical, and tortured in syntax and strange in vocabulary. Jonathan Smith[1] describes Leontes' language as composed of "an 'exsufflicate' vocabulary, extraordinary in every way." There are polysyllabic latinisms, and such words as "distinguishment" and "federary" are used by Shakespeare only in this passage. Posthumus, not being royal himself and not speaking before courtiers, does not need to be afraid of using barbarous language, so he uses the repulsive simile of the full-fed German boar. Both husbands are distracted, but it is noteworthy that the speeches do not so much characterize the speakers as dramatize the occasion.

The language of the romances is often used for purposes other than characterization. This has led to a misunderstanding of the quality of the last plays, and especially of *Cymbeline.* Imogen's expression of her love for Posthumus immediately after his departure is strained and curious:

> *Imogen:* I would have broke mine eye-strings, crack'd them but
> To look upon him, till the diminution
> Of space had pointed him sharp as my needle;
> Nay, followed him till he had melted from
> The smallness of a gnat to air, and then
> Have turn'd mine eye and wept. But, good Pisanio,
> When shall we hear from him?
> *Pisanio:*   Be assur'd, madam,
> With his next vantage.
> *Imogen:* I did not take my leave of him, but had
> Most pretty things to say. Ere I could tell him
> How I would think on him at certain hours
> Such thoughts and such; or I could make him swear
> The shes of Italy should not betray
> Mine interest and his honor; or have charg'd him
> At the sixt hour of morn, at noon, at midnight,
> T'encounter me with orisons, for then
> I am in heaven for him; or ere I could
> Give him that parting kiss which I had set
> Betwixt two charming words, comes in my father,
> And, like the tyrannous breathing of the north
> Shakes all our buds from growing.

(I. iii. 17-37)

The scene exists solely for the sake of this speech, and its purpose is not at all to characterize Imogen. It is to sharpen the audience's awareness of the situation. In the preceding scene we have beheld the witless and cowardly Cloten complaining that he had not had a chance to defeat Posthumus in a duel and lamenting that "She should love this fellow and refuse me!" In the scene following, Posthumus is enticed into the wager on his wife's chastity. Imogen's baroque or mannered speech is therefore in support of the conviction the audience must have of her ingrained and thorough fidelity and an awareness of her precarious position — she is threatened from both sides.

Sometimes Shakespeare destroys the syntax purposely to indicate a combination of excitement and uncertainty, as in Imogen's speech when she reads the letter telling her that Posthumus is coming to Milford Haven:

> Hear'st thou, Pisanio?
> He is at Milford-Haven. Read, and tell me
> How far 'tis thither. If one of mean affairs
> May plod it in a week, why may not I
> Glide thither in a day? Then, true Pisanio,
> Who long'st like me to see thy lord; who long'st
> (O, let me bate!) — but not like me — yet long'st,
> But in a fainter kind — O, not like me,
> For mine's beyond beyond — say, and speak thick
> (Love's counsellor should fill the bores of hearing
> To th' smothering of the sense), how far it is
> To this same blessed Milford. And by th' way
> Tell me how Wales was made so happy as
> T'inherit such a haven. But first of all,
> How we may steal from hence; and for the gap
> That we shall make in time, from our hence-going
> And our return, to excuse. But first, how get hence.
> Why should excuse be born or ere begot?
> We'll talk of that hereafter. Prithee speak,
> How many [score] of miles may we well rid
> 'Twixt hour and hour?

(III. ii. 48-68)

James Sutherland[2] finds this kind of speech not special to the character speaking it, but typical of Shakespeare himself in this last period. He is "thinking rapidly, breaking off, making fresh starts"; he is "forcing the pace" in a situation where competition breeds exaggeration. The opening expository dialogue in *Cymbeline* is, Sutherland thinks, an example of this. Shakespeare was writing at speed and without care or correction. Perhaps it was the manuscripts of these late plays which Heminge and Condell had in mind when they said they had scarce received a blot from him in his papers. B. Ifor Evans[3] calls attention to the breaking up of the sentence into quick, short phrases, as in Imogen's soliloquy before the cave of Belarius:

> Milford,
> When from the mountain top Pisanio show'd thee,
> Thou wast within a ken. O Jove, I think
> Foundations fly the wretched: such, I mean,
> Where they should be reliev'd. Two beggars told me
> I could not miss my way. Will poor folks lie,
> That have afflictions on them, knowing 'tis
> A punishment or trial? Yes; no wonder,
> When rich ones scarce tell true. To lapse in fullness
> Is sorer than to lie for need; and falsehood
> Is worse in kings than beggars. My dear lord,
> Thou art one o' th' false ones. Now I think on thee
> My hunger's gone; but even before, I was
> At point to sink for food. But what is this?
> Here is a path to't; 'tis some savage hold.
>
> (III. vi. 4-18)

"This effect of breaking up the verse," says Evans, "while bold and original, is used with no easily definable dramatic purpose." One might suggest that again the nature of the speech may be appreciated if one looks at the dramatic context. It is a moment of terrific excitement and suspense. In the preceding scene Cloten has made his plans to dress up in Posthumus' clothes, meet him at Milford Haven, kill him and rape Imogen on his dead body and then whip her back to the court. Immediately following her soliloquy she is discovered by **Guiderius** and her long-lost brothers. The event is of course as improbable as any that could be invented, but it is very powerful theatrically and it is the uniting of the two separate strands of plot which Shakespeare had chosen to put into the same play — the story of what happened to Imogen and the story of what happened to her brothers. The nervousness of the style is entirely appropriate to the feelings the audience is supposed to have, assuming, of course, that the audience is willing to accept the improbable events of romance fiction.

A most remarkable instance of Shakespeare's special use of language in the late plays is Posthumus' report of the battle in Act V, scene iii. The only action in the scene comes at the end, when Posthumus, who has helped the old man and two boys defeat the Roman army, now identifies himself as a Roman and is taken prisoner. But for some ninety lines before that Posthumus describes the battle to a silly British lord who had fled from the action. It is as if Hotspur had taken a whole scene to describe the battle of Holmedon to that popinjay who pestered him about the prisoners. Nosworthy comments that the account of the battle in *Cymbeline* is "extremely involved." "Excitement and indignation render him incoherent, and it is probable that Shakespeare here employed incoherence with calculated dramatic effect, as he had already done in *Coriolanus*."[4]

Posthumus is in disguise as a peasant. Jachimo, whom he has defeated, refers to him as "this carl, a very drudge of Nature's" and "this lout" (V. ii. 4-9); the Second Captain says he was dressed in "a silly habit" (V. iii. 86). He has fought in the battle seeking death, in repentance for having caused, as he supposes, the death of Imogen. But he has failed to find it:

> I, in mine own woe charm'd,
> Could not find death where I did hear him groan
> Nor feel him where he strook. Being an ugly monster,
> 'Tis strange he hides him in fresh cups, soft beds,
> Sweet words; or hath moe ministers than we
> That draw his knives i' th' war.   (V. iii. 68-73)

Accordingly, Posthumus' situation is completely paradoxical, both with respect to himself and his own fate and to the curious role he is now playing as the narrator of brave victory to a coward. He answers the question about the narrow lane:

Close by the battle, ditch'd, and wall'd with turf,
Which gave advantage to an ancient soldier
(An honest one, I warrant), who deserv'd
So long a breeding as his white beard came to,
In doing this for's country. Athwart the lane,
He, with two striplings (lads more like to run
The country base than to commit such slaughter,
With faces fit for masks, or rather fairer
Than those for preservation cas'd, or shame),
Made good the passage, cried to those that fled,
"Our Britain's harts die flying, not our men.
To darkness fleet souls that fly backwards. Stand,
Or we are Romans and will give you that
Like beasts, which you shun beastly, and may save
But to look back in frown. Stand, stand!" These three,
Three thousand confident, in act as many —
For three performers are the file when all
The rest do nothing — with this word "Stand, stand!"
Accommodated by the place, more charming
With their own nobleness, which could have turn'd
A distaff to a lance, gilded pale looks;
Part shame, part spirit renew'd, that some, turn'd coward
But by example (O, a sin in war,
Damn'd in the first beginners!), gan to look
The way that they did, and to grin like lions
Upon the pikes o' th' hunters. Then began
A stop i' th' chaser; a retire; anon
A rout, confusion thick. Forthwith they fly
Chickens, the way which they [stoop'd] eagles; slaves,
The strides [they] victors made: and now our cowards,
Like fragments in hard voyages, became
The life o' th' need. Having found the back door open,
Of the unguarded hearts, heavens, how they wound
Some slain before, some dying, some their friends
O'erborne i' th' former wave. Ten chas'd by one
Are now each one the slaughter-man of twenty.
Those that would die or ere resist are grown
The mortal bugs o' th' field.

                                        (V. iii. 14-51)

Since he is disguised as a peasant, his speech is full of homely expressions: the two lost princes are "lads more like to run the country base than to commit such slaughter" and the Romans retreat like frightened chickens down the route they had come as conquering eagles; the cowardly Britons finally stand, at the urging and example of the old man and two boys, and like a hard dry remainder biscuit on a long voyage they become "the life o' the need." Everything that has happened is paradoxical; the cowards (all except the lord who is listening) become champions, slaughter-men of twenty, the mortal bugs o' th' field. But the naive response of the foppish lord, to marvel at the strange events he has heard of, "This was strange chance: / A narrow lane, an old man, and two boys" is rebuked by the jaded and irritated Posthumus, who, as Nosworthy puts it, "tells him not to wonder at fact since he was born to wonder at fiction."

Posthumus is beyond human concerns. His account of the battle is the preparation for his soliloquy in the next scene, where he is chained to one of the stage posts (not in prison, as many editions say, though he has been placed there by jailers) and welcomes bondage and tries with penitence to unlock the fetters on his conscience. His language can only approximate his meaning, so after offering his life in payment for his wife's, he concludes:

> If you will take this audit, take this life,
> And cancel these cold bonds. O Imogen,
> I'll speak to thee in silence.   *{Sleeps.}*   (V. iv. 27-29)

This is a very subtle and delicate language, possibly demanding more of an actor than he can be expected to deliver, but it is not the result of haste or mental exhaustion. Posthumus' soliloquy is prefigured faintly by Shakespeare earlier in the play when he shows Imogen opening the letter:

> Good wax, thy leave. Blest be
> You bees that make these locks of counsel! Lovers
> And men in dangerous bonds pray not alike;
> Though forfeiters you cast in prison, yet
> You clasp young Cupid's tables. Good news, gods!
>
> (III. ii. 35-39)

That the language given to a character to speak may sometimes serve for other purposes than characterization is no very startling discovery, though it is not always kept in mind by editors and critics. One of the remarkable uses of language in *Cymbeline* is the overheard — and intentionally overheard — soliloquy of Jachimo when he first tries to defame Posthumus to Imogen:

> What, are men mad? Hath nature given them eyes
> To see this vaulted arch and the rich crop
> Of sea and land, which can distinguish 'twixt
> The fiery orbs above, and the twinn'd stones
> Upon the number'd beach, and can we not
> Partition make with spectacles so precious
> 'Twixt fair and foul?
>
> . . . .
>
> It cannot be i' th' eye; for apes and monkeys,
> 'Twixt two such shes would chatter this way, and
> Contemn with mows the other; nor i' th' judgment,
> For idiots in this case of favor would
> Be wisely definite; nor i' th' appetite:
> Sluttery, to such neat excellence oppos'd,
> Should make desire vomit emptiness,
> Not so allur'd to feed.
>
> . . . .
>
>   The cloyd will —
> That satiate yet unsatisfied desire, that tub
> Both fill'd and running — ravening first the lamb,
> Longs after for the garbage.
>
>   (I. vi. 32-50)

Shakespeare here puts into the seductive technique of his Italian villain some of the images and even some of the phrases that haunt the mind of Hamlet as he considers his mother's behavior. Though Imogen does hear what he says, it makes no impression on her and Jachimo has to change his strategy, to make out that Posthumus is merry while absent from her and scornful of a Frenchman who sighs for his love at home.

Again, Jachimo's speech in the bedchamber is one of the most remarkable in all of Shakespeare: It begins with an almost magical evocation, capable of countering the absurdity of a man who has just popped out of a trunk:

> The crickets sing, and man's o'er-labor'd sense
> Repairs itself by rest. Our Tarquin thus
> Did softly press the rushes ere he waken'd
> The chastity he wounded. Cytherea,
> How bravely thou becom'st thy bed! fresh lily,
> And whiter than the sheets! That I might touch!
> But kiss, one kiss! Rubies unparagon'd.
> How dearly they do't! 'Tis her breathing that
> Perfumes the chamber thus. The flame o' th' taper
> Bows toward her, and would under-peep her lids,
> To see th' enclosed lights, now canopied
> Under these windows, white and azure lac'd
> With blue of heaven's own tinct.
>
> (II. ii. 11-23)

Then this suddenly shifts to action, which is guided by the language, so the actor can make no mistake:

> But my design —
> To note the chamber, I will write all down:
> *{Takes out his tables.}*
> Such and such pictures; there the window; such
> Th' adornment of her bed; the arras, figures,
> Why, such and such; and the contents o' th' story.
> Ah, but some natural notes about her body,
> Above ten thousand meaner moveables
> Would testify, t' enrich mine inventory.
> O sleep, thou ape of death, lie dull upon her,
> And be her sense but as a monument,
> Thus in a chapel lying! Come off, come off!
> *{Taking off her bracelet.}*
> As slippery as the Gordian knot was hard!
> 'Tis mine, and this will witness outwardly,
> As strongly as the conscience does within,
> To th' madding of her lord.
>
> (II. ii. 23-37)

Not only do the lines direct the actor, but they are dramatic and psychologically persuasive in their metrical irregularity. At this point the verse returns to its descriptive, emblematic tone and ends with a rhetorical flourish reminiscent of *Macbeth* and Marlowe's *Dr. Faustus* as Jachimo gets back into the trunk:

> On her left breast
> A mole cinque-spotted, like the crimson drops
> I' th' bottom of a cowslip. Here's a voucher,
> Stronger than ever law could make; this secret
> Will force him think I have pick'd the lock and ta'en
> The treasure of her honor. No more: to what end?
> Why should I write this down, that's riveted,
> Screw'd to my memory? She hath been reading late
> The tale of Tereus; here the leaf's turn'd down
> Where Philomele gave up. I have enough;
> To th' trunk again, and shut the spring of it.
> Swift, swift, you dragons of the night, that dawning
> May bare the raven's eye! I lodge in fear;
> Though this a heavenly angel, hell is here.
>   *{Clock strikes.}*
> One, two, three. Time, time!
>
>   (II. ii. 37-51)

Jachimo's confession in Act V, scene v, is another long speech. It is interrupted frequently by Cymbeline, who is eager to get to the heart of the matter. But it is also interrupted by Jachimo himself, who breaks in with parenthetical remarks, rephrasings, contradictions, and explanations. He is relieved, glad, as he says, to be constrained to utter that which torments him to conceal. Yet what he has to tell is against himself. Nosworthy comments that Jachimo's story is at once boastful and apologetic. He thinks this is because Shakespeare is conflating two confessions (both Boccaccio and *Frederick of Jennen* have two) "the first of which is voluntary and self-glorifying." But Jachimo is truly in a paradoxical situation. He must show himself to be clever — how else could he have deceived Imogen and Posthumus so successfully? — and at the same time repentant, so that he can be forgiven.

185

Upon a time — unhappy w.s the clock
That strook the hour! — it was in Rome — accurs'd
The mansion where! — 'twas at a feast — O would
Our viands had been poison'd, or at least
Those which I heav'd to head! — the good Posthumus
(What should I say? He was too good to be
Where ill men were, and was the best of all
Amongst the rar'st of good ones), sitting sadly,
Hearing us praise our loves of Italy
For beauty that made barren the swell'd boast
Of him that best could speak. . . .   (V. v. 153-63)

And he proceeds to describe the wager, being careful always to de-
nounce himself and praise Posthumus at any mention of him. Finally,
his account of his practice at the court of Cymbeline ends in the theatrical materializing of Posthumus himself:

                    Well may you, sir,
Remember me at court, where 1 was taught
Of your chaste daughter the wide difference
'Twixt amorous and villainous. Being thus quench'd
Of hope, not longing, mine Italian brain
Gan in your duller Britain operate
Most vildly; for my vantage, excellent;
And, to be brief, my practice so prevail'd,
That I return'd with simular proof enough
To make the noble Leonatus mad,
By wounding his belief in her renown
With tokens thus, and thus; averring notes
Of chamber hanging, pictures, this her bracelet
(O cunning, how I got['t]!) nay, some marks
Of secret on her person, that he could not
But think her bond of chastity quite crack'd,
I having ta'en the forfeit. Whereupon —
Methinks I see him now —

                                   (V. v. 192-209)

If we consider the language of *Cymbeline* from the point of view of its contribution to theatrical effect, we may well conclude that "It is no act of common passage, but / A strain of rareness."

Sometimes the language in the romances is in that middle ground between prose and verse. In *The Winter's Tale,* after the indictment against Hermione is read, she begins with calm matter-of-factness which will lead in time to heightened rhetorical and poetical expression when she refers herself to the oracle and cries "Apollo be my judge!" She begins, "Since what I am to say must be but that which contradicts my accusation, and the testimony on my part no other but what comes from myself, it scarce shall boot me to say 'Not guilty' " (III. ii. 22-25). The editors all print this as verse, but when it is printed as prose one doesn't feel the necessity to separate it into lines of blank verse.

Contrarily, a passage in *Hamlet* always printed as prose has some right to be considered verse:

> If it be now, 'tis not to come; if it
> Be not to come, it will be now; if it
> Be not now, yet 'twill come: the readiness
> Is all. Since no man knows aught of what he leaves,
> What is't to leave betimes?[5]

But the question of whether a passage is prose or verse cannot be decided without reference to the actor and what Shakespeare expected of him. As an illustration, George Rylands printed as prose the following speech of Imogen:

> Thou told'st me, when we came from horse, the place
> Was near at hand. Ne'er long'd my mother so
> To see me first, as I have now. Pisanio! man!
> Where is Posthumus? What is in thy mind
> That makes thee stare thus? Wherefore breaks that sigh
> From th' inward of thee? One but painted thus
> Would be interpreted a thing perplex'd
> Beyond self-explication. Put thyself
> Into a havior of less fear, ere wildness
> Vanquish my staider senses. What's the matter?
>
> (III. iv. 1-10)

"This is in fact blank verse and not (as printed) a rather incompetent specimen of prose," says Rylands. "As blank verse it is in motion, as prose it stumbles and stands still.... As Shakespeare became more experimental and more expert in his handling of line and sentence length, of verse paragraph, of stress, pace and rhythm, so his language became more audacious and eccentric, his grammar more telegraphic, his panache more splendiferous. All the more essential therefore in the latest plays to hang on to the blank verse line as a drowning man to a spar and let the imperious surge of conceit and metaphor break over one's head."[6]

In the trial scenes of accused queens Shakespeare uses a stately language which has a certain similarity, whether it is spoken by Katherine of Aragon or Hermione:

> Sir,
> I am about to weep; but thinking that
> We are a queen (or long have dreamed so), certain
> The daughter of a king, my drops of tears
> I'll turn to sparks of fire.
> *(King Henry the Eighth* II. iv. 69-73)

> Good my lords,
> I am not prone to weeping, as our sex
> Commonly are, the want of which vain dew
> Perchance shall dry your pities; but I have
> That honorable grief lodg'd here which burns
> Worse than tears drown.
> *(Winter's Tale* II. i. 107-12)

or, again,

> Please you, sir,
> The King your father was reputed for
> A prince most prudent, of an excellent
> And unmatched wit and judgment. Ferdinand,
> My father, King of Spain, was reckon'd one
> The wisest prince that there had reign'd by many
> A year before. It is not to be question'd
> That they had gathered a wise council to them
> Of every realm, that did debate this business,
> Who deemed our marriage lawful;
> *(H8* II. iv. 42-51)

The Emperor of Russia was my father.
O that he were alive, and here beholding
His daughter's trial! that he did but see
The flatness of my misery, yet with eyes
Of pity, not revenge!

(*WT* III. ii. 119-23)

The directness of the language in these situations has been noticed before. Oliver Elton quotes from De Quincey: "No woman in this world, under a movement of resentment from a false accusation . . . ever was at leisure to practice vagaries of caprice in the management of her mother tongue: strength of feeling shuts out all temptation to the affectation of false feeling."[7]

Though *Cymbeline* may offer the best examples of the late style of language used primarily for accenting the situation rather than character and supplying for the audience a feeling appropriate to that situation, it is of course also notable for its lyric beauty. (It was Tennyson's favorite Shakespeare play.) The aubade which the crude Cloten provides for Imogen, "Hark, hark the lark" is rightly considered to be the finest aubade in the English language. Its beauty and delicacy contrast in the strongest possible way with the scenes coming just before and after it, yet the song is functional (in giving Imogen time to change costume), and its emphasis on morning supports a reiterated theme in the play. The dirge for the supposedly dead Fidele, "Fear no more the heat o' th' sun," is peerless. It encompasses the sceptre, learning, physic; it recognizes the hardships of weather, of slander and censure, the stroke of the tyrant, thunder and lightning; it subsumes all — golden lads and girls, chimney sweepers, all lovers young — into dust.

This lyric vein is not confined to songs in the romances. It appears strongly in the last three acts of *Pericles*. The opening speech of Act III, by Pericles on shipboard, announces a new music: "The god of this great vast, rebuke these surges." And it continues, while evoking the storm in language, to convey the tenderest feelings related to the childbirth that is taking place:

> The seaman's whistle
> Is as a whisper in the ears of death,
> Unheard.

The pathos of Pericles' address to his supposedly dead wife is expressed in the most delicate manipulation of pauses:

> A terrible child-bed hast thou had, my dear,
> No light, no fire . . .

$$\text{(III. i. 57-58)}$$

And the imagery of burial at sea begins that lovely development which will culminate in Ariel's song in *The Tempest;* Pericles continues:

> Th' unfriendly elements
> Forgot thee utterly, nor have I time
> To give thee hallow'd to thy grave, but straight
> Must cast thee, scarcely coffin'd, in [the ooze],
> Where, for a monument upon thy bones,
> And [e'er-] remaining lamps, the belching whale
> And humming water must o'erwhelm thy corpse,
> Lying with simple shells.

Pericles' patience under adversity is expressed in a very Shakespearian gnomic way:

> We cannot but obey
> The powers above us. Could I rage and roar
> As doth the sea she lies in, yet the end
> Must be as 'tis.

$$\text{(III. iii. 9-12)}$$

Marina's flower-maiden speech is only the first of several in the romances. In *Cymbeline* it is spoken by Arviragus, and his brother comments on his wench-like words (IV. ii. 219-31) and in *The Winter's Tale* it is Perdita's. Marina's speech is really a soliloquy; although she enters to Dionyza and Leonine, she does not notice them and speaks her speech as though no one were present:

No; I will rob Tellus of her weed,
To strow thy green with flowers. The yellows, blues,
The purple violets, and marigolds
Shall as a carpet hang upon thy grave
While summer days doth last. Ay me! poor maid,
Born in a tempest when my mother died,
This world to me is a lasting storm,
Whirring me from my friends.

(IV. i. 13-20)

The situation is sensational: Dionyza has just persuaded Leonine to murder Marina, so the dying fall of her final remark is doubly poignant. Curiously enough, the flower-maiden speech is printed as prose in the Quarto, but Dionyza's following speech, which is hardly metrical at all, is printed in verse.

Marina's protestation to Leonine of her innocence has some characteristic versification:

Why would she have me kill'd now?
As I can remember, by my troth,
I never did her hurt in all my life.
I never spake bad word, nor did ill turn
To any living creature. Believe me law,
I never kill'd a mouse, nor hurt a fly;
I trod upon a worm against my will,
But I wept for't.

(IV. i. 72-79)

The fifth line in this passage is an example of George Rylands' Type I: "a pause after the ninth syllable and a short conjunction or other monosyllable dovetailing the two lines together."[8] His Type II, the paradoxical superlative, is perhaps best seen in the rich environment of the reunion of Pericles and Marina in Act V: "Thou that beget'st him that did thee beget" (V. i. 195). But there are many fine poetic passages in this great scene. Pericles' discourse on Patience:

Tell thy story;
If thine, consider'd, prove the thousand part
Of my endurance, thou art a man, and I
Have suffered like a girl. Yet thou dost look
Like Patience gazing on kings' graves, and smiling
Extremity out of act.

(V. i. 134-39)

And later, the extraordinary mingling of dramatic and lyric expression:

O, stop there a little!
This is the rarest dream that e'er dull'd sleep
Did mock sad fools withal. This cannot be
My daughter — buried! — Well, where were you bred?
I'll hear you more, to th' bottom of your story,
And never interrupt you.

(V. i. 160-65)

Finally, the resolution of the marvelous reunion in music which only those experiencing it can hear:

Pericles: Give me my robes; I am wild in my beholding.
O heavens bless my girl! But hark, what music?
Tell Helicanus, my Marina, tell him
O'er, point by point, for yet he seems to dote,
How sure you are my daughter. But what music?
Helicanus: My lord, I hear none.
Pericles: None?
The music of the spheres! List, my Marina.
Lysimachus: It is not good to cross him; give him way.
Pericles: Rarest sounds! Do ye not hear?
Lysimachus: Music, my Lord? I hear.
Pericles: Most heavenly music!
It nips me into list'ning, and thick slumber
Hangs upon my eyes; let me rest.   *{Sleeps.}*

(V. i. 222-35)

Frank Kermode comments that "the last plays might be expected to, and do, exhibit a control of language and imagery formerly unequaled."[9] Moreover there is a development, from *Pericles* through *Cymbeline* and *The Winter's Tale* into *The Tempest*. This development I see as the elevation of language and imagery into music. Short as *The Tempest* is, it contains more songs than any other play in the canon. It has much instrumental music, which is functional in the play. Ferdinand is first brought onstage by Ariel's song "Come unto these yellow sands" and led on by "Full fadom five thy father lies." He asserts that the music that crept by him on the waters allayed both their fury and his sorrow. Caliban is witness that "The Isle is full of noises, / Sounds and sweet airs, that give delight and hurt not." And, thing of darkness that he is, as disproportion'd in his manners as his shape, yet he is a part of the poetry, the music, of the island.

In the romances Shakespeare's style achieves a new complexity and beauty. The effect is elaborate because the plays of this group offer more theatrical displays, suitable for the kind of romance material being handled; because the relative importance of character and situation has changed; and because this theatrical emphasis provides more opportunity for music of all kinds. It brings about in the audience a heightened awareness of the improbable, the incredible, the marvelous.

Appendices

Appendix A

MYTH, SYMBOL AND POETRY

How easy is a bush supposed a bear!

A Midsummer Night's Dream

In the incomparable flower scene, Act IV scene iv of *The Winter's Tale,* Perdita turns from her argument with Polixenes about art and nature to the task which that argument interrupted, the welcoming of all the guests, young and old, to the sheepshearing feast. She wishes that she had some flowers of the spring that might suit the age, or "time of day," as she calls it, of Florizel, "and yours," she says, turning to the girls,

> That wear upon your virgin branches yet
> Your maidenheads growing. O Proserpina,
> For the flow'rs now, that, frighted, thou let'st fall
> From Dis's waggon! daffadils,
> That come before the swallow dares, and take
> The winds of March with beauty; violets, dim,
> But sweeter than the lids of Juno's eyes
> Or Cytherea's breath; pale primeroses,
> That die unmarried, ere they can behold
> Bright Phoebus in his strength (a malady
> Most incident to maids); bold oxlips and
> The crown imperial; lilies of all kinds,
> The flow'r-de-luce being one.[1]

It must have been passages like this that Milton had in mind when he spoke of "Sweetest Shakespeare, fancy's child / Warbling his native woodnotes wild." And Milton's own art is consummately expressed in his passage evoking the Proserpina legend to give an impression of Eve in paradise:

> Not that fair field
> Of *Enna,* where *Proserpin* gath'ring flow'rs
> Herself a fairer *Flow'r* by gloomy *Dis*
> Was gather'd, which cost *Ceres* all that pain
> To seek her through the world.[2]

There is something ominous about the comparison in Milton; the maiden Proserpina was ravished off to hell by gloomy Dis, and innocent Eve will shortly be seduced by the wiles of the infernal serpent.

The role of Eve as a Proserpina figure in *Paradise Lost* is discussed with great clarity by Maud Bodkin. She points out that "Milton does not in his main intention view Eve as a fated innocent victim, but as a responsible being, duly warned of danger, and in her act illustrating not so much the pathos of human destiny as the culpable 'levity and shallowness' of the human mind."[3] This is inconsistent with the Proserpina role, she admits, but in poetry we should not look for consistency, because feeling, not logic, dictates the blending. "Moreover," she says, "we are here studying the poem not distinctively with reference to the mind of its author, but as it lives in our experience today ... *Paradise Lost,* in my experience, presents the figure of Eve in several different aspects having affinity with different type-figures powerful and deep-seated in men's minds. Among these, one is the Proserpine-figure of virginal youth, lovely in its doomed transience." But Shakespeare has no such associations. He is interested in the flowers — they are the physical occasion for all this poetry, since Perdita is distributing flowers to her guests — and in the fragility of youth, beauty, and maidenhead. There is an interesting transition from the mythical beauty of the flowers, associated with Juno's eyes and Cytherea's breath, to the imagery of anemic girls who die unmarried and are compared to the pale primroses which are gone before midsummer — bright Phoebus in his strength.[4]

Some of the same associations are present in the masque in *The Tempest* (which should reinforce the conviction that the masque is not by another hand than Shakespeare's). Ceres, the mother of Proserpina, is addressed by Iris:

> Ceres, most bounteous lady, thy rich leas
> Of wheat, rye, barley, fetches, oats, and pease;
> Thy turfy mountains, where live nibbling sheep,

And flat meads thatch'd with stover, them to keep;
Thy banks with pioned and twilled brims,
Which spungy April at thy hest betrims
To make cold nymphs chaste crowns

(IV. i. 60-66)

and Ceres replies, a few lines later,

Tell me, heavenly bow,
If Venus or her son, as thou dost know,
Do now attend the Queen? Since they did plot
The means that dusky Dis my daughter got,
Her and her blind boy's scandall'd company
I have forsworn.

(IV. i. 86-91)

Perhaps the most influential of modern critics, Northrop Frye, sees the Proserpina myth as most pervasive and fundamental in Shakespeare's late plays, and indeed, in much other literature. It is a ritual of death and rebirth and of course Hermione is a representation of it. But so are, according to him, Hero in *Much Ado,* Imogen in *Cymbeline,* Spenser's Florimell, Esther Summerson with her attack of smallpox in *Bleak House,* Lorna Doone, Richardson's Pamela, and Pope's Belinda in *The Rape of the Lock.*[5] One trouble is that the passage in *The Winter's Tale* seems to connect Proserpina with Perdita, in that they are both flower girls, but it is not Perdita, but her mother, Hermione, who goes "underground" for a time and then reappears when almost everyone thought she was dead. As Abrams says, though, "the odd thing about evidence for an archetype is not that you cannot prove that it is present, but that you cannot help proving it, and that there is no way of disproving it."

Nevertheless there are some ways of seeing what the Proserpina myth meant to Shakespeare's contemporaries, and to get a little closer to the state of mind in which deeper meanings may be discerned without distorting the surface. It is as clear as can be that Shakespeare's principal knowledge of the Proserpina story came from Ovid, as so much else in his mind and memory did. The emphasis upon spring, upon the flowers, upon "frighted," all reflect Golding's translation:

A wood enuirons euery side the water round about,
And with his leaues as with a vaile doth keepe the sun heat out.
The boughes doo yeeld a coole fresh aire; the moistnesse of the
    ground

199

Yeelds sundrie flowers: continual spring is all the yeare there
    found,
While in this garden Proserpine was taking her pastime
In gathering either violets blew, or lillies white as lime,
And while of maidenlie desire she filled her maund and lap,
Endeuouring to out-gather her companions there. By hap
Dis spide her, lou'd her, caught her vp, and all at once well neere:
So hastie, hot, and swift a thing is loue, as may appeere.
The ladie with a wailing voice afright did often call
Her mother and her waiting maids, but mother most of all.
But as she from the upper part her garment would have rent,
By chance she let her lap slip downe, and out the flowers went.[6]

Golding does not force an explanation of the myth on his translation, though he particularizes the flowers somewhat and provides the lead for Shakespeare's romantic catalogue. Dr. Jenijoy LaBelle, who thinks there is more to myth interpretation than I do, notices other lines in Golding which clearly influenced Shakespeare. When Ceres discovers that Proserpina has been taken by Dis:

> Hir [Proserpine's] mother stoode as starke as stone, when she
>   these newes did heare,
> And long she was like one that in another world had beene.
>
> (V. 631-32)

And in line 643

> Behold our daughter whom I sought so long is found at last.

Jove says "My daughter is a *Jewell dear* and leefe: A *collup of mine* own flesh" (650-51). Mamillius is called "the jewel of children" (V. i. 116) and Leontes calls him *"most dear'st! my collop!"* (I. ii. 137).

Leonard Digges, a friend and admirer of Shakespeare's,[7] published a translation of Claudian's *Rape of Proserpine* in the year after Shakespeare's death; for the benefit of his sister, to whom the translation was dedicated, he gave three explanations of the story — the historical, the natural, and the allegorical. In the historical sense, Ceres, the wife of Siculus, King of Sicily, was the first domesticator and cultivator of wheat "and for this cause the blinde Gentiles adored her as a goddesse, and consecrated that Island of Sicilie vnto her, as to the inuentresse of Haruest."[8] Proserpina, her daughter, was stolen away by Orion King of Epirus and the Molossiand, and Ceres, in searching for her, sowed the rest of the world with wheat. "This story," says Digges, "gave matter to the Poets to faine, that Pluto stole away Proserpina from Sicilia in her mother's absence ... and knowing that she was in hell with Pluto, requested of Iupiter, that she might remaine with her one halfe of the yeare vpon Earth, and the other with her Husband Pluto" (Bʳ).

In the natural sense, Digges explains, "By the person of *Ceres* is signified *Tillage*. By *Proserpine,* the seedes which are sowed, by *Pluto,* the earth that receiues them." In the allegorical sense, Digges declares, "By Proserpine left alone in her mothers absence at her worke, is noted the good education of Children, to which mothers are bound, that are honest and carefull. By Ceres leauing her alone, and Pluto's stealing her away is put (as an example): that Mothers ought not to be so carelesse of their children, as to expose them to so great a hazard of their honours."

Abraham Fraunce explained the Proserpina myth as follows:

> Pluto, then, you see, the third brother, rauished Proserpina: the naturall efficacie and vertue of the earth (sayth Cicero, 2. de natura deorum) draweth vnto it the rootes of corne, growing & increasing in the bowels of the earth. ... Six moneths she lies with her husband: all the winter time, whilest the sunne doth soiourne in the southerne signes: six aboue with her mother, when the sunne returneth to the northerne signes: bringing corne to ripenes and maturities. She had this name Proserpina, of the latine word Proserpo, which is to creep forwards, because the rootes creepe along in the body of the earth. She was gathering flowers when Pluto took her away, and kept her below; for then is that naturall vertue of the seede working, to produce afterwards the fruit and flowre accordingly.[9]

More remote from Shakespeare, one could learn from the *Ovide Moralisé* that Proserpine represents the Church which seeks to bring back the strayed souls of sinners, or from John Ridewall's interpretation of Fulgentius that Proserpina represents Beatitudo. None of this is germane to Shakespeare's two passages on Proserpina, and none of it supports the critics of the archetype school. It looks as if Shakespeare deliberately shied away from the explanations of the sort we have been noticing. For it is demonstrable that he knew and used Thomas Cooper's *Thesaurus,* particularly the *Dictionarium Historicum et Poeticum* at the end of the book. The Ixion centaur images in *King Lear* IV. vi. 112-32 and IV. vii. 45-48 are very close to Cooper, and it is from this dictionary that Shakespeare quite evidently got the word *dotage,* which he uses twice to describe Antony's passion for Cleopatra.[10] But he rejects Cooper's help on Proserpina. Cooper identifies her: "The wyfe of Pluto, daughter to Jupiter and Ceres: she is taken sometyme for the Moone."

This myth and archetype criticism goes back essentially to Jane Harrison, whose *Prolegomena to the Study of Greek Religion* (Cambridge, 1912) was a landmark in classical studies. She substituted an interest in ritual and the implications of ritual for the fictional and largely artificial figures of the Olympian gods, and, according to Gilbert Murray, "she was so eager to penetrate beneath the surface that she almost grew to dislike the surface itself and to love what lay below — and the deeper below the better."[11] Harrison's disciple was F. M. Cornford, also of Cambridge, and he in turn influenced Maud Bodkin, whose *Archetypal Patterns in Poetry* (London, 1934) brought in Jungian psychology to supplement the classics and anthropology already there. E.M.W. Tillyard, one of the founders of the Cambridge English tripos, followed Miss Bodkin, somewhat untypically for him, when he came to write his little book on Shakespeare's last plays.

He objects to the way Perdita is acted: "It has been far too much the property of young women doing eurhythmics at Speech Days or on vicarage lawns; and when it is acted professionally, the part of Perdita is usually taken by some pretty little fool or pert surburban charmer." When Perdita refers to "bright Phoebus in his strength" in her flower speech, she is really referring to Apollo, who "appears as the bridegroom, whom the pale primroses never know, but who visits the other flowers. Not to take the fertility symbolism as intended would be a perverse act of caution. Perdita should be associated with them, as a symbol both of the creative powers of nature, physical fertility, and of healing and re-creation of the mind."[12]

And so we come around again to Northrop Frye and the Proserpina myth. In his highly influential *Anatomy of Criticism* he writes,

> Or, again, we have, in myth, the story of Proserpina, who disappears in the underworld for six months every year. The pure myth is clearly one of death and revival; the story as we have it is slightly displaced, but the mythical pattern is easy to see. The same structural element often recurs in Shakespearian comedy, where it is adapted to a roughly high mimetic level of credibility. Hero in *Much Ado* is dead enough to have a funeral song, and plausible explanations are postponed until after the end of the play. Imogen in *Cymbeline* has an assumed name and an empty grave, but she too gets some funeral obsequies. But the story of Hermione and Perdita is so close to the Demeter and Proserpina myth that hardly any

serious pretense of plausible explanations is made. Hermione, after her disappearance, returns once as a ghost in a dream, and her coming to life from a statue, a displacement of the Pygmalion myth, is said to require an awakening of faith, even though, on one level of plausibility, she has not been a statue at all, and nothing has taken place except a harmless deception."[13]

There have been several objections to Frye's myth criticism as reductive[14] and of ignoring the particularity of a work in favor of its supposed relationships to underlying motifs.[15] Is it really profitable to be told that the most significant thing about *Lycidas* is that it is a version of the Adonis myth?[16]

How we regard myth criticism will have to depend upon our total evaluation of its contribution to the understanding and appreciation of all of the late plays, but the conclusion to be reached about the Proserpina myth in *The Winter's Tale* may best be expressed in the judicious words of Ernest Schanzer:

> Perdita, like Proserpina, is separated from her mother and later reunited with her, and is emblematic of spring. But here the resemblance ends, and the two stories are utterly different: in the one we have the abduction of a young woman by Pluto, and her mother's search for her through the world; in the other the exposure of an infant, her upbringing by a shepherd, and her mother's self-sequestration for sixteen years. The importance of symbolism of the cycle of the seasons throughout the play is evident. But there is no warrant for finding a specific myth shadowed in its events.[17]

That the myth-allegory kind of interpretation is a matter of mode and fashion is suggested by Philip Edwards in his survey of criticism of the romances in the period 1900-57.[18] He says, "There is little point at this stage in the waning of the century in speaking once more of the tremendous impact of anthropology and comparative religion on criticism, but it must be said that interest in the last plays would have been a shadow of what it has been in fact, if vegetation rites and royal deaths and resurrections, and the symbolic patterns in which the inner realities of human experience display themselves, had been less enthusiastically received into the small-talk of the age."

This sounds as if myth interpretation is a savior for those critics who cannot understand the plays they are trying to criticize. Indeed, as Wallace W. Douglas has pointed out, "Myth" legitimizes paraphrase, it opposes facts, the logic of ordinary knowledge, the finite, the logos, the intelligence and the will, and, of course, consciousness. It originates "in the unconscious, the dream; in memories of the primordial, the Mystery, the primordial Mystery; in the world of spirit, of value, of an extra dimension; in the imagination; or in man's now suppressed or denied awareness of his sin."[19]

Another seminal essay is Morton Bloomfield's "Symbolism in Medieval Literature."[20] It is particularly impressive because of its demonstration that even in medieval literature the method is distorting. "It misunderstands the nature of meaning and of literature. It neglects the concrete for the universal and assumes that the concrete exists only for the universal in a work of art, which is not true even of the Bible. It is as if one were to love a woman because she represented eternal beauty or eternal good."

The myth-archetype critics rely ultimately, as we have seen, on anthropology. But anthropologists differ about as much as literary critics. Whether one follows Frazer, or Jane Harrison, or Cornford makes a difference. The most important recent authority figure is the structural anthropologist Lévi-Strauss. His works have caused a plethora of commentary among social anthropologists, though their concerns are not of course always the same as those of literary critics and scholars. Sometimes they are. Lévi-Strauss contends that a myth is a "work of art arousing deep aesthetic emotion," but he rejects the idea that myth is a kind of primitive poetry, and he maintains that "Myth should be placed in the gamut of linguistic expressions at the end opposite to that of poetry. . . . Poetry is a kind of speech which cannot be translated except at the cost of serious distortions; whereas the mythical value of the myth is preserved even through the worst translation."[21]

The critics may be muddled about the meaning of myth, and they may be on shaky ground from the point of view of the anthropologist, but these conditions do not necessarily disqualify them as commentators on these plays as pieces for the theater. One editor of a late play, R. A. Foakes, has faced up to the question of whether the myth-symbol element derives from the stage or the study: *Pericles* and *Cymbeline* are rarely performed now, he notes, and *The Winter's Tale* and *The Tempest* present serious problems of staging. So the romances are not currently successful in the theater:

> In seeking to show a perspective of life, Shakespeare seems to have relied on myth and magic to knit together the many strands, the great distances and time-spans of these plays, especially the last two, perhaps after a greater reliance on intricacies of plot in the earlier two had not proved successful. In doing this, providing an allegorical frame of refer-

ence, he made use of extra-dramatic themes and values. These plays were written at a time when masques had developed into a sophisticated and complex art under the genius of Ben Jonson and Inigo Jones.... Possibly in this wholesale use of symbolism, rather than in the increase of scenic effects and pageantry, may lie the most crucial influence of this new development in courtly entertainments on Shakespeare. But in a masque symbolism is the natural vehicle, for scenery and dance and movement are of primary importance, and symbolic values secondary, liable to go unnoticed, or if observed, to mystify an audience unfamiliar with their particular frame of reference. In their time these plays of Shakespeare's were perhaps highly successful (it is on record that Pericles was a great "hit") but by the introduction of extra-dramatic values, the likelihood of their permanent popularity on the stage was reduced. On the stage now, the symbolism, the fertility pattern in *The Winter's Tale* for instance, the correspondence between Perdita and Proserpine, and the restoration of summer when each is found, or the conflict between Art and Nature which has recently been detected in *The Tempest,* tend to remain unrealized, or obtrude to spoil the action. Most of these correspondences or interpretations belong to the former category, and are only found at all after close pursuit in the study; yet here the secret of these plays is said to lie.[22]

Now there is no evidence whatever that anybody in the first quarter of the seventeenth century saw any myth or symbol in Shakespeare's romances. *Pericles* was indeed popular, but if we count the number of quarto editions as an index of popularity, the most popular play in Shakespeare's whole lifetime was the apocryphal *Mucedorus,* and no one has, to my knowledge, succeeded in finding any myth or symbol in it. The truth is that myth and symbol do not appear when these plays are acted because myth and symbol are not really there; they have been imported into the plays by the critics.

A variant of the myth-archetype school of criticism, and perhaps growing out of it, is the allegorical school, which may for convenience be divided into two groups, the psychological and the religious. I will discuss the latter first. The most prominent pioneer of this group was Colin Still, who published in 1921 a book called *Shakespeare's Mystery Play: A Study of "The Tempest."* According to Still "the inner theme of *The Tempest* is one which is expressed not only in the pagan initiatory rites, but also in such works as Dante's *Divina Commedia,* Virgil's *Aeneid VI,* Milton's *Paradise Regained* and Bunyan's *Pilgrim's Progress"* (p. 84). Prospero, in this reading, represents the "prototypical Supreme Being" or God. Accordingly, "the expulsion of the dragon Caliban from the cell of Prospero is a version of the fall of Satan from Heaven" (p. 202). Stephano and Trinculo re-enact the Fall of Man. Ariel is the Old Testament Angel of the Lord or the pagan Hermes. In this interpretation the allegory can be both Christian and pagan, in fact it has to be because all of these stories have the same meaning. Miranda stands for Wisdom or is the Persephone of the Eleusinian *cultus*, i.e. the planted seed itself: the Proserpina legend again!

These views would seem to characterize themselves as patently absurd or whimsical, but they are praised by G. Wilson Knight and followed by such religiously oriented scholars as S. L. Bethell and Roy Battenhouse. Una Ellis-Fermor dared not be quite so doctrinally specific, for she said that "Shakespeare's utterance in this play is, I believe, like that of the mystics, definite but comprehensible only to the initiate."[23] But the editor of *The Tempest* in the New Arden edition, Frank Kermode, had no such reticence, for he testified "I believe that Shakespeare offers an exposition of the themes of Fall and Redemption by means of analogous narrative."[24]

Another character in Shakespeare who is sometimes likened to God is the Duke in *Measure for Measure;* this is perhaps a little more plausible, since the Duke's purposes are hidden while those of Prospero are as open as daylight. But when G. Wilson Knight says "Like Prospero, the Duke tends to assume proportions evidently divine. Once he is actually compared to the Supreme Power," Knight refers to the words of Angelo to the Duke after he has been detected:

> I should be guiltier than my guiltiness
> To think I can be undiscernible,
> When I perceive your grace, like power divine,
> Hath looked upon my passes.
>
> (V. i. 365-68)

The error and folly of this are well pointed out by Mary Lascelles, who says "So to argue is to misunderstand the nature and usage of imagery — which does not liken a thing to itself."[25] And finally Northrop Frye, who is so devoted to the myth-archetype approach, delivers us out of the hands of the religious allegorists by saying, *"The Tempest* is not an allegory or religious drama; if it were Prospero's great 'revels' speech would say, not merely that all things will vanish, but that an eternal world will take their place."[26]

It is instructive and gratifying that the most learned and industrious expositor of allegorical imagery in Renaissance literature, the late Rosemond Tuve, in commenting on Spenser's secular allegory, says, "Thorough, sincere and devoted Christian that he was, it is noteworthy that he did not choose to write Christological allegory into his romance; in this I think him firmly typical, for I do not believe Shakespeare or most contemporaries did either, modern interpreters to the contrary."[27]

Approaching the subject from another direction, Madeleine Doran considers various ways in which Ovid was read allegorically and typologically or symbolically in the Renaissance and comes to the conclusion that these ways of reading Ovid were obsolete in Shakespeare's time. So, she asks modestly "whether, in view of the demonstrable fading of an analogical habit of mind in the reading of Ovid, the notion that anyone would see or read Shakespeare in this way is not wholly anachronistic. If not Ovid, then who else could possibly qualify?"[28]

The routing of the allegorical critics does not clear the field, however. There remain those, who, not professing to read the play as a spiritual or religious allegory, nevertheless see in it some kind of symbolic picture of the soul. This is a canker of romantic criticism, and it can be traced back to the German philosopher Schlegel in 1811. Schlegel was not naturally disposed to allegorical readings, but the juxtaposition of Ariel and the airy elements with Caliban and the earthy elements aroused his interest, "thus opening the doors to an allegory of the soul in terms of seventeenth century psychology."[29]

The major nineteenth-century romantic allegorist was James Russell Lowell, who supposed that Prospero represented Imagination, Ariel stood for Fancy, and Caliban, of course, was mere Brute Understanding. Once the allegorical itch is yielded to, the scratching must continue; Miranda represents Womanhood and Ferdinand represents Youth. As the philosopher Nuttall remarks, Lowell's fallacy is that he "thinks of certain universals as if they were very important instances of themselves."

One might suppose that such fancies would disappear with the Romantic Movement, but a psychological interpretation of *The Tempest* is to be found as late as the four hundredth anniversary year, 1964, and in the *Shakespeare Quarterly*, the most respectable of scholarly journals in this field. In this paper, James E. Phillips maintains that Prospero represents the Rational Soul, Ariel the Sensitive Soul, and Caliban the Vegetative Soul.[30] The odd thing about it is that Phillips cites passages from Sir John Davies' *Nosce Teipsum* to illustrate the points about the function and nature of the various kinds of soul, and indeed *Nosce Teipsum* is about this general subject, but it would be hard to imagine two works more unlike each other than *Nosce Teipsum* and *The Tempest*.

It is very instructive to find a myth critic who changes his mind. An impressive example is Herbert Weisinger, who traces his own belief in myth in literature from a high-water mark in *Tragedy and the Paradox of the Fortunate Fall* in 1953 to a low-water mark seven years later, in an essay called "An Examination of the Myth and Ritual Approach to Shakespeare."[31] The first problem, Weisinger concedes, is that there is no agreement as to what the myth and ritual pattern really is. "As a matter of fact no myth and ritual pattern as such ever exists or existed in any real sense; it is a modern, scholarly reconstruction of diverse materials drawn from divergent sources" and, he goes on, "assuming for the moment that such a pattern as the myth and ritual pattern does in fact exist, there is no satisfactory way of explaining how Shakespeare got at it."

Yet, true as this may be, there remains the problem of explaining why so many critics see the pattern there, or think they do. Weisinger lists fourteen of them, plus the *"Scrutiny-Penguin* group." There are some things there which look like myth and ritual, he says: "In no other plays of Shakespeare do the elements of the myth and ritual pattern occur so frequently as they do in the last four plays, but their very profusion is a sign of the breakup of the pattern in Shakespeare. Never does the sea storm so often and so violently, never is magic music heard so much, never do so many magicians practice their art, . . . they remind me of nothing so much as Mozart's *Magic Flute* which sounds in much the same grotesque mockeries of the myth and ritual elements. But the measure of distance between *The Magic Flute* and *The Marriage of Figaro* is precisely the same as that between the high comedies and the late romances; the spirit is gone, leaving only the dry bones of stunning technique."

This astonishing critical judgment was not a momentary lapse; it is repeated, in more emphatic terms, later on: "As for the four final romances, I am more than willing to concede the presence in them of all the ritual devices; indeed, there are more deaths, rebirths, magical musics, spirits, visions, sorcerers, doctors, storms, caskets, rescues, reconciliations, illuminations and the like in them than in all the plays before them, and that precisely is the trouble. These plays are all ritual and no myth; the spirit is gone from them, and only the letter remains. The last plays are the mere machinery of ritual, functioning beautifully no doubt, but to no end."[32]

So Weisinger has lost his belief in the myth and ritual interpretation of the last plays only to end up in a Lytton Strachey position, that there is nothing in the last plays but poetry and beauty — mere, empty beauty. But we may find content in the last plays where Weisinger failed to find it, and we owe him something for his characterization of the myth and ritual critics: "It is a committed point of view and so cantankerous, obstreperous, irritating, wrong on details and dictatorial, but it is passionate and alive and has something to say."[33]

A different lineage for myth and ritual criticism from the one I have outlined, and accordingly a different refutation of it, is to be found in John Holloway's "The Concepts of 'Myth' and 'Ritual' in Literature."[34] He takes his departure from Cassirer's *Philosophy of Symbolic Forms,* especially the second volume called *Mythical Thought.* Holloway points out that the conception of myth in Cassirer's work is totally at odds with the understanding of myth that comes from the actual field studies of Malinowski and others, and that all the philosopher has done is to call attention to an analogy which may, in certain circumstances, be less than helpful. But he goes on to say that there are other resemblances between a literary work and a ritual: "Ritual must, at every stage, be perfectly authentic. A defective version is no version: the virtue has gone out of it. Moreover, the authentic version must be executed through from beginning to end; it must not be abridged, its parts must not be transposed. To modify it in any such way is not an imperfect performance of the ritual, so much as an attack upon it, an affront, a blasphemy."[35] These comments might be applied to Weisinger's description of the last plays as "empty" ritual.

What is important about a ritual, Holloway says, is that it is supposed to *do* something, to bring about a result, and that it involves *participation.* The analogy with a play is incomplete. But here Holloway's concern is to tie up some of the ideas in his chapter on "Shakespearean Tragedy and the Idea of Human Sacrifice." His conclusion is that "plays such as we have been examining *(Macbeth, Lear, Antony and Cleopatra)* do not (like the rituals themselves) suspend life in order to stage a ritual. They embed the essential movement of that ritual in life's common fabric. They *ritualize reality."*[36]

Here is a fundamental difference between the tragedies and the late plays. The late plays, by their "distancing," by their constant reminders of artifice, by their theatrical contrasts and displays, break up this participation which is so essential to ritual or, for that matter, to tragedy. These romances are not ritualizing reality; they are hinting at something beyond it — some mysterious music of the spheres.

𝕬𝖕𝖕𝖊𝖓𝖉𝖎𝖝 𝕭

THE TOPICALITY OF
CYMBELINE AND *THE WINTER'S TALE*

'Twere to consider too curiously, to consider so.

Hamlet

In writing *King Lear* Shakespeare took up two narratives and fused them together. One was from romance, the story of the Paphlagonian king in Sidney's *Arcadia;* the other was the story of an English king of the pre-Christian period, as told by Holinshed and Spenser and an old play, *King Leir.* The king was the focus — the romantic material, which echoed the theme of parents and children became the subplot. In writing *Cymbeline,* Shakespeare likewise picked up two narratives and fused them together. One was from romantic fiction — the story of a wager on a wife's chastity and her wandering in disguise as a page (like Julia in *Two Gentlemen,* or Viola in *Twelfth Night*). The other was a patchwork of motifs drawn from Holinshed's accounts of early kings — Cymbeline and his son Guiderius and the still earlier Brutus — plus an episode in Holinshed's Scottish history which Shakespeare had found no use for when writing *Macbeth.* He practised the same economy of left-overs in writing his next play, *The Winter's Tale;* the punishment for the villain in the wager story was not needed because the play has a happy ending and everybody will be pardoned, but it could be used as a threat in *The Winter's Tale* to frighten the clown.

It is obvious enough that the historical part of *Lear* is the main plot, and the romantic material from the *Arcadia* is the subplot. This works very well because the themes of the two are so similar. But in *Cymbeline* the main plot is the separation of Posthumus and Imogen — the wager story and its consequences; the story about Cymbeline and his sons, the question of tribute and the Roman invasion, constitutes the subplot. Shakespeare was not repeating the technique he used in *Lear* — the structural technique, that is. He had to merge the two stories so the accused innocent bride becomes the King's daughter. The two plots are thus linked, as they are again when Imogen stumbles upon her unknown brothers in the wilds of Wales and when Posthumus and Jachimo participate in the battle, as do the rustic exiles, so the threads can be conveniently tied together at the end. There is so much to tie up that the final scene has struck many audiences as fantastic and absurd[1] — they would prefer Shaw's substitute fifth act — and others as Shakespeare's finest piece of craftsmanship.

The critical issues resulting from this mixture and the way it is done are the business of every editor and commentator. Those who dismiss the play as a poor thing save themselves trouble. But those who think it not unworthy of its author, though perhaps not his greatest achievement, must find its justification. The two most recent editors, J. M. Nosworthy and J. C. Maxwell, have stressed that the play is experimental. Granville-Barker saw it as an example of "sophisticated artlessness" and Maxwell goes further in pointing out "deliberate incongruity" and "comic exploitation of conventions." Perhaps the most fervent admirer of the play among recent scholarly critics is Bertrand Evans, who finds in it splendid examples of the "discrepant awareness" he specializes in. "Considered from the point of view of its uses of awareness, *Cymbeline* IV, ii, is beyond question Shakespeare's finest dramatic achievement."[2] It is the scene of Imogen's apparent death, of Cloten's execution, of the dirge, of Imogen's awakening and her rescue by Lucius. John Wain declares that *Cymbeline* has more experimental daring than any other romance of Shakespeare's; in fact "it is his most avant-garde work."[3]

G. Wilson Knight considers *Cymbeline* to be "a peculiarly studied work" and "mainly an historical play."[4] He considers that in it Shakespeare was trying to reconcile his two great loyalties, to Rome and to Britain, in a plot which brings these nations into conflict, but reaches a serene and peaceful resolution when Cymbeline, having won the battle against Caius Lucius' Roman army, decides to pay tribute to Rome anyway. But Knight thinks the last plays "are to be read as parables or myths" and that "in *Cymbeline* ... Shakespeare tries to body forth his hard-won religious conviction in personal symbols."[5] Now, it is self-proclaimed that Knight does not expound the meaning of a writer's work by reference to what meaning it would have had for the age in which it was written; he believes that we should "interpret an age in the light of its great books and men of visionary genius, not the men of genius in the light of their age."⁶ Accordingly, there must be a great deal of the subjective in his interpretations, and this is not necessarily a vice. But to make the play a British-Roman one, as he does, involves some difficulties. Take Jachimo, for instance. Is he a Roman, like the Romans of *Julius Caesar, Antony and Cleopatra,* and *Coriolanus?* Of course not; he is a Roman only in the sense that he lives in Rome, but he is actually a Renaissance Italian. He is in the romance plot, not the history. In fact there is very little material in the history plot — some names, the argument over tribute, and the battle, which is partly based on Scottish history of many centuries later. Imported from somewhere is the Welsh scenery and sojourn. Nosworthy thinks the cave is related in some curious way to Timon's cave in *Timon of Athens,* written not long before Cymbeline.⁷

The mountains of Wales were synonymous with rough wild country; Hotspur charges that King Henry, in refusing to ransom Mortimer from Glendower's stronghold in Wales, "wish'd him on the barren mountains starve." Milford Haven is of course the greatest port in Wales. It indents the coast of Pembrokeshire for ten miles and is two miles wide. Drayton praises it in *Poly-Olbion* as that harbor "which this isle her greatest port doth call." Furthermore, it had appeared in a romantic-historical play before. In Peele's *Edward I* Lluellen brings his friends in disguise to Milford Haven to await the landing of Lady Elinor from France.

Some critics, at the opposite extreme from G. Wilson Knight, interpret small details from the age and then use these to maintain they have discovered a new, topical significance which may alter the whole interpretation of the play and disclose the occasion for its writing or production. One such is Emrys Jones, who took the occasion of a review of Maxwell's edition to propose that *Cymbeline* is directly pointed at King James.⁸ Milford Haven is not mentioned in the sources, he says, but it is prominent in the play. Why? Well, the only other time Shakespeare mentions the place is in *Richard III* (IV. iv. 534), where it is noted that the Earl of Richmond (who became Henry VII) has landed there. Now of course Henry VII was King James's great-grandfather, and the two monarchs are celebrated together in part of Dekker's *Magnificent Entertainment* designed for the coronation in 1603. Therefore Imogen's reference to "this same blessed Milford" would have been readily understood by Shakespeare's audience as referring to Henry VII and his modern counterpart James VI and I.

Whether Shakespeare mentioned Milford Haven only one other time or not, and that one time in association with the invasion of the Earl of Richmond, it is clear that Milford Haven was widely recognized as the port anyone would choose if he wished to invade England. In III. iv Imogen is thinking that it is possible to live elsewhere than in England and Pisanio encourages her:

> I am most glad
> You think of other place. Th' ambassador,
> Lucius the Roman, comes to Milford-Haven
> Tomorrow.
>
> (140-43)

Pisanio speaks of Lucius because the last time he was present at Cymbeline's court he was the ambassador, negotiating about the tribute due. But that being denied he delivers his defiance:

> Receive it from me, then: war and confusion
> In Caesar's name pronounce I 'gainst thee: look
> For fury, not to be resisted.
>
> (III. i. 65-67)

Cymbeline's kingdom is to be invaded by the Romans. And Milford Haven was the only logical place to land and begin the campaign. Foreign enemies knew it, as is evidenced from a Spanish document drawn up in 1597 for the use of the admiral of an invading force:

> It is a protected harbor and is six or seven
>   leagues round about.
> There is room for countless ships.
> There is no fortress, but one tower at the entrance.
> On the right side it is not strong, it usually has
>   two pieces of artillery, which cannot prevent an
>   entry. It is six leagues to the head of the river.
> There is an open village.
> It has water, meat and grain in abundance.
> There are many Catholics and the people are naturally
>   enemies of the English and do not speak their language.[9]

The peace motif at the end of the play would, argues Jones, be especially pleasing to King James, who regarded himself as a peacemaker. No doubt,

214

but there is much about peace in the Holinshed treatment of Cymbeline, and it is difficult to see how anyone dramatizing that material could avoid some peace propaganda. In fact Shakespeare uses very little of it, and that only at the very end. Kymbeline in the chronicle wanted peace with Rome so British youth could be brought up there as he had been, to "learne both to behave themselves like civill men, and to attain the knowledge of feats of warre."[10] But there was a more general situation, a *pax Romana:* "it pleased the almightie God so to dispose the minds of men that present, not onlie the Britains, but in manner all other nations were contented to be obedient to the Romane empire." In fact the embassy in Holinshed's Cymbeline is a peaceful one; the tribute embassy Shakespeare transferred from the reign of Guiderius in the source. "About the same time also there came vnto Kimbaline king of the Britains an ambassador from Augustus the emperor, with thanks, for that entring into the governement of the British state, he had kept his allegiance toward the Romane empire; exhorting him to keepe his subiects in peace with all their neighbors, with the whole world, through meanes of the same Augustus, was now in quiet, without all warres or troublesome tumults." If anything, Shakespeare seems to have toned down the peace propaganda in his source rather than emphasizing it.

An additional clue, Jones finds, is that Cymbeline in the play has one daughter and two sons, whereas in the chronicle he has only two sons. But *King James* had a daughter and two sons! This suggests a degree of identification of Cymbeline and the King which one would think embarrassing. Cymbeline is stupid, and tyrannical, unduly under the sway of his wife, and he survives only by the merest luck. The English Solomon would not be flattered. And Queen Anne for the wicked mother of Cloten? Oh, no, the critic maintains, Shakespeare prevented too close identification by making his Queen an obvious fairy-tale character.

The play is dated 1610. That was the year of Prince Henry's installation as Prince of Wales, at the age of 16, and of ceremonies celebrating that event. And 1610, says Jones, was the only year in this whole period in which all Europe was at peace. But James's biographer, David Harris Willson, notes that "James joined this warlike coalition in 1610 by promising 4,000 troops, not from England, but from English and Scottish forces serving with the Dutch."[11] All of the alleged reasons for supposing that *Cymbeline* had particular topical significance pointing to King James in 1610 fail to demonstrate their point, either because they are not true or because there are alternative explanations.[12]

The most obvious connection between *Cymbeline* and *The Winter's Tale* is that both plays deal with a wife wrongly suspected of infidelity who disappears, is thought to be dead, and returns for a vindication and reunion with her husband. It is generally agreed (with Wilson Knight dissenting) that *The Winter's Tale* is the later of the two, although Nosworthy[13] guesses "that the composition of the two plays was more or less simultaneous, or, at any rate, that both had been written, revised and prepared for the stage before either was actually performed, with consequent cross-fertilization." The use of the leftover passage about the punishment of the villain in *W.T.* IV. iv. 783-91 suggests that *The Winter's Tale* followed *Cymbeline*. The dates conventionally given are 1609-10 for the first and 1610-11 for the second. The theaters were closed because of the plague from the summer of 1608 to December, 1609, but Shakespeare might well have been writing during that period.

Glynne Wickham maintains[14] that *The Winter's Tale* was "written for performance in the autumn of 1610 before the King and the Heir Apparent then aged sixteen"; he undertakes "to reveal it as a drama which figures the mystical marriage of Prince Henry (Florizel) to the three kingdoms whose original unity was lost but has been found (Perdita) thanks to 'Time' and King James' own 'piaculous action'; and finally to show that, by substituting for the dead Queen of Greene's novel the living statue of Hermione in his own play, Shakespeare created a work of art which was as effective an emblem for his court audience as it was enjoyable dramatic romance for his wider public in the city."

Wickham's worry about a topical meaning for the play seems to have been connected earlier with an attempt to explain the structure, particularly the sixteen-year gap in time between Acts III and IV. That this gap of time is necessary to allow Perdita to grow from a baby to a marriageable girl would seem to explain everything, but no, Wickham will have it that the sixteen-year gap has some external significance. "Shakespeare is more than usually careful" he says "to state on three occasions that the gap between the deaths of Hermione and Mamillius and the betrothal of Perdita and Florizel was sixteen years."[15] As a matter of fact, Shakespeare was *not* very careful. The first of the three references is in the speech of Time, the Chorus, who says he slides o'er sixteen years (IV. i. 4-6). The second reference is by Camillo, who says it is *fifteen* years (IV. ii. 4). The third reference is by Paulina, who says the time lapse is "some sixteen years" — not very exact (V. iii. 30-31).

But Wickham goes on to suggest that *The Winter's Tale*, like the Lord Mayor's show of 1605, Anthony Munday's *Triumphs of Reunited Bri-*

tannia, celebrates the reunification of Scotland and England under King James I and VI. And where do the sixteen years come in? Why, "Mary Queen of Scots was executed in 1587 and James I accepted the English crown in 1603. The time gap is precisely sixteen years. As coincidences go, this is at least remarkable." It is not at all remarkable. In three of Shakespeare's last plays there is a gap of some sixteen years between the tragic events and the happy ending: *Pericles, The Winter's Tale,* and *The Tempest.* Sidney said that back in the eighties "ordinary it is" that in contemporary plays two young princes fall in love, "she is got with childe, deliuered of a faire boy; he is lost, groweth a man, falls in loue, and is ready to get another child; and all this in two hours space." Sixteen years is about the right time.[16]

In his earlier article, Wickham explicitly disclaims any specific topical identifications in the play: "It is against some background of this sort that I believe Shakespeare set to work on the construction of this remarkable comedy. I do not wish to suggest that any direct parallel was intended between particular characters in the play and particular characters at King James's court: but I would maintain that Shakespeare did invite his audience to compare events in the Sicilia and Bohemia of his play with events in living memory in England and Scotland. In other words, it is through the structure rather than through the details of characterization and incident that the emblematic nature of the play is revealed" (pp. 260-61). But by the time of his *TLS* article, Wickham had noticed two other things. The first was that Henry Frederick, King James's elder son, was created Prince of Wales in 1610, at the age of sixteen, and many masques, dedications, and congratulatory poems marked the occasion. The other was that James commissioned two marble statues, one of Queen Elizabeth and one of his mother, Mary, Queen of Scots, for installation in the Henry VII chapel in Westminster Abbey. Shakespeare of course changed his source, Greene's *Pandosto,* to keep Hermione alive and invented the statue scene. Now if King James's royal statues had anything to do with *The Winter's Tale,* it would seem to be Mary's, not Elizabeth's; Mary could in some sense be thought to be resurrected by the investiture of her grandson as Prince of Wales. The trouble is that Mary's statue was not finished until 1612, when James had his mother's body disinterred at Peterborough Cathedral and reburied under the statue in the Abbey, and by this time *The Winter's Tale* had been on the stage for two years. But Wickham, undismayed, says the sculptors lived in Southwark, not far from the Globe, and Shakespeare could have dropped in at their studio any time from 1606 to 1610 to see how the statue was coming. On this frail evidence we are asked to believe that Florizel represents Prince Henry.

E. K. Chambers, in his salad days, wondered whether Shakespeare could have got the models for his innocent but high-hearted heroines, like Perdita and Imogen, from the country, since it was unlikely that they would be found at the court of Anne of Denmark. But "there is no doubt a temptation," Chambers wrote, "to trace the lineaments of the gallant and too early lost Prince Henry" in "Florizel, the unstained shepherd."[17] I take the expression "there is no doubt a temptation" to imply the conclusion that the temptation may be recognized but can well be resisted.

Prince Henry was 16 years old in 1610. Florizel is of course older. He was almost the exact age of Mamillius (V. i. 117), and Mamillius was no infant at the time of his death. Leontes implies that Florizel is 21 (V. i. 126). Prince Henry, unlike his father, detested hunting, but was extremely fond of martial sports, spending five or six hours a day in armor. All we know about Florizel before he adopted a pastoral disguise, is that he, like his prototype, Dorastus, went hawking.[18]

I rejoice in the statement by Alfred Harbage, in discussing the suggestions that *A Midsummer Night's Dream* was written for a particular noble wedding, *The Merry Wives of Windsor* for an installation feast of the Order of the Garter, *Troilus and Cressida* for some feast at an inn of court, and the like: "The trouble is that there is nothing to support any of these hypotheses except the other hypotheses, now functioning as ghostly precedents. There is no supporting external evidence to prove that any regular play performed by any regular company, juvenile or adult, was originally written for a special occasion during the whole reign of Elizabeth and lifetime of Shakespeare."[19]

Topical significance in ordinary scholarly usage means a reference which would be understood by the original audience to refer to some current person, event, or situation. A very famous instance is the one in the chorus before the fifth act of *Henry V*:

> As, by a lower but loving likelihood
> Were now the general of our gracious Empress
> As in good time he may, from Ireland coming,
> Bringing rebellion broached on his sword,
> How many would the peaceful city quit,
> To welcome him!

(29-34)

It was long supposed that this was a clear reference to the unfortunate, or perhaps disastrous, expedition of Essex to Ireland from April to September of 1599. It is certainly a topical allusion. But Warren D. Smith has shown reasons to believe that the choruses in *Henry V* were written later than the publication of the Quarto in 1600. They are not in the Quarto and if they were written later they must refer to Charles Blount, Lord Mountjoy, who succeeded Essex in the Irish command.[20] An example of the opposite kind — a topical significance which is not obvious and agreed to by all — could be one of Lillian Winstanley's identifications. She makes out that *Hamlet* is a play about the Scottish Succession: Hamlet's mother married the man who murdered her husband, and so did King James's mother, Mary, Queen of Scots. "It would be, I think, unfair to say that Hamlet is the portrait of anyone; he is more subtle, more many-sided than any human being ever has been or could be."[21] But Hamlet, in her view, is clearly modeled on King James and the Earl of Essex, and Polonius is a combination of Burleigh and Rizzio. This method of showing topical significances (or what Miss Winstanley calls "symbolic mythology") can be applied anywhere. "Shakespeare is doing in *Macbeth* what he did in *Hamlet*; he is dealing with the events of most immediate interest to his audience and he is working to a pre-existent unity in the minds of that audience."[22] Shakespeare, she thinks, works the way Spenser did; everything he writes has a political allegory, whatever else it has. So *Othello* becomes a play about Spain (the Moor) and Venice (Desdemona). More specifically Philip II of Spain was alleged to have killed his wife Elizabeth of Valois with his bare hands because he was convinced that a courtier who picked up her handkerchief was her lover.[23]

Here we have the extreme case. Miss Winstanley's views are not taken seriously by Shakespeare scholars now, (though Emrys Jones mentions her with approbation) but they are based upon a conviction which was honestly held and which, if it is a wrong one, dictated the erroneous conclusions she reached. That conviction was that Shakespeare was just like Spenser. It is our concern to find out what kind of writer Shakespeare was and on the basis of that knowledge judge whether the late plays are at all likely to be plays of topical significance.

Some other topical significances, not quite so plain as the reference to the general in *Henry V*, nor so conjectural as Miss Winstanley's, should be considered. In *A Midsummer Night's Dream* Oberon gives a lovely and elaborate description of the flower called Love-in-Idleness which he wishes to use on Titania:

That very time I saw (but thou could'st not),
Flying between the cold moon and the earth,
Cupid all arm'd. A certain aim he took
At a fair Vestal, throned by [the] west,
And loos'd his love-shaft smartly from his bow,
As it should pierce a hundred thousand hearts.
But I might see young Cupid's fiery shaft
Quench'd in the chaste beams of the wat'ry moon
And the imperial vot'ress passed on
In maiden meditation, fancy free.

(II. i. 155-64)

This is evidently a compliment to the Queen — what other "fair Vestal, throned by the west" was there? And in a Scottish play Shakespeare offered some flattery to a Scottish king by glamorizing his ancestors, the descendants of Banquo. Furthermore, there is a passage on touching for the King's Evil, scrofula, by King Edward the Confessor, which is so unnecessary to the dramatic context that it has long been suspected to be a topical reference to King James. That sovereign was at first reluctant to touch, believing that miraculous power to cure disease belonged to God alone, but he was persuaded to at least hang angels (ten shilling gold pieces) around the neck of sufferers and offer prayers. This is what King Edward does in the play, and Malcolm says that he can pass on the gift to his successors on the English throne:

he cures,
Hanging a golden stamp about their necks,
Put on with holy prayers, and 'tis spoken,
To the succeeding royalty he leaves
The healing benediction.

(IV. iii. 152-56)

Some editors have suspected that these lines, and others in the same scene, are interpolations put in specifically for a performance at court, possibly during the visit of King James's brother-in-law, King Christian of Denmark, in August, 1606. That such interpolations occurred may be suggested by the "some dozen or sixteen lines" which the players were willing to insert into *The Murther of Gonzago* at Hamlet's request.

A play produced soon after the theaters reopened in 1604, *Measure for Measure,* was also presented at court on St. Stephen's night. Recent students of the play have restated the old case about similarities between the Duke and King James. "To see the Duke in *Measure for Measure* as an exact replica of James I would be to misunderstand both Shakespeare's dramatic methods and the practice of the contemporary stage" writes J. W. Lever (New Arden ed., p. 1), but he agrees with Ernest Schanzer, D. L. Stevenson and others that the play contains some passages compatible with the views expressed in the king's book *Basilikon Doron* and that the character of the Duke, based upon legends about the Emperor Severnus, has some traits which were recognizable in King James. On the other hand Mary Lascelles, the most perceptive of all the critics of the play, says "It is surely time that we heard the last of that supposed connection between the Duke's sagacity and *Basilikon Doron,* and with it the notion of a dramatist deeply disquieted by the corrupting influence of power, yet intent on flattering, in the person of his patron, the highest representative of that power."[24]

This is just about the extent of the generally admitted topical reference in the plays of Shakespeare. The extraordinary thing is that there is so little of it. Shakespeare, unlike most Elizabethan writers, did not commemorate the death of Queen Elizabeth or the accession of King James. Those who think that he referred to the Gunpowder Plot or the trial of Father Garnet have to rely upon very slight bits of evidence. He was a writer who drew very little of contemporary concerns, public affairs, gossip, sensations into his plays. One who wishes to learn the social history of Elizabethan England would do far better to read the works of Ben Jonson, Thomas Dekker, or Thomas Heywood than the works of William Shakespeare. "He was not of an age" as Ben Jonson well knew.

Perhaps the most notable of the hunters for topical significances was G. B. Harrison, whose collections of news, rumors, and gossip published as *The Elizabethan Journals* give such a rich picture of life in those times. Harrison's essays on *King John* and on the Earl of Essex related current events to the history plays.[25] Harrison was particularly interested in Essex and the public excitement about him. He did, however, make a distinction: "Direct topical allusions are not very common in Shakespeare, but topical *significances* abound. ... a *caveat* is here needed against the assumption that 'Hotspur is Essex' or that Shakespeare meant him so to be taken. Shakespeare finds opportunities in the character of Hotspur for significant speeches and takes them, but he is writing a play and not an allegory of the times."[26] Moreover, in his elaborated treatment of the subject three years later Harrison described it as "personal interpretation," "conjectural reconstruction" and, for the most part, "sheer guess work."[27]

Notes

Notes

My Shakespeare references and quotations are based upon G. Blakemore Evans's text in the New Riverside Shakespeare, which was in press at Houghton Mifflin Co., Boston, when this book was written. The same text is the basis for Marvin Spevack's *A Complete and Systematic Concordance to the Works of Shakespeare*, which I have also used. In some Shakespeare quotations I have italicized words which I later discuss.

Preface

[1]Only three of the five plays are included in the First Folio. *The Tempest* is there the first of the comedies, and *The Winter's Tale* is the last. *Cymbeline, King of Britain* is the last of the tragedies, and the last play in the volume.

[2]Annual Shakespeare Lecture of the British Academy, 1953.

[3]"What do we do with Shakespeare?" *Shakespeare Jahrbuch,* 96 (1960), 45.

[4]*Shakespeare Quarterly,* 8 (1957), 535.

[5]*Shakespeare Quarterly,* 9 (1958), 301-06.

Chapter 1. The Romance Tradition as it Influenced Shakespeare

[1]R. M. Dawkins, "Modern Greek Oral Versions of Apollonius of Tyre," *MLR,* 37 (1942), 172-84.

[2]Analyses of the plot material, some account of its possible sources, and the conclusion that it is an original Latin work of the third century and not a translation of a lost Greek original, are found in Philip H. Goepp, 2nd., "The Narrative Material of *Apollonius of Tyre*" *ELH,* 5 (1938), 150-72, and in greater detail in Appendix II, "The Latin Romance of *Apollonius of Tyre*" in Ben Edwin Perry, *The Ancient Romances: A Literary-Historical Account of their Origins* (Berkeley, 1967), pp. 294-324.

[3]*ELH,* 5 (1938), 168.

[4]R. S. Crane in *MP* 11, (1913), 271. Ashley was born in 1565. For his biography, see V. B. Heltzel, ed. *Of Honour* (San Marino, 1947), pp. 1-19.

[5]Arthur Dickson, *Valentine and Orson: A Study in Late Medieval Romance* (New York, 1929), pp. 4-5.

[6]J. Rendel Harris in *Contemporary Review,* 126 (1924), 331, cited by Dickson in his edition of *Valentine and Orson, EETS.* Original Series No. 204, (1937), lix.

[7]*Ibid.,* lxi.

[8]Sophie Trenkner, *The Greek Novella in the Classical Period* (Cambridge, 1958), p. 101.

[9]*Ibid.,* pp. 107-08.

[10]*Ibid.,* p. 109, which includes an extensive bibliography.

[11]J. M. Manly, "The Miracle Play in Mediaeval England," *Essays by Divers Hands,* RSL, n.s. 7 (1927), 133-53.

[12]Geoffrey Bullough, *Narrative and Dramatic Sources of Shakespeare* (London and New York, 1957-66), II, 7-11, 283-84. His utilization of the Apollonius and Silla story from Riche is made doubly certain by the fact that he uses four words from other parts of the book which are to be found nowhere else in his works: "coisterell," "garragascoynes," "pavion," and "galliarde." Kenneth Muir, *Shakespeare's Sources* (London, 1957), p. 70.

[13]D. T. Starnes, "Barnabe Rich's 'Sappho Duke of Mantona': A Study in Elizabethan Story-Making," *SP*, 30 (1933), 455. For the story in full, and a commentary on the *Farewell* as a whole, see the edition by Thomas M. Cranfill (Austin, 1959).

[14]*Playes Confuted in Five Actions*, D5ᵛ.

[15]*Elizabethan Critical Essays*, ed. Gregory Smith (Oxford, 1904) I, 160.

[16]*The Sad Shepherd*, I. v. 94-97.

[17]J. Q. Adams, "Hill's List of Early Plays in Manuscript," 4 *Library* 20 (1940), 80-81.

[18]"Robert Greene and Greek Romance," Chapter V of *Idea and Act in Elizabethan Fiction* (Princeton, 1969), pp. 138-88.

[19]The edition of *Pan His Syrinx* by Wallace A. Bacon (Evanston, 1950), has a long introduction on the relationship of the work to Greek romance and to Elizabethan drama.

[20]*The Greek Romances in Elizabethan Prose Fiction* (New York, 1912), pp. 370 ff.

[21]*Idea and Act*, p. 144.

[22]*Idea and Act*, pp. 171-72, and Wolff, *The Greek Romances*, pp. 444-45.

[23]Sig E4ᵛ. O.E.D. This is the first usage of the world in English cited there.

[24]See Juan B. Avalle-Arce, "The *Diana* of Montemayor: Tradition and Innovation," *PMLA*, 74 (1959), 1-6; and Bruce W. Wardropper, "The *Diana* of Montemayor: Re-valuation and Interpretation," *SP*, 48 (1951), 126-244.

[25]*The Greek Romances*, pp. 312-13.

[26]The literature is extensive. It includes William R. Elton, *"King Lear" and the Gods* (San Marino, 1966), especially Chapter III; Fitzroy Pyle, *"Twelfth Night, King Lear,* and *Arcadia,"* *MLR*, 43 (1948), 449-55; Kenneth Muir, ed. *King Lear*, New Arden ed. (Cambridge, Mass., 1952), pp. xxxvii-xlii; D. M. McKeithan, "*King Lear* and Sidney's *Arcadia,"* *Studies in English*, University of Texas Bulletin No. 14 (1934), 45-49; Hardin Craig, "Motivation in Shakespeare's Choice of Materials," *Shakespeare Survey*, 4 (1951), 32-33; Muir and Danby, *"Arcadia* and *King Lear,"* *N&Q*, 195 (Feb. 4, 1950), 49-51; William A. Armstrong, *"King Lear* and Sidney's *Arcadia,"* *TLS*, Oct. 14, 1949, p. 665.

[27]*King Lear*, ed. Muir, pp. 245-46.

[28]*Greek Romances*, p. 365.

[29]See C. R. Baskervill, "Some Evidence for Early Romantic Plays in England," *MP*, 14 (1916-17), 492-49; Lee Monroe Ellison, *The Early Romantic Drama at the English Court* (Chicago, 1917); and Betty J. Littleton, ed. *Clyomon and Clamydes* (The Hague, 1968), pp. 53-64, 195-98.

[30]*From Mankind to Marlowe* (Cambridge, Mass., 1962), pp. 62, 194-96. Some similarities between *Clyomon* and *Cymbeline* are noted in R. S. Forsythe, "Imogen and Neronis" *MLN*, 40 (1925), 313-14.

[31]Lee Monroe Ellison, *The Early Romantic Drama at the English Court*, pp. 91-93. David Bevington analyzes the structure of *Common Conditions* in *From Mankind to Marlowe*, pp. 191-94. Oddly enough, he does not realize that Leostines and Galiarbus are the same man. The author, to be sure, stupidly forgets to make this clear, but Ellison, perhaps instructed by Tucker Brooke's note to line 509 in his edition, establishes the identity.

[32]J. M. Nosworthy, ed. *Cymbeline*, New Arden ed. (London, 1955), p. xxv.

[33]See C. R. Baskervill, *MP*, 14 (1916-17), pp. 272-73. Shakespeare's debt to *Love and Fortune* was first suggested by R. W. Boodle in *N&Q*, 7th Series, vol. iv (1887) 404-05.

[34]"The Texts of *Mucedorus,"* *MLR*, 50 (1955), 1-5.

[35]"*Mucedorus*, Most Popular Elizabethan Play?" *Studies in the English Renaissance*

Drama in Memory of Karl Julius Holzknecht, (New York, 159), pp. 248-68.
[36]*Ibid.,* p. 253.
[37]J. C. Maxwell, ed. *Pericles,* New Cambridge edition, (1956), p. xxv.
[38]Gesner, p. 102. I think this is clearly a mistake, in view of Posthumus' words at
II. v. 9-13:

> Me of my lawful pleasure she restrain'd,
> And pray'd me oft forbearance; did it with
> A pudency so rosy, the sweet view on't
> Might well have warm'd old Saturn; that I thought her
> As chaste as unsunn'd snow.

Chapter 2. Innocence and the Pastoral World

[1]See Bruno Snell, "Arcadia: This Discovery of a Spiritual Landscape" in *The Discovery of the Mind: Greek Origins of European Thought,* Harper Torchbook (New York, 1960), pp. 281-309. He says "His Arcadia is set half way between myth and reality: it is also a no-man's land between two ages, an earthly beyond, a land of the soul yearning for its distant home in the past" (p. 301).
[2]Tr. Thorney-Edmonds, Loeb ed. Book I, section 9.
[3]C. G. Osgood, *Boccaccio on Poetry* (Princeton, 1930), pp. 56-57.
[4]Ed. Albert Feuillerat (Cambridge, Eng., 1922), I. 13.
[5]*Twelfth Night,* IV. i. 52-53. This whole subject, and the vocabulary of it, are admirably treated in Madeleine Doran, "Yet Am I Inland Bred," *Shakespeare 400,* ed. J. G. McManaway (New York, 1964), pp. 99-114. I draw on this essay here and elsewhere.
[6]"Yet Am I Inland Bred" pp. 113-14.
[7]D. S. Brewer, "The Ideal of Feminine Beauty in Medieval Literature, Especially 'Harley Lyrics,' Chaucer, and Some Elizabethans," *MLR,* 50 (1955), 269.
[8]H. B. Charlton, *Shakespearean Comedy* (London, 1938), p. 40 *n1.* E. C. Pettet essentially agrees: *Shakespeare and the Romance Tradition* (New York, 1949), p. 40.
[9]L. G. Salingar, "The Design of *Twelfth Night,*" *Shakespeare Quarterly* 9 (1958), 122.
[10]*Friar Bacon and Friar Bungay,* ed. Daniel Seltzer, (Lincoln, Nebraska, 1963), i, 72-81.
[11]vi, 104-07.
[12]vi, 120-24.
[13]viii. 93-98. Harold Brooks in the New Arden *TGV* (London, 1969), suggests that this passage may have influenced "The uncertain glory of an April day" in that play at I. ii. 85.
[14]xiv, 86-92.
[15]*Winter's Tale* IV. iv. 116-24. The criticism is in Kenneth Muir, "Greene as a Dramatist," *Essays on Shakespeare and Elizabethan Drama in Honor of Hardin Craig.* ed. Richard Hosley (Columbia, Missouri, 1962), p. 49.
[16]*Friar Bacon and Friar Bungay,* pp. xvii-xviii.
[17]Muir, *Op. cit.,* p. 52.
[18]Malone Society Reprint (Oxford, 1921), ll. 1025-34.
[19]*Ibid.,* ll. 2327-34.
[20]*FQ* VI, ix, 9-10. See Pafford, ed. *Winter's Tale,* (London, 1963) p. lxxvii; A. Thaler, "Shakespeare and Spenser" *SAB,* 10 (1935), 204; E. Gleenlaw, "Shakespeare's Pastorals," *SP,* 13 (1916), 145.
[21]John Arthos defends the brothel scenes as follows: "They were in his sources, but more than that the brothel was traditionally the scene in the old romances and in the lives of the saints where the power of innocence and trust could be most powerfully asserted, and perhaps there is no better way of showing the obtuseness of so much of life"

(*The Art of Shakespeare*, Philadelphia, 1964, pp. 136-57). J. C. Maxwell comments that "It is in the brothel scenes that the play adds most to its sources." New Cambridge Edition, p. 162. A story of a nun in a brothel who preserves her chastity is in Seneca's *Sententiae*, whence it was taken in Lazarus Pyott's *The Orator*, 1596, sometimes cited as a source for *Pericles*. See Eugene M. Waith, "*Pericles* and Seneca The Elder" *JEGP*, 50 (1951), 180-82.

[22]I. iii. 59-82. For a demonstration that this passage is in a scene written by Shakespeare, not Fletcher, see Kenneth Muir, "Shakespeare's Hand in *The Two Noble Kinsmen*" *Shakespeare Survey*, 11 (1958), 57-58. The discussion of this play in the edition by G. R. Proudfoot (Lincoln, Nebraska, 1970), is valuable.

[23]Charles and Mary Cowden-Clarke. *Recollections of Writers* (New York, n.d.), p. 126. I owe this reference to Stuart Ende.

[24]*The Sovereign Flower* (London, 1958), p. 197.

Chapter 3. From Comedy to Romance

[1]*Narrative and Dramatic Sources of Shakespeare* (London and New York, 1957-66), I, 10.

[2]V. i. 307-19. G. K. Hunter comments that "it is the threat of lost identity that draws forth the most powerful poetry in the play." *John Lyly* (London, 1962), p. 303.

[3]V. i. 206-13. See L. G. Salingar, "Time and Art in Shakespeare's Romances." *Renaissance Drama*, 9 (1966), 19.

[4]Northrop Frye, *A Natural Perspective* (New York, 1965), p. 74.

[5]G. K. Hunter, in the New Arden ed. of *All's Well* (London, 1959), comments sensitively on this "forshadow of the world of the last plays," (pp. xxxvii-xxxviii).

[6]*Samuel Johnson, Editor of Shakespeare*, ed. A. Sherbo, Yale Edition, pp. 7, 173.

[7]Clifford Leech, in his New Arden edition, inclines to the "stratification" theory of the play's composition, though he was not able to persuade one of the General Editors of the Arden Series, Harold Brooks. Stanley Wells thinks that the peculiar geography of the play and its internal inconsistencies "might almost be regarded as a normal feature of romance." "The Failure of *The Two Gentlemen of Verona*," *Shakespeare Jahrbuch*, 99 (1963), 162.

[8]See Mozell Scaff Allen, "Broke's *Romeus and Juliet* as a Source for the Valentine-Silvia Plot in *The Two Gentlemen of Verona*," *University of Texas Studies in English*, No. 18 (1938), 25-46.

[9]"Nothing was lost in Shakespeare's experience. Traces of his reading remained below the surface of his mind, waiting for an opportunity to float up as images or names or incidents or ideas maybe years later" Geoffrey Bullough, *Narrative and Dramatic Sources of Shakespeare*, (London and New York, 1957-66) I, 453-54. This "sense of thrift" is commented on by Ralph M. Sargent, "Elyot and the Integrity of *The Two Gentlemen of Verona*," *PMLA*, 65 (1950), 1179*n*.

[10]"Shakespeare's *Twelfth Night*," *Rice Institute Pamphlet* 45 (January 1959), 31.

[11]Ed. Judith M. Kennedy (Oxford, 1968), p. 87.

[12]Ed. J. J. Munro (London, 1908), ll. 1620-22, 1681-82, 2483-84.

[13]II. iii. 10-12.

[14]"The Argument of Comedy" in *English Institute Essays*, ed. Alan Downer (New York, 1948), pp. 58-73.

[15]*Cymbeline* V. i. 2-11; *Much Ado* V. i. 284-85. This is pointed out by Homer Swander, "*Cymbeline* and the 'Blameless Hero'" *ELH*, 31 (1964), 268.

[16]New Arden ed. (London, 1959), p. xxiv.

[17]*All's Well* II. iii. 1-6. G. Wilson Knight remarks on these two resemblances and says the LaFew's speech "might be read as a text for *The Winter Tale*." The Crown

228

of Life (New York, 1966), pp. 127-28.

[18]Walter Raleigh, *Shakespeare* (London, 1908) p. 53.

[19]New Arden ed. (Cambridge, Mass., 1965), p. xcviii.

Chapter 4. From Tragedy to Romance

[1]J. F. Danby, *Poets on Fortune's Hill* (London, 1952), p. 107.

[2]Fitzroy Pyle " 'Twelfth Night,' 'King Lear' and 'Arcadia' "*MLR*, 43 (1948), 449-55, and Kenneth Muir, New Arden edition of *King Lear* (London, 1952), pp. xxxviii-xli, and his *Shakespeare's Sources* (London, 1957), I, 146-47.

[3]D. S. Bland, "The Heroine and the Sea: An Aspect of Shakespeare's Late Plays," *Essays in Criticism*, 3 (1953), 39-44. I am not sure whether Dr. Johnson, who found the death of Cordelia so painful, would agree. He remarked that in preferring Tate's version to Shakespeare's "the publick has decided."

[4]*Shakespearean Tragedy* (London, 1904), pp. 443-45; *Timon* IV. iii. 82-166; *Lear* IV. vi. 112-32.

[5]*Shakespeare's Tragedies and Other Studies in Seventeenth Century Drama* (New York, 1950), p. 113.

[6]*A Natural Perspective* (New York, 1965), p. 98.

[7]*"King Lear" in Our Time* (Berkeley, 1965), pp. 63-65.

[8]F. D. Hoeniger, ed. *Pericles,* New Arden ed. (London and Cambridge, Mass., 1963), p. lxxxvi; J.M.S. Tompkins, "Why *Pericles?,*" RES n.s. 3 (1952), 320-21. Besides these, Danby, Stauffer, Muir, Arthos and Traversi all consider Pericles an example of patience. They are challenged by Thelma N. Greenfield, "A Re-examination of the 'Patient' Pericles," *Shakespeare Studies* 3, ed. Barroll, (1967), 51-61. Ernest Schanzer, Signet Classic ed. (New York, 1965), pp. xxxiii-xxxiv, argues that Pericles is not a model of patience.

[9]W. W. Greg, "The Date of 'King Lear' and Shakespeare's Use of Earlier Versions of the Story," 4 *Library* 20 (1940), 388.

[10]V. ii. 489-94. Dekker, *Dramatic Works* ed. Bowers (Cambridge, 1955), II, 108.

[11]IV. ii. 169-81. William R. Elton, *"King Lear" and the Gods* (San Marino, 1966), pp. 188-89, points out that invocations to nature are common in plays with a pre-Christian setting, and cites examples from *Gorboduc.*

[12]IV. i. 38-39. According to W. A. Armstrong, *TLS* Oct. 14, 1949, the *Lear* passage, like so many others, is derived from Sidney's *Arcadia.*

[13]New Arden ed. (London, 1955), p. 50.

[14]*The Complete Works of Shakespeare* (Boston and New York, 1936), p. 1332.

[15]*Shakespeare's Roman Plays* (Cambridge, Mass., 1961), p. 141.

[16]F. E. Halliday, *The Life of Shakespeare* (London, 1961), p. 205.

[17]H. B. Charlton, *Shakespearian Tragedy* (London, 1948), p. 240.

[18]Theodore Spencer, "Shakespeare's Last Plays" *MP*, 39 (1941-42), 265-74.

[19]"The Note of Shakespeare's Romances' in *Lectures on Poetry* (London and New York, 1911), p. 227.

Chapter 5. *As You Like It* and *Rosalynde*

[1]"The Relation of *As You Like It* to Robin Hood Plays," *JEGP*, 4 (1902), 59-60.

[2]*Pastoral Poetry from the Beginnings to Marvell* (London, 1952), p. 38 n1.

[3]*Elizabethan Prose Fiction*, ed. Merritt Lawlis (New York, 1967), p. 288.

[4]John Shaw, "Fortune and Nature in *AYLI*," *Shakespeare Quarterly*, 6 (1955), 45-50.

[5]*Elizabethan Prose Fiction*, p. 299.

[6]*Ibid.*, p. 301. There is much ado about Hercules in Richard Knowles, "Myth and Type in *As You Like It*," *ELH*, 33 (1966), 1-22.

[7]*Ibid.*, p. 301.

[8]*Ibid.*, p. 305.

[9]*Ibid.*, p. 311.

[10]*Shakespeare and the Idea of the Play* (London, 1962), p. 219 *n3*.

[11]*Lawlis*, p. 339.

[12]*Ibid.*, p. 335.

[13]*Ibid.*, p. 366.

[14]"The Argument of Comedy," *English Institute Essays* (New York, 1949), p. 68.

[15]*"King Lear" in Our Time* (Berkeley, 1965), pp. 64-65.

[16]"The Oaten Flute," *Harvard Library Bulletin*, 11 (1957), 180-82.

[17]Ed. Over and Bell (London, 1967), p. 13.

[18]C. H. Hobday, "Why the Sweets Melted," *Shakespeare Quarterly*, 16 (1965), 3-17.

[19]*Ben Jonson and the Language of Prose Comedy* (Cambridge, Mass., 1960), p. 29.

[20]Whiter, p. 76.

[21]*Narrative and Dramatic Sources of Shakespeare* (London and New York, 1957-56), II, 143-57.

[22]*Ibid.*, p. 318.

[23]*Ibid.*, p. 369.

[24]"As You Like It" in *More Talking of Shakespeare*, ed. John Garrett (New York, 1959), pp. 17-32.

[25]"As You Like It," *Shakespeare Survey*, 8 (1955), 40-51.

[26]Yale Ed. VII, 264.

[27]"What Shakespeare did to Rosalynde," *Shakespeare Jahrbuch*, 96 (1960), 78-89.

[28]"Masking in Arden: the Histrionics of Lodge's *Rosalynde*" SEL, 5 (1965), 151-63.

[29]P. 28. After writing this chapter I read Robert B. Pierce's "The Moral Languages of *Rosalynde* and *As You Like It*" SP, 68 (1971), 167-76. It is a perceptive essay.

Chapter 6. *The Winter's Tale* and *Pandosto*

[1]For a discussion with quite different purposes from mine, see John Lawlor, *"Pandosto* and the Nature of Dramatic Romance," *PQ*, 41 (1962), 96-113. Lawlor emphasizes differences of plot and characterization, generally ignoring verbal echoes and image-associations, in order to provide help in assessing the characteristics of romance as a dramatic form.

[2]*Elizabethan Prose Fiction*, ed. Merritt Lawlis (New York, 1967), p. 254.

[3]*Idea and Act in Elizabethan Fiction* (Princeton, 1969), p. 169.

[4]Ed. Lawlis, pp. 251-52.

[5]*Shakespeare's Sources* (London, 1957), I, 241.

[6]Lawlis, p. 246.

[7]*"The Winter's Tale": A Commentary on the Structure*, (London, 1969), p. 159.

[8]*The Winter's Tale*, New Penguin ed. (Baltimore, 1969), p. 12.

[9]*Ibid.*, p. 13.

[10]Lawlis, p. 277.

[11]See *Shakespeare Quarterly*, 14 (1963), 163-66.

[12]Lawlis, p. 233.

[13]*"The Winter's Tale": A Commentary*, p. 39.

[14]Lawlis, pp. 234-35.

[15]New Penguin ed., p. 36.

[16]Lawlis, p. 234.

[17]New Penguin ed., p. 30.

[18]*Shakespeare's Wordplay* (London, 1957).

[19]In *Pandosto* the image comes from the game of backgammon, with perhaps a second-

ary sexual meaning: "In the meantime, Pandosto's mind was so far charged with jealousy that he did no longer doubt, but was assured (as he thought) that his friend Egistus had entered a wrong point in his tables and so had played him false play." (ed. Lawlis, pp. 234-35).

²⁰That there are some theatrical images in the last act must be admitted. The sharp observation of Dr. Jenijoy LaBelle has noticed one at V. i. 55-60 and V. ii. 86-87, but she agrees that there are none in the statue scene.

²¹Lawlis, pp. 258-59.

²²Fitzroy Pyle thinks she is the germ of the character of Paulina. *"The Winter's Tale": A Commentary*, p. 40.

²³See John Robert Moore, "Ancestors of Autolycus in the English Moralities and Interludes," *Washington University Studies*, Humanistic Series, Vol. 9, No. 2 (1922), 157-64.

²⁴Lee Sheridan Cox, "The Role of Autolycus in *The Winter's Tale*," *Studies in English Literature*, 9 (1969), 283-301.

²⁵*The Winter's Tale*, New Arden ed. (Cambridge, Mass., 1963), p. 165.

²⁶*Shakespeare: The Final Plays* (London, 1963) p. 35.

²⁷*"The Winter's Tale": A Commentary*, p. 117. It means "a valiant fighter." See *The Merry Wives of Windsor* I. iv. 26.

²⁸"Shakespeare's Pastorals" *SP*, 13 (1913), 145-46.

²⁹"Shakespeare's Pastoral Comedy" in *More Talking of Shakespeare*, ed. John Garrett, (London, 1959), 70-86.

³⁰"The Final Scene of *The Winter's Tale*," *English Studies*, 33 (1952), 193-208.

³¹"Secondary Sources of *The Winter's Tale*," *PQ*, 34 (1955), 37 *n*23. In so far as Hermione is the model of a *patient* woman, there is an association in Shakespeare's mind between *patience* and *statues*. See *Twelfth Night* II. v. 117-18 and *Pericles* V. i. 138-40.

³²See Michael Jamieson, "Shakespeare's Celibate Stage" in G. E. Bentley, ed., *The Seventeenth Century Stage*, (Chicago, 1968), p. 81.

³³Lawlis, p. 238.

³⁴IV. ii. 22-25. For interesting comments on this passage, by T. S. Eliot and Robert Speaight, see *Studies in The Arts*, ed. Francis Warner, (Oxford, 1968) p. 42.

³⁵For a sensitive and fascinating examination of vocabulary shift as a part of characterization, see Jonathan Smith, "The Language of Leontes," *Shakespeare Quarterly*, 19 (1968), 317-27.

³⁶*Shakespeare's Last Plays* (London, 1938), p. 77.

³⁷III. iv. 6-11. *The Crown of Life*, (London, 1947), p. 98.

³⁸"Nature and Art in *The Winter's Tale*," *SAB*, 18 (1943), 114-20.

³⁹*Primitivism and Related Ideas in Antiquity* (Baltimore, 1935), p. 207. Lovejoy calls Montaigne's passage the *locus classicus* of primitivism in modern literature, and says that "Shakespeare's own extreme antipathy to the passage is shown by the fact that he wrote two replies to it — a humorous one in *The Tempest*, a serious and profound one in *The Winter's Tale*." *Essays in the History of Ideas*, 1948, p. 238. Margaret T. Hodgen shows that Shakespeare could have easily got his material from sources other than Montaigne. "Montaigne and Shakespeare Again," *HLQ*, 16 (1952-53), 23-41. Harry Levin clarifies matters when he says "Shakespeare was clearly not a primitivist, though Gonzalo may well have been. It was Shakespeare's gift to envisage many viewpoints, to endow conflicting purposes with words." *The Myth of the Golden Age in the Renaissance*, (Bloomington, Ind., 1969), p. 127.

⁴⁰*Elizabethan Critical Essays*, ed. G. *Gregory Smith* (London, 1950), II, 188.

⁴¹"*The Winter's Tale*." *Scrutiny*, 5 (1936-37), 345.

⁴²*The Slave of Life: A Study of Shakespeare and the Idea of Justice* (London, 1955), p. 185.

⁴³*Shakespeare: The Last Phase* (New York, 1953), p. 119.

44 "Recognition in *The Winter's Tale*" in *Essays on Shakespeare and Elizabethan Drama: in Honor of Hardin Craig*, ed. R. Hosley (Columbia, Mo., 1962), p. 239.

45Ed. Lawlis, p. 239.

46"*The Winter's Tale*": *A Study* (London, n.d.) pp. 117-18.

47"The Meaning of *The Winter's Tale*," *University of Toronto Quarterly*, 20 (1950-51), 11-26.

48"Shakespeare's Allegory: *The Winter's Tale*," *Sewanee Review*, 63 (1955), 202-22.

49*REL*, 5 (1964), 83-100.

50"The Structural Pattern of *The Winter's Tale*," *REL*, 5 (1964), 72-82.

51*The Greek Romances and Elizabethan Fiction* (New York, 1912), pp. 376, 432, 456.

Chapter 7. *A Midsummer Night's Dream* and *The Tempest*

1This point, and many others of critical significance, are discussed by R. W. Dent, "Imagination in *A Midsummer Night's Dream*," *Shakespeare Quarterly*, 15 (1964), 115-29. Bullough says that *Romeo and Juliet* in style "goes with the sonnets, and with *A Midsummer Night's Dream*, in which the Pyramus and Thisbe playlet may be a whimsical burlesque of Shakespeare's first experiment in romantic tragedy" (*Narrative and Dramatic Sources in Shakespeare*, London and New York, 1957-66, I, 269). Bullough also considers that *A Midsummer Night's Dream* "may be in part a whimsical revulsion against the sentimental love and friendship which colour the *Knightes Tale* as well as *Two Gentlemen of Verona*" (I, 369).

2IV. iv. 459-60; V. v. 52-55; V. ii. 74-78, 93-100.

3*Comic Characters of Shakespeare* (London, 1946), pp. 92-109.

4R. W. Dent, "Imagination in *A Midsummer Night's Dream*," *Shakespeare Quarterly*, 15 (1964), 121. Dent drily remarks, "It used to be customary to see no significance whatever in this echo."

5V. ii. 93-99. There is a useful commentary on this passage in Maurice Charney, *Shakespeare's Roman Plays: The Function of Imagery in Drama* (Cambridge, Mass., 1961), p. 21.

6IV. ii. 7; "discharge" is ambiguous.

7III. ii. 114-15. Kittredge cites the parallel of *As You Like It* III. iv. 55-58:

> If you will see a pageant truly play'd
> Between the pale complexion of true love
> And the red glow of scorn and proud disdain,
> Go hence a little, and I shall conduct you.

8This discovery was made by John Dover Wilson in a paper read to the Bibliographical Society in December, 1918. *Transactions*, 15 (1920) 137-38. It is challenged, unsuccessfully I think, by Hazelton Spencer in *MLR*, 25 (1930), 23-29, and by Leo Kirschbaum in *MLN*, 61 (1946), 44-49.

9"The Mature Comedies" in *Early Shakespeare* (Stratford-upon-Avon Studies 3, 1961), p. 219.

10*Something of Great Constancy* (New Haven, 1966) p. 113.

11"The Argument of *A Midsummer Night's Dream*," *Shakespeare Quarterly*, 8 (1957), 307-10.

12"The Ritual and Rhetoric of *A Midsummer Night's Dream*," *PMLA*, 83 (1968), 380-91.

13"*A Midsummer Night's Dream* and the Meaning of Court Marriage," *ELH*, 24 (1957), 109.

14*The Winter's Tale: A Commentary on the Structure* (London, 1969), pp. 142-43.

15Bonamy Dobree, "The Tempest" in *Twentieth Century Interpretations of The Tempest* (New Jersey, 1969), pp. 47-59, and C. J. Sisson, "The Magic of Prospero," *Shakespeare Survey*, 11 (1958).

Notes

[16]D. G. James, *The Dream of Prospero* (Oxford, 1967).

[17]P. 327.

[18]Harry Berger, Jr., "Miraculous Harp: A Reading of Shakespeare's *Tempest,*" *Shakespeare Studies,* 5 (1970), 253-83.

[19]"The Macbeth Murder Mystery," in *My World and Welcome To It.*

[20]III. iii. 18-33. The point is not affected by whether one agrees with Kermode that "living drollery" means a puppet show with living actors, or "an animated grotesque picture" or an imitation of an Indian dance. See *New Arden* ed. (London, 1954), p. xxxiii, *n.*4.

[21]*New Arden* ed., pp. 133-34.

[22]"Shakespeare's Last Plays," reprinted in *Twentieth Century Interpretations of The Tempest,* p. 45, *n.*2.

[23]*L'inspiration Personelle et l'Esprit du Temps chez Les Poètes Métaphysiques Anglais* (Paris, 1960), III, 60.

[24]Cited by Christopher Hill, *Intellectual Origins of the English Revolution* (Oxford, 1965), p. 147.

[25]"Ceremonial Magic in *The Tempest,*" Chapter VI of *Shakespeare and the Outer Mystery* (Lexington, Ky., 1968), pp. 82-83. There are, I think, some errors in C. J. Sisson's "The Magic of Prospero" in *Shakespeare Survey,* 2 (1958), 70-77. For example, he says that Prospero draws no circles, but the stage direction after V. i. 57, which is in the Folio, shows clearly that he does. Excellent accounts, in addition to West's, are Harry Levin's "Two Magian Comedies: 'The Tempest' and 'The Alchemist,' " *Shakespeare Survey,* 22 (1969), 47-58, and Robert Silhol, "Magie et Utopie dans La Tempête," *Etudes Anglaises,* 17 (1964), 447-56.

[26]Kermode's account of this is muddled. He calls Richard Eden Robert; he remarks that Setebos is borrowed from the *History of Travaile* and "I believe Shakespeare also knew Eden's version of Peter Martyr, though much of that might seem relevant in the work was repeated countless times elsewhere." The *History of Travaile* and the translation of Peter Martyr are the same book, STC 649 and 650. The editions of 1577 and 1612 have the same pagination, though one is in black letter and the other in Roman. The reviser of 1577 is given as Willes and of 1612 as Lok.

[27]f 431ᵛ for 432ᵛ.

[28]f 433 ʳ.

[29]f 434ᵛ.

[30]f 15 ʳ.

[31]*The Age of Reconnaissance* (Cleveland, 1963), p. 31.

[32]f 55ʳ.

[33]f 96 ʳ misnumbered 86.

[34]f 34 ʳ.

[35]*Science and Imagination* (Ithaca, 1956).

[36]*Essays of John Dryden,* ed. P. W. Ker, I, 187 and 219. The semantic importance of this word is not apparent from the OED; it is developed in Logan Pearsall Smith, *Words and Idioms* (London, 1925), 90-91.

Chapter 8. Scenery and "Landscape"

[1]What I have called "landscape" would include several of the topics of invention according to Elizabethan rhetorical labelling. *Pragmatographia* is vivid description of an action or event. It is, as Sister Miriam Joseph observes, particularly useful in reporting events that take place offstage (*Shakespeare's Use of the Arts of Language,* New York, 1947, p. 129). She cites as an example the meeting between Leontes and Polixenes in *The Winter's Tale* V. ii. 47-63 and the discovery that Perdita is Leontes' long-lost

daughter. *Chronographia* is the description of times of day, *Topographia* is the name given to description of places, for which she cites *Cymbeline* III. i. 18 ff. where the Queen describes the English coast, while *Topothesia* is the description of imaginary places, for which she can find no examples in Shakespeare except some minor ones in *A Midsummer Night's Dream*.

[2]*Samuel Johnson on Shakespeare,* ed. W. K. Wimsatt, p. 113.

[3]See Geoffrey Bullough, *Narrative and Dramatic Sources of Shakespeare* (London and New York, 1957-66), VI, 225-50.

[4]*Shakespeare's Tragedies* (New York, 1950), p. 113.

[5]*Narrative and Dramatic Sources,* VI, 250.

[6]*"King Lear" in Our Time* (Berkeley, 1965), p. 20.

[7]*New Arden* ed. (London & Cambridge, Mass., 1965), p. 258; and *N&Q,* 200 (1955), 15.

[8]The best demonstration of this, I think, is George F. Reynolds' "Two Conventions of the Open Stage (As Illustrated in *King Lear?*)" *PQ,* 41 (1962), 82-95.

[9]This is elaborately demonstrated in William R. Elton, *"King Lear" and the Gods* (San Marino, 1966).

[10]The statement frequently made that Shakespeare was influenced by a real-life case, that of Brian Annesley, of Lee in Kent, who was declared insane and was cared for by his daughter Cordell against the opposition of her two sisters is examined judiciously by Geoffrey Bullough in *Festschrift Rudolf Stamm,* 1969, pp. 43-49. Bullough concludes that Shakespeare may have known of the case but "we have no reason to conclude that he thought of the Annesley affair at all."

[11]Ed. Kenneth Muir, pp. 31-32.

[12]IV. i. 51-64. This passage, like much else in the romances, derives from Sidney's *Arcadia.* Marina's account, by report, of her father's behavior in the storm depends upon the account of Pyrocles' actions before the shipwreck. See Ernest Schanzer, ed. *Pericles,* Signet ed. (New York, 1965), pp. xxxiv-xxxv.

[13]*The Staging of Elizabethan Plays at the Red Bull Theater 1605-1625* (New York, 1940), pp. 181-82.

[14]*Pericles,* Signet ed. p. xxx

[15]Norman Rabkin, *Shakespeare and the Common Understanding* (New York, 1967), p. 211.

[16]J. M. Nosworthy, New Arden ed. (London, 1966), pp. lxxix-lxxx.

[17]*"Cymbeline:* Crude Dramaturgy and Aesthetic Distance" *Renaissance Papers* (1966), ed. G. W. Williams, pp. 39-47.

[18]J. P. Brockbank, "History and Histrionics in *Cymbeline*" *Shakespeare Survey,* 11 (1958), 42-49.

[19]*Shakespeare at the Globe* (New York, 1962), p. 94.

[20]Irwin Smith, *Shakespeare's Blackfriars Playhouse, Its History and Its Design* (New York, 1964), p. 247.

[21]See Clifford Leech, "The Structure of the Last Plays," *Shakespeare Survey,* 11 (1958), 19-30.

[22]Edmond Malone, *An Account of the Incidents, from which the Title and Part of the Story of Shakespeare's Tempest were Derived; and its True Date Ascertained* (London, privately printed, 1808), pp. 2-3.

[23]*Adventurer* No. 93, September 25, 1753. Quoted by G. W. Stone, Jr., in *Shakespeare Quarterly,* 7 (1956), 1.

[24]V. i. 221-40. An example of critical bewilderment at the way in which the storm is "landscape" is the recent comment of D. G. James, in *The Dream of Prospero.* James thinks there are two storms in the play — the one Miranda sees and the one in which everybody was saved, pp. 30, 147.

Notes

[25]These shows all owe something to the technique of the masque, but they are not masques, nor do I think it is proper to refer to the hunting scene as anti-masque. The commentary on this subject is extensive. See Enid Welsford, *The Court Masque* (Cambridge, Eng., 1927); Paul Reyher, *Les masques anglais,* (Paris, 1909) and the relevant passages in Kermode's New Arden edition (London, 1954), lxxi-lxxxi and Appendix E.

Chapter 9. Language and Style

[1]"The Language of Leontes," *Shakespeare Quarterly,* 19 (1968), 317-27.

[2]"The Language of the Last Plays" in *More Talking of Shakespeare,* ed. John Garrett, (New York, 1919), 144-58.

[3]*The Language of Shakespeare's Plays* (London, 1952), p. 179.

[4]*Cymbeline,* New Arden ed. (London, 1955), p. 156 *n*3.

[5]V. ii. 231-35. Walter Morris Hart, "Shakespeare's Use of Verse and Prose," in *Five Gayley Lectures* (1947-1954), p. 6. Hart attributes the suggestion to Edward Rowland Sill, himself a poet.

[6]"The Poet and the Player" *Shakespeare Survey,* 7 (1954), 32-33.

[7]"Style in Shakespeare," British Academy Shakespeare Lecture, 1936, p. 12.

[8]*Words and Poetry* (New York, 1928), pp. 212-17. The word "law" is often emended to "la."

[9]*The Tempest,* New Arden ed. (London, 1958), p. lxxviii.

Appendix A. Myth, Symbol, and Poetry

[1]115-27. A medieval rendering of the rape of Proserpina is reproduced from a Paris manuscript in Jean Seznec, *The Survival of the Pagan Gods* (New York, 1953), pl. 8, p. 33. Pluto is in armor as a knight; he is accompanied by Cerberus, his three-headed-dog servant who walks on foot; he reaches for "Preserpine" from his chariot, but as Shakespeare's Perdita says, it is not so much a chariot as "Dis's waggon"; it is a regular four-wheeled farm wagon, drawn by two horses.

[2]*Paradise Lost,* IV, 268-72.

[3]*Archetypal Patterns in Poetry* (London, 1934), p. 166.

[4]J. H. P. Pafford has an enlightening appendix in his New Arden ed. (London and Cambridge, Mass., 1958), pp. 170-72 in which he cites poems by Herrick, including "How Primroses Came Green."

[5]M. H. Abrams, review of Frye's "Anatomy of Criticism" in *University of Toronto Quarterly,* 28 (1958-59), 190-96.

[6]V. 487-500. Certainty that Shakespeare is echoing Golding is expressed by Kenneth Muir, *Shakespeare's Sources* (London, 1957), I, 250.

[7]Friend and admirer is perhaps an understatement. John Freehafer, in "Leonard Digges, Ben Jonson, and the Beginning of Shakespeare Idolatry," *Shakespeare Quarterly,* 21 (1970), 63-75, shows clearly the position of Digges in the early establishment of Shakespeare's reputation.

[8]A4[v].

[9]*The Third part of the Countesse of Pembrokes Yuychurch, Entituled Amintas Dale. Wherein are the most conceited tales of the Pagan Gods in English Hexameters together with their aunciént descriptions and Philosophicall explications,* (1592), Sig G4[v].

[10]I. i. 1 and I. ii. 121. It is not in Plutarch.

[11]*Proc. Brit. Acad.,* 29 (1943), 422.

[12]*Shakespeare's Last Plays* (London, 1938), 42-46.

[13]*Anatomy of Criticism* (Princeton, 1957), p. 138.

[14]Rudolf Gottfried, "Our New Poet: Archetypal Criticism and *The Faerie Queene,*" *PMLA,* 83 (1968), 1362-77; Frank Kermode, "Spenser and the Allegorists," *Proc. Brit.*

Acad., 48 (1962), 262; John Holloway, *The Story of the Night: Studies in Shakespeare's Major Tragedies*, Appendix B, "The Concepts of 'Myth' and 'Ritual' in Shakespeare," pp. 166-83, (1961); and several essays in *Northrop Frye in Modern Criticism*, ed. Murray Krieger, (New York, 1966).

[15]Helen Gardner, *The Business of Criticism* (Oxford, 1959), 127-57.

[16]This is an exaggeration of the view put forth in Northrop Frye "Literature as Context: Milton's *Lycidas*," in *Fables of Identity* (New York, 1963), 119-29.

[17]New Penguin ed. (Baltimore, 1969), pp. 42-43.

[18]*Shakespeare Survey*, 11 (1958), 6.

[19]Wallace W. Douglas, "The Meanings of 'Myth' in Modern Criticism," *MP*, 50 (1952-53), 235. Douglas' article also illustrates the various meanings of the word "myth" as currently used and the confusion which results from critics' failure to realize its ambiguity.

[20]*MP*, 56 (1958), 73-81.

[21]Cited in Mary Douglas, "The Meaning of Myth" in *The Structural Study of Myth and Totemism*, ed. Edmund Leach, (New York, 1907), p. 62.

[22]*Henry VIII*, New Arden ed. (Cambridge, Mass., 1957), pp. xl-xli.

[23]*Jacobean Drama* (London, 1936) p. 269.

[24]P. lxxxiii. A few pages earlier. (p. lxxx) Kermode has remarked that "It is not surprising that *The Tempest* has sent people whoring after strange gods of allegory."

[25]*Shakespeare's "Measure for Measure"* (London, 1953), p. 99.

[26]*The Tempest*, Pelican ed. (Baltimore, 1959), p. 18.

[27]*Allegorical Imagery* (Princeton, 1966), p. 417.

[28]"Some Renaissance 'Ovids' " *Literature and Society*, ed. Bernice Slote, (Lincoln, Neb., 1964), 44-62.

[29]A. D. Nuttall, *"The Tempest* and its Romantic Critics," *Two Concepts of Allegory: A Study of Shakespeare's "The Tempest" and the Logic of Allegorical Expression* (London, 1967).

[30]"*The Tempest* and the Renaissance Idea of Man," *Shakespeare Quarterly*, 15 (1964), 147-59.

[31]In *Myth and Mythmaking*, ed. Henry A. Murray, (Boston, 1960), pp. 132-40; reprinted in *The Agony and the Triumph*, (Ypsilanti, Mich., 1963).

[32] *Ibid.*, p. 239.

[33]"Examination," p. 140.

[34]Appendix B to *The Story of the Night: Studies in Shakespeare's Major Tragedies* (London, 1961), pp. 166-83.

[35]*Ibid.*, p. 177.

[36]*Ibid.*, p. 154.

Appendix B. The Topicality of *Cymbeline* and *The Winter's Tale*

[1]Dr. Johnson, for example, declared that "To remark the folly of the fiction, the absurdity of the conduct, the confusion of the names and manners of different times, and the impossibility of the events in any system of life, were to waste criticism upon unresisting imbecility, upon faults too evident for detection, and too gross for aggravation." (Yale edition VIII, 908.)

[2]*Shakespeare's Comedies* (Oxford, 1960), p. 272.

[3]*The Living World of Shakespeare* (New York, 1964), p. 209.

[4]*The Crown of Life* (London and New York, 1957), p. 129.

[5]*Shakespeare and Religion* (New York, 1967), pp. 48, 49. Knight violently, almost hysterically, objects to Roland Mushat Frye's characterization of him as a Christianizer of Shakespeare, but it seems to me that Frye's description is a fair one. See his *Shakespeare*

and Christian Doctrine (Princeton, 1964), and Knight's "Christian Doctrine" in *Shakespeare and Religion*, pp. 293-303.

[6]*Shakespeare and Religion*, p. 294.

[7]New Arden ed. (London, 1955), pp. liii-liv. He warns against drawing a false analogy.

[8]*Essays in Criticism*, 2 (1961), 84-99.

[9]A. J. Loomie, "An Armada Pilot's Survey of the English Coastline, 1597" *Mariner's Mirror*, 49 (1963), 288-300, cited in Joel Hurstfield, *The Elizabethan Nation* (New York, n.d.), p. 78.

[10]*Shakespeare's Holinshed*, ed. W. G. Boswell-Stone, (London, 1896), p. 8.

[11]*King James VI and I* (London, 1956), p. 279.

[12]Bernard Harris declares that "Jones's discussion of the topical references in the play are *(sic)* both convincing and speculatively enticing." " 'What's past is prologue': *Cymbeline* and *Henry VIII*," *Later Shakespeare* (Stratford-upon-Avon Studies 8, 1966), p. 209.

[13]*Cymbeline*, New Arden ed., p. xvi.

[14]"Shakespeare's Investiture Play: The Occasion and Subject of 'The Winter's Tale,'" *TLS*, December 18, 1969, p. 1456.

[15]"*The Winter's Tale*: A Comedy with Deaths" in *Shakespeare's Dramatic Heritage* (London, 1969), p. 265.

[16]*Elizabethan Critical Essays*, ed. Gregory Smith, (London, 1950), I, 197.

[17]*Shakespeare: A Survey* (London, 1925), p. 303, but these chapters merely reprint Chambers' introductions to the Red Letter Shakespeare, which appeared 1904-1908.

[18]See D. H. Willson, *King James VI and I*, pp. 280-81. Elkin Calhoun Wilson, in his *Prince Henry and English Literature* (Ithaca, 1946), finds no connection with Shakespeare.

[19]"Love's Labor's Lost and the Early Shakespeare," *PQ*, 41 (1962), 19-20.

[20]"The *Henry V* Choruses in the First Folio," *JEGP*, 53 (1954), 38-57.

[21]"*Hamlet*" and the Scottish Succession (Cambridge, Eng., 1921), p. 176.

[23]"*Macbeth*," "*King Lear*," "*Othello*" as the Tragedy of Italy (London, 1924).

[23]*Othello as the Tragedy of Italy* (London, 1924).

[24]*Shakespeare's "Measure for Measure"* (London, 1953), p. 109.

[25]*TLS* November 13 and 20, 1930. Reprinted in *Shakespeare Criticism 1919-1935*, ed. Anne Bradby (London, 1936).

[26]Bradby, pp. 271, 286.

[27]*Shakespeare at Work 1592-1603* (London, 1933), Preface.

INDEX

Index

241